ADDRESSES

UPON

THE AMERICAN ROAD

1950–1955

ADDRESSES BY HERBERT HOOVER

The New Day: Campaign Speeches of Herbert Hoover, 1928
(Stanford University Press)

Addresses upon the American Road, 1933–1938
Further Addresses upon the American Road, 1938–1940
Addresses upon the American Road, 1940–1941
(Charles Scribner's Sons)

Addresses upon the American Road, 1941–1945
Addresses upon the American Road, 1945–1948
(D. Van Nostrand Company)

Addresses upon the American Road, 1948–1950
Addresses upon the American Road, 1950–1955
(Stanford University Press)

ADDRESSES

UPON

THE AMERICAN ROAD

BY

HERBERT HOOVER

1950-1955

1955
STANFORD UNIVERSITY PRESS
STANFORD, CALIFORNIA

STANFORD UNIVERSITY PRESS
STANFORD, CALIFORNIA

PUBLISHED IN GREAT BRITAIN, INDIA, AND
PAKISTAN BY GEOFFREY CUMBERLEGE,
OXFORD UNIVERSITY PRESS,
LONDON, BOMBAY, AND KARACHI

———

THE BAKER AND TAYLOR COMPANY
HILLSIDE, NEW JERSEY

HENRY M. SNYDER & COMPANY, INC.
440 FOURTH AVENUE, NEW YORK 16

W. S. HALL & COMPANY
510 MADISON AVENUE, NEW YORK 22

———

PRINTED AND BOUND IN THE UNITED STATES
OF AMERICA BY STANFORD UNIVERSITY PRESS

———

Library of Congress Catalog Card Number: 55-7136

Contents

PART II:
ADDRESSES AND COMMENT ON DOMESTIC ISSUES

PART III: ENGINEERING MATTERS

xi

PART I
FOREIGN RELATIONS

Our National Policies in This Crisis

Nation-wide Broadcast from New York City
[December 20, 1950]

MY FELLOW Americans:
I have received hundreds of requests that I appraise the present situation and give my conclusions as to our national policies.

I speak with a deep sense of responsibility. And I speak tonight under the anxieties of every American for the nations' sons who are fighting and dying on a mission of peace and the honor of our country.

No appraisal of the world situation can be final in an unstable world. However, to find our national path we must constantly re-examine where we have arrived and at times revise our direction.

I do not propose to traverse the disastrous road by which we reached this point.

THE GLOBAL MILITARY SITUATION

We may first survey the global military situation. There is today only one center of aggression on the earth. That is the Communist-controlled Asian-European land mass of 800,000,-000 people. They have probably over 300 trained and equipped combat divisions with over 30,000 tanks, 10,000 tactical planes, and further large reserves they can put in action in ninety days. But they are not a great sea power. Their long range air power is limited. This congeries of over thirty different races will some

3

day go to pieces. But in the meantime they furnish unlimited cannon fodder.

Facing this menace on the Eastern front there are about 100,000,000 non-Communist island people in Japan, Formosa, the Philippines, and Korea. Aside from Korea, which I discuss later, they have probably only 12 effective combat divisions with practically no tanks, air, or navy.

Facing this land mass on the south are the Indies and the Middle East of about 600,000,000 non-Communist people. There are about 150,000,000 further non-Communist people in North Africa and Latin America. Except Turkey and Formosa, these 850,000,000 non-Communist people have little military force which they would or could spare.

But they could contribute vital economic and moral strength.

Facing this menace on the Continental European front there are about 160,000,000 further non-Communist people who, excluding Spain, have less than 20 combat divisions now available, few tanks, and little air or naval force. And their will to defend themselves is feeble and their disunities are manifest.

Of importance in military weight at this moment there is the British Commonwealth of 150,000,000 people, with probably 30 combat divisions under arms, a superior navy, considerable air force, and a few tanks.

And there are 150,000,000 people in the United States preparing 3,500,000 men into a gigantic air force and navy, with about 30 equipped combat divisions.

Thus there are 1,310,000,000 non-Communist people in the world, of whom today only about 320,000,000 have any military potency.

SOME MILITARY CONCLUSIONS

If we weigh these military forces as they stand today we must arrive at certain basic conclusions.

a) We must face the fact that to commit the sparse ground forces of the non-Communist nations into a land war against this Communist land mass would be a war without victory, a war without a successful political terminal.

The Germans failed with a magnificent army of 240 combat divisions and with powerful air and tank forces. That compares with only 60 divisions proposed today for the North Atlantic Pact Nations.

Even were Western Europe armed far beyond any contemplated program, we could never reach Moscow.

Therefore any attempt to make war on the Communist mass by land invasion, through the quicksands of China, India, or Western Europe is sheer folly. That would be the graveyard of millions of American boys and would end in the exhaustion of this Gibraltar of Western Civilization.

b) Equally, we Americans alone with sea and air power can so control the Atlantic and Pacific Oceans that there can be no possible invasion of the Western Hemisphere by Communist armies. They can no more reach Washington in force than we can reach Moscow.

c) In this military connection we must realize the fact that the Atomic Bomb is a far less dominant weapon than it was once thought to be.

d) It is obvious that the United Nations have been defeated in Korea by the aggression of Communist China. There are no available forces in the world to repel them.

Even if we sacrifice more American boys to hold a bridge-head, we know we shall not succeed at the present time in the mission given to us by the fifty members of the United Nations.

OUR ECONOMIC STRENGTH

We may explore our American situation still further. The 150,000,000 American people are already economically strained by government expenditures. It must not be forgotten that we are carrying huge burdens from previous wars including obligations to veterans and $260 billions of bond and currency issues from those wars. In the fiscal year 1952, federal and local expenditures are likely to exceed $90 billions. That is more than our total savings. We must finance huge deficits by further government issues. Inflation is already moving. The dollar has in six months fallen 15 or 20 percent in purchasing power. But we might with stern measures avoid the economic disintegration of such a load for a very few years. If we continued long on this road the one center of resistance in the world will collapse in economic disaster.

We may also appraise the diplomatic front. Our great hope was in the United Nations. We have witnessed the sabotage of its primary purpose of preserving peace. It has been, down to last week, a forum for continuous smear on our honor, our ideals, and our purposes.

It did stiffen up against raw aggression last July in Korea. But in its call for that military action, America had to furnish over 90 percent of the foreign forces and suffer over 90 percent of their dead and injured. That effort now comes at least to a measurable military defeat by the aggression of Communist hordes.

Whether or not the United Nations is to have a moral defeat and suffer the collapse of its whole moral stature now depends on whether it has the courage to:

a) Declare Communist China an aggressor.

b) Refuse admission of this aggressor to its membership.

c) Demand that each member of the United Nations cease to furnish or transport supplies of any kind to Communist China that can aid in their military operations. Such a course honestly carried out by the non-Communist nations is not economic sanctions nor does it require military actions. But it would constitute a great pressure for rectitude.

d) For once, pass a resolution condemning the infamous lies about the United States.

Any course short of such action is appeasement.

WHAT SHOULD OUR POLICIES BE?

And now I come to where we should go from here.

Two months ago I suggested a tentative alternate policy for the United States. It received a favorable reception from the large majority of our press.

Since then the crisis in the world has become even more acute. It is clear that the United Nations are defeated in Korea. It is also clear that other non-Communist nations did not or could not substantially respond to the United Nations call for arms to Korea. It is clear the United Nations cannot mobilize substantial military forces. It is clear Continental Europe has not in the three years of our aid developed that unity of purpose and that will power necessary for its own defense. It is clear that our British friends are flirting with appeasement of Communist China. It is clear that the United Nations is in a fog of debate and indecision on whether to appease or not to appease.

In expansion of my proposals of two months ago, I now propose certain principles and action.

First. The foundation of our national policies must be to preserve for the world this Western Hemisphere Gibraltar of Western Civilization.

Second. We can, without any measure of doubt, with our own air and naval forces, hold the Atlantic and Pacific Oceans with one frontier on Britain (if she wishes to co-operate); the other, on Japan, Formosa, and the Philippines. We can hold open the sea lanes for our supplies.

And I devoutly hope that a maximum of co-operation can be established between the British Commonwealth and ourselves.

Third. To do this we should arm our air and naval forces to the teeth. We have little need for large armies unless we are going to Europe or China. We should give Japan her independence and aid her in arms to defend herself. We should stiffen the defenses of our Pacific frontier in Formosa and the Philippines. We can protect this island chain by our sea and air power.

Fourth. We could, after initial outlays for more air and navy equipment, greatly reduce our expenditures, balance our budget, and free ourselves from the dangers of inflation and economic degeneration.

Fifth. If we toil and sacrifice as the President has so well asked, we can continue aid to the hungry of the world. Out of our productivity, we can give aid to other nations when they have already displayed spirit and strength in defense against Communism. We have the stern duty to work and sacrifice to do it.

Sixth. We should have none of appeasement. Morally there is no appeasement of Communism. Appeasement contains more dangers than Dunkirks. We want no more Teherans and no more Yaltas. We can retrieve a battle but we cannot retrieve an appeasement. We are grateful that President Truman has denounced such a course.

Seventh. We are not blind to the need to preserve Western Civilization on the Continent of Europe or to our cultural and religious ties to it. But the prime obligation of defense of Western Continental Europe rests upon the nations of Europe. The test is whether they have the spiritual force, the will, and acceptance of unity among them by their own volition. America cannot create their spiritual forces; we cannot buy them with money.

You can search all the history of mankind and there is no parallel to the effort and sacrifice we have made to elevate their spirit and to achieve their unity.

To this date it has failed. Their minds are confused with fears and disunities. They exclude Spain, although she has the will and means to fight. They higgle with Germany, although she is their frontier. They vacillate in the belief that they are in little danger and the hope to avoid again being a theater of war. And Karl Marx has added to their confusions. They still suffer from battle shock. Their highly organized Communist parties are a menace that we must not ignore.

In both World War I and World War II (including West Germany) those nations placed more than 250 trained and equipped combat divisions in the field within sixty days, with strong air and naval forces. They have more manpower and more productive capacity today than in either one of those wars. To warrant our further aid they should show they have spiritual strength and unity to avail themselves of their own resources. But it must be far more than pacts, conferences, paper promises, and declarations. Today it must express itself in organized and equipped combat divisions of such huge numbers as would erect a sure dam against the red flood. And that before we land another man or another dollar on their shores. Otherwise we shall be inviting another Korea. That would be a calamity to Europe as well as to us.

Our policy in this quarter of the world should be confined to a period of watchful waiting before we take on any commitments.

NATIONAL UNITY

There is a proper urge in all Americans for unity in troubled times. But unless unity is based on right principles and right action it is a vain and dangerous thing.

Honest difference of views and honest debate are not disunity. They are the vital process of policy making among free men.

A right, a specific, an open foreign policy must be formulated which gives confidence in our own security before we can get behind it.

CONCLUSIONS

American eyes should now be opened to these hordes in Asia.

These policies I have suggested would be no isolationism. Indeed they are the opposite. They would avoid rash involvement of our military forces in hopeless campaigns. They do not relieve us of working to our utmost. They would preserve a stronghold of Christian civilization in the world against any peradventure.

With the policies I have outlined, even without Europe, Americans have no reason for hysteria or loss of confidence in our security or our future. And in American security rests the future security of all mankind.

It would be an uneasy peace but we could carry it on with these policies indefinitely even if the Communists should attack our lines on the seas.

We can hope that in time the more than a billion of other non-Communist peoples of the world will rise to their dangers.

We can hope that sometime the evils of Communism and the crumbling of their racial controls will bring their own disintegration. It is a remote consolation, but twice before in world history Asiatic hordes have swept over a large part of the world and their racial dissensions dissolved their empires.

Our people have braved difficult and distressing situations in these three centuries we have been on this continent. We have faced our troubles without fear and we have not failed.

We shall not fail in this, even if we have to stand alone. But we need to realize the whole truth and gird ourselves for troubled times. The truth is ugly. We face it with prayer and courage. The Almighty is on our side.

We Should Revise Our Foreign Policies*

Nation-wide Broadcast from New York City
[February 9, 1951]

FELLOW Americans:

I have been urged by many thousands of you to again discuss with you our foreign policies.

A responsibility rests upon me to speak out from fifty years of personal experience with most of the peoples of the free world and with Russia and China. I have been entrusted during thirty-five years with high responsibilities by my countrymen.

I should like to address you through the rose-colored spectacles of idealism and the need of free nations to defend free men.

But I would be doing my country a disservice if I did not take into account the realities in this endangered world.

There is nothing sacrosanct about foreign policies, as witness the tombstones which have been erected over many of them in the last ten years. They bear the inscriptions Undeclared War, The Alliance with Stalin, Teheran, Yalta, Potsdam, Dismantling of German Peacetime Industry, The Promoting of Mao Tse-tung.

---

* In delivering this address Mr. Hoover announced he was compelled to condense it to come within the radio time and that the full text could be had in print.

This is the full address. It also includes a small amount of rephrasing for greater clarity.

Many men, including myself, have demanded the revision of these policies at each wrong turning.

The rightness of our many proposals has been proved by time. I shall recall only two of them for your test.

Seventeen years ago, as President, I refused recognition of the Soviet Government. I knew from ample experience, and their own documents, that this bloody conspiracy against mankind would flood our country through this open door with Fifth Columns and spies; that they would sabotage our national life and government. Every American knows they have done just that.

About ten years ago, on June 29, 1941, in a great crisis I urged the revision of our policies to meet the greatest danger that had come to the American people.

Mr. Roosevelt had proposed a tacit alliance of the United States with Stalin and his Communist Russia. Britain was then safe because of the diversion of Hitler's armies to an attack on Russia. A few sentences from my address were:

... Now we find ourselves promising aid to Stalin and his militant Communist conspiracy against the whole democratic ideals of the world. ...

It makes the whole argument of our joining the war to bring the four freedoms to mankind a gargantuan jest. ...

If we go further and join the war and we win, then we have won for Stalin the grip of Communism on Russia and more opportunity for it to extend in the world.

I said these two dictators—Stalin and Hitler—were locked in deadly combat, that statesmanship required the United States to stand aside in watchful waiting, armed to the teeth; that the day would come when these nations

... will be sufficiently exhausted to listen to the military, economic, and moral powers of the United States and at that moment and that moment only can the United States promote a just and lasting peace.

Remember this was in June 1941, almost ten years ago. Need I remind you that the grip of Communism in this decade has spread slavery from 200,000,000 to 800,000,000 people? And we have no peace.

I could recall a dozen more instances, some within the past twelve months.

OUR PROBLEMS NOW

In order to reach any conclusions as to the wise course for America to pursue in the critical issues which confront us we must again and again appraise the constantly shifting forces moving in the world.

The problems which we face are of far larger dimensions than the current discussion on sending contingents of American boys to Europe.

Their appraisal must also include:

1. Land war strengths.
2. The defense of the American people and the Western Hemisphere.
3. Our economic capacity over a long period.
4. The United Nations.
5. Our policies in the Far East.
6. The North Atlantic Military alliance.

Policies in these six categories cannot be separated from each other—they are all interlocked.

We must appraise the somber facts around these points before we can map a national direction. We must not shrink from clear-minded appraisal of our strengths, our weaknesses and the attainment of the purposes to which the Congress has committed us.

LAND WAR STRENGTHS

The first grim reality is the military strengths for land war in the world.

I am fully aware of the shortcomings of the term "divisions" as a measuring device for comparative military strength, but it is the nearest to a common descriptive unit that we have.

The Kremlin-directed horde has under arms and in reserves

probably 300 combat divisions, with 30,000 tanks. I am now told they have over 20,000 mostly tactical planes and they have with their satellites 50,000,000 men available for cannon fodder.

In World War II, when Russia was without the satellites, the Germans failed with 240 well-equipped divisions to overcome her. With her allies of General Manpower, General Space, General Winter, and General Scorched Earth, she had stopped the Germans even before Lend-Lease had reached her.

The nations of Europe in the Atlantic Pact have at the present moment less than 20 equipped and trained combat divisions available for European action.

There is here a stark reality upon which our foreign policies must be based. With any seeable land forces from non-Communist nations, even including the United States, a land offensive against the Communists could bring no military victory, no political conclusion. But that does not mean that there are no other methods of stopping the Kremlin's ambitions.

THE DEFENSE OF OUR GIBRALTAR
OF WESTERN CIVILIZATION

The second stark realism upon which our foreign policies must be based is the defense of the Western Hemisphere. Its defense is not only in our interests but in the interests of free men everywhere.

Much criticism is offered even to a discussion of this question. An atmosphere of hurry, rush, anxiety is being developed, the effect of which is to make it difficult, if not impossible, for the American people to judge their own situation.

I may say at once that with proper economic action this Hemisphere can be made self-contained in critical raw materials. From a long professional career and from years as Secretary of Commerce dealing with such questions, I might qualify as something of an expert in this field.

Also, unless we so dissipate our strength as to become a beaten and crushed people, we will be able to keep sea lanes open.

Moreover, this Hemisphere can be defended from Communist armies come what will. It is still surrounded with a great moat. To transport such invading armies either 3,000 miles across the Atlantic or 6,000 miles across the Pacific would require transport ships and naval protection which the Russians do not possess and could not build or seize, no matter what further countries they occupy. If we have a proper naval and air strength, we could sink them in mid-ocean. With somewhat more attention paid to our defense, this would apply to invasion by way of the Bering Straits. Hitler's armies could not even cross the English Channel. Bering Straits are much wider. Atomic bombs can do us damage but they do not transport troops over the ocean.

Communist armies can no more get to Washington than any allied armies can get to Moscow.

No responsible military man denies these two conclusions.

The American people should not be frightened into rash action by fear that we cannot survive. I am not advocating isolationism. But if other nations should fail, we may be isolated by force of circumstance and against our will.

We might go into a period hard to endure, but this nation can stick it out.

OUR AMERICAN ECONOMIC CAPACITY

The third stark realism upon which our policies must be built is our economic capacity. The bleak outlook of the world may well last more than a decade—possibly two of them.

The new budget calls for federal spending of over $71.6 billion. This $71 billions alone, plus state and local expenditures, is about 37 percent of our national income.

That is beyond the long endurance of any nation and fatal to the preservation of a system of free men.

The President has asked for a large increase of taxes. We will need also to increase state and local government taxes.

This burden is going to fall on people with smaller incomes. The proof of this is easy.

If all personal incomes above the level of a United States

Senator were confiscated it would yield only about $2.5 billion of additional revenues. But confiscation would stop most people earning the $2.5 billion. We must also remember that excise and corporation taxes in most part are ultimately passed on to the consumer or these milch cows would die.

Grim austerity must enter the door of every American home.

Even before these burdens are actually imposed there are stark signs of economic strain. The purchasing power of the dollar has fallen 20 percent in six months. The stock boom indicates that many people are seeking flight from inflation. Our already gigantic government debts permit little expansion without inflation of credit. Two wars prove economic controls cannot wholly stop inflation. The surest road away from inflation is to accept the President's wise proposal to "Pay-as-you-go."

But we simply cannot carry this expenditure or such tax load for long.

Spending, taxing, and inflating ourselves into economic exhaustion are the routes by which Stalin hopes to overcome the United States.

THE UNITED NATIONS

The fourth focal point of our thinking must be the United Nations.

Our stark reality here is the lack of cohesion and unity in the free nations. The representatives of 40 percent of all of the people in the free nations voted against us on Chinese aggression while their armies were killing thousands of American men. Even some of our European Allies are anxious to appease the Chinese branch of the Kremlin on policies of the United Nations.

Despite this, we must not forget that the aspiration of mankind for over a century has been to find peace by collective action against aggressors. The United Nation was built on this same central idea as were the Concert of Europe and the League of Nations. Halting and faulty as it may be, we cannot abandon this idea and this hope.

But it must be clear that the U.N. for the present will not be a substantial protection from Communist aggression.

OUR POLICIES IN THE FAR EAST

Our men are holding heroically to the mission assigned us by the United Nations in Korea. We are suffering great losses. General Marshall says we must send 15,000 men a month. We cannot yet see the end. But if we were to drive all the enemy out of Korea, how much of our armies must remain there to protect it?

Japan, Formosa, and the Philippines are vital links in our national security. This must not be minimized by nations anxious to direct our energies to Europe. We will need retain much military strength in the Pacific to protect those areas.

Certainly there is little stark reality in talking about American ground divisions in Europe at present in view of our involvement in Asia and our needs in Alaska.

THE NORTH ATLANTIC PACT

The sixth consideration in our decisions revolves around the North Atlantic Pact and the proposals to start another American expeditionary land army to Europe.

Current statements stretch this Pact far beyond its text. The Pact provides that the nations shall aid each other in case of attack. There has been no attack.

Moreover, at the time of ratification of that Alliance the Administration, through the Secretary of State and the Chairman of the Foreign Relations Committee, gave positive assurances that under the Pact no expeditions of American ground troops would be sent to Europe. That certainly meant no forces to Europe prior to attack. Our participation, prior to an attack, was to be limited to munitions. The Pact being the will of the American people through the Congress, and in the faith of the text and those promises, I subsequently supported the Alliance.

But last fall it became evident that the Administration was contemplating sending ground troops to Europe. It was also evident that after years of gigantic American subsidies the European Atlantic Pact nations had done nothing of consequence toward their own defense. Former Prime Minister Churchill had repeatedly and forthrightly stated this fact—the last occasion being only a few weeks ago.

I made two addresses in protest. Judging by the scolding of the European press, I may have helped to start them thinking.

Then General Eisenhower was appointed to organize their military strength. And the General has become the potent symbol of the policy of at once sending American ground troops to Europe.

The American people are indebted to General Eisenhower for many great services. He has magnificent fitness both for the command and the stimulation of spirit and action among the Allies in Europe.

But his appointment does not commit the American people as to policy.

The stark realities in Western Continental Europe are their large Communist parties and the disunities which gnaw at their vitals. Their prejudices prevent taking Spain into the Alliance with 20 divisions and the most defensible area in Europe. For some reason Turkey and Greece are excluded from the Alliance.

Equally vital is the fact that there is little hope of adequate land defense of Europe without West German participation. Two months ago detailed plans and great progress were announced. Now it is decided that West German military participation is out or can wait.

From press reports based on information from European officials and from General Eisenhower's statements, it would appear that his army, including the 2 American divisions now in Germany, will start with 9 or possibly 10 divisions; by the end of two years, including American divisions, it would seem to be 35 or 40 divisions.

The stark reality is that such an army is not one-third the strength of the enemy.

America is at present the major deterrent to the Kremlin's ambitions of world conquest. There is nothing that Stalin would like more than to get the United States into his clutches by fighting us on the ground in Europe. There lies his overwhelming strength.

Disaster could thus come to the American Hemisphere with no salvation to Europe.

THE AMERICAN PEOPLE NEED ANSWERS
TO SOME QUESTIONS

The American people should have more information before they risk trying a third expedition of ground troops to Europe.

Any defense line in Europe must be over 400 miles long. Will our responsible leaders make a public statement that the forces so far proposed, can defend this line against odds of three or four to one? We have tried this in Korea.

Is Stalin likely to remain quiet while large American armies are built up against him?

Will our responsible leaders tell us whether they contemplate the proposed American contingent as only an installment? Does not this contribution and our huge increase in the Army budget imply many more American divisions? Do the American people know all the facts?

ALTERNATIVE POLICIES

Despite all these stark realities and these problems, I have believed there is a way to at least an uneasy peace for the world.

In my address of six weeks ago, I stated that we should not land men or send money to Europe until large European forces were in sight. I was well aware of the obligation assumed by Congress to give aid in case of attack. It was my view that we should hold to the text of the Pact and the promises. I urged "arming our air and navy to the teeth."

I suggest that air power and the navy are the alternative to sending American land divisions to Europe. With our gigantic productive capacity and within our economic strength we can build and sustain overwhelming air and sea forces held on our home ground ready in case of attack.

Stalin well knows we could carry on that kind of war for his destruction for indefinite years.

The air threat has been during four years the most powerful deterrent to any attack on Western Europe. It is far more powerful than pouring American divisions into the reach of this

Asiatic horde. I am suggesting no attack from us. I am suggesting the very protection for Western Europe and our own defense which the Senate contemplated when it ratified the Atlantic Pact.

There are other reasons for such a policy—both military and economic.

Manifestly, if attack on Europe came, the free world would be inferior in ground forces. Such a ground war would at best be a war of defense. In the air we would have the offensive. An Air Force has range, speed, flexibility, and striking power which can come nearer gaining a decision than allied ground armies. Especially is this true, for in an air war the Communist horde would be without a large part of its ground allies, that is, General Manpower, General Space, General Winter, and General Scorched Earth.

The whole Korean tragedy is developing proof that the way to punish aggressors is from the air and sea and not by land armies. It would be infinitely less costly in dead and disaster.

The unbearable strain on our economic system will come from trying to do five things at the same time. That is, to maintain armies in the Pacific; to build up an air force; to build up a naval force; to furnish munitions to nations who are determined to defend themselves; and beyond that to send large armies to Europe. That is a greater burden than our economy can bear for long.

I can give you an indication of the lesser economic strain to attain the same or more power by air than by ground forces.

To train, equip, place in Europe, and maintain for one year 10 of the usual combinations of American divisions would cost about $4.5 billion. This same sum would, for example, purchase and man 390 B-36 long-range bombers, compared to the 60 of them which we now have. If neither went into battle, the annual cost of the 10 divisions would be about $3 billion and that of such a segment of the air force less than $1 billion.

POINTS OF REVISION OF OUR FOREIGN POLICIES

I can most clearly state the points of foreign policies in which many of us believe at this time by summarizing a program. No program can be perfect—none without risk. For the present I suggest:

1. We should devote our overwhelming productive power to air and naval strength and supply of munitions.

2. If the Europeans are attacked, and if they request it, we should be prepared to use such overwhelming air and naval power and to keep it up until the aggressor has had enough.

The Kremlin knows that we are committed by the Congress to do so. I believe that reserve, if large enough, is Europe's real protection.

3. We should supply munitions to nations doing their utmost to defend themselves.

4. From the starkly realistic, economic, political, and military reasons which I have given you, my personal conviction is that we should not create land armies for expeditions into the quicksands of either Europe or China. I do not want to even start on the road to another Korea.

5. There are those who think we should send more divisions to Europe before there is an attack. To them, I urge watchful waiting until much more will to prepare has been developed within Europe itself and until there is more evidence they have resolved their disunities.

6. We must reduce our national expenditures to a level we can carry over a long term of years, and thus avoid economic disaster which can destroy freedom in America.

Senator Byrd estimates that $8.6 billion of proposed non-defense expenditures in the budget could be reduced or postponed. We should spend all we can afford on air, navy, and munitions rather than on large armies.

7. We can and must defend Formosa, the Philippines, and Japan. We can do it by naval and air forces.

As to Korea, we should demand of the United Nations that they call for a stop of supplies to Communist China by the non-Communist nations.

Since Red China is making war on our American armies, we should free Chiang Kai-shek to do what he wishes in China and furnish him munitions.

8. I proposed three years ago that we should give full inde-

pendence to Japan and Western Germany under representative governments. During one hundred years these nations were the great dams against these Russian-controlled hordes. In the last war we may have been engaged in a great crusade for freedom of mankind, but we certainly destroyed these two dams. The sooner they are given their independence the sooner, for their own security, they will resume their ancient role.

9. Recently I proposed that if the nations of Europe failed we should, as a prudent nation, have in mind a second line of air and naval defense based upon the foreign shores of the Pacific and Atlantic oceans, both north and south, and I may add the Mediterranean and Indian oceans.

10. Congress should recover its constitutional authority over starting wars. There are resolutions before Congress to do this.

IN CONCLUSION

I have proposed no retreat, no withdrawal. I have proposed no repudiation of treaties or obligations. Rather I have proposed that the pledges to the Congress and the American people be kept. I have proposed that we stop, look, and listen before we start on a road of land war that risks the loss of all civilization.

I propose no good to Stalin. His greatest hope is to get us into a land war.

Before we go off the deep end of steps toward another land war in Europe, let us remember that we fought two such wars hoping to bring peace and we have no peace. We should be prepared to make heavy sacrifices to help. But we should do it with common sense, within our strength, with the long view of history in our minds.

The essence of the program I have proposed is to effectively restrain our enemies from attack upon our allies or ourselves. It is the best chance of peace—even if it is an uneasy peace.

If we pursue the lines of our own genius and resources, we can meet this—the greatest menace of a century.

And being in the right the Almighty is on our side.

On Defense of Europe

*Statement Before the Senate Committees
on Foreign Relations and the Armed Services
[February 27, 1951]*

I HAVE gone through the records of these hearings as carefully as I could and so far as they have included the testimony of military, Executive, and Congressional officials.

We can get at the heart of this national problem most effectively if I state the matters upon which there seems to be general agreement and afterward take up the areas of disagreement.

I believe it is agreed:

First. Our primary purpose must be to hold some sort of peace in the world—even an uneasy peace.

Second. There should be no preventive war.

Third. We must show a strength that will deter the aggression from this Communist-controlled mass.

Fourth. Up to date the major deterrent has been our air and naval potential.

Fifth. It is insisted by all the Air Force Officers—General Vandenberg, General Spaatz, General LeMay, General Whitehead, General George, and Major Seversky—that with sufficient increase in our air force we can ultimately destroy the war potential of Soviet Russia and her European satellites.

Sixth. I think it is agreed by all the high military officers who have testified here that we could not gain victory over the Communist land mass by ground troops without prior protracted air destruction of Soviet war potential.

23

Seventh. There is a limit to the economic and military burden that the United States can bear.

Eighth. That Western Europe, both the North Atlantic Pact and other non-Communist nations, should make the utmost effort on their own behalf.

THE MILITARY SITUATION

To make the military situation clear and before I get into the points of differences in views, it is necessary that we should briefly review the military strengths of the North Atlantic Pact nations with their 300 million people on one side and the Communist land mass of 800 million people on the other.

A State Department listing of respective military strengths, furnished you under date of February 15, requires a realistic analysis. It gives the armed forces of the North Atlantic Pact nations, including reserves, as 7,100,000 men, and those of the Communist nations, including China, as 5,965,000, thus conveying an impression of the overpowering military strength of the North Atlantic Pact nations.

While "organized reserves" were included in the men available in the North Atlantic Pact nations, this State Department statement obviously omitted the trained reserves available in the Communist nations. If the reserves were included, the Communist forces would probably exceed 10,000,000 men.

If we analyze this State Department statement from the point of view of ground armies, the numerical disparity becomes overwhelming against the North Atlantic Pact nations. The Soviet active ground forces, with tanks and tactical air strength, is given as 175 divisions, to which must be added about 50 European satellite divisions, and probably 50 Chinese divisions, or a total of some 275 divisions. And to these must be added probably as many reserve divisions.

The State Department statement gives the North Atlantic Pact nations 2,632,000 ground forces and 2,724,000 "organized reserves," which includes naval and air reserves. The effectiveness of these ground forces for use in Europe must be reduced by a large amount. Many of them must be retained for home defense of these nations and for defenses in other parts of the world. If the situation be examined from the point of view of the actual "battleworthy" divisions available for European action, it diminishes still further. For instance, France is quoted as having now 600,000 armed ground forces and 1,500,000 reserves. But General Eisenhower has informed your committees that France can contribute to his army two years hence either 15 or 25 battleworthy divisions, or 400,000 men. Even if it is 25 divisions, that is a far different picture from 2,100,000 armed forces and reserves. In fact, the evidence before your committees points to the European composition of General Eisenhower's army at the present moment (exclusive of American divisions) as only 13 divisions, with about 40 divisions total expected in two years.

The proposed United States ground army will include the equivalent of about 27 combat ground divisions, of which at least 17 divisions will likely be required to defend Alaska and the United States and to keep Far Eastern commitments. Thus, unless the United States raises large armies in addition to those announced at present, we can hardly supply Europe with more than 10 divisions. The total of General Eisenhower's army, with this addition, might reach 50 divisions.

THE FOUR-DIVISION PROPOSAL

It is proposed that 4 divisions be now added to our 2 divisions already in the occupation of Germany, making General Eisenhower's army at the start say 19 divisions. The Administration representatives have repeatedly refused before your committees to take a commitment limiting this contingent to 4 divisions only. They demand no restrictions. Therefore, this seeming proposal of 4 divisions is not limited. In fact, it is probably only the first installment of American troops.

The strategic purposes of these 4 additional divisions are argued as, first, to lift the morale of Western Europe; second, to protect our 2 divisions of occupation troops in Germany; and, third, to protect our "nearby" air bases on the Continent of Europe.

It seems generally agreed that, as air power takes time for attrition, the Communists with their huge armies and accumulated supplies can at the present time overrun this initial army and all Europe before the Russian war potential could be destroyed.

PROTECTING AIR BASES

As to the argument that these 4 American divisions could protect our nearby air bases on the Continent of Europe, one of our most eminent air officers expressed the conviction that he wanted these bases "protected by a strip of water." That means the English Channel, the Mediterranean, or the Atlantic Ocean or parts thereof. He seemed to believe that, with the British Air forces, we could protect bases in England. Certainly General Eisenhower's initial army—or his army two years hence—could not protect these Continental bases in case of a Russian ground avalanche.

MORALE BUILDING

We should examine this question of morale building both from the evidence before your committees and the common knowledge from many reliable observers.

It must be acknowledged that the will to preparedness of the European Atlantic Pact nations (outside of Britain) has been most discouraging. Aside from the Marshall Plan subsidies over four years, it has now been two years since the North Atlantic Pact was published. Under Article III of this Pact, each member agreed to develop its own armed forces to resist attack. So far as is known, despite our supplies of resources, hardly a battleworthy division has been created by any of the Continental European members in these two years. There has been some evidence of more action recently, but it does not represent a burst of speed.

These European North Atlantic Pact nations, which today have less than 15 battleworthy divisions available, did, in both World War I and World War II, place 170 such divisions in the field in sixty days. Their manpower and industrial potential are greater today. And we might add to this proven capacity of 170 divisions say 50 to 60 possible divisions from West Germany, or a total of 220 to 230 divisions.

The problem of summoning of Continental armies is much deeper than can be cured by encouragement. These peoples are weary from the horrors of war and their sufferings under enemy occupations. Deeper still are the forces of internal and international disunities. These underlying forces need more objective examination on the ground. They would include:

1. Many non-Communist persons on the Continent hold a dread of racial destruction. They fear that their people will be further bled white, their homes and cities again destroyed, and they would prefer an unopposed Soviet occupation to seeing their homelands become another European battlefield.

2. The 20- to 30-percent Communist vote in France and Italy is not only virtually impervious to "morale building" against Soviet Russia, but these nations are in positive danger from disloyalties in battle and the sabotage from the Communist-controlled labor unions in their strategic industries.

3. The left wing of the large Socialist vote of Continental countries is probably less unsympathetic to Communist ideology than to what they call capitalism.

4. Italy is limited by treaty to about 3 or 4 divisions of troops which, as the testimony before your committees indicated, will be kept within their own borders.

5. Large elements in all the parliaments of the European North Atlantic Pact nations continue to oppose the incorporation of Spain in the alliance. Even were this agreed to, my information is that Generalissimo Franco, having no confidence in the present plans for ground forces, would not take his armies out of Spain.

6. West Germany could make a critical addition to the Western European forces. The French have three times in the lives of living men been brutally invaded by the Germans. They so far refuse to agree to such a rearming of Germany as would command German support.

7. As to the building up of European morale, we have given three great impulses already.

First. Our treaty obligations under the North Atlantic Pact.

Second. The gigantic effort we are making in the United States for common protection in case of attack.

Third. The fact that the United States is bearing 85 percent to 90 percent of the whole military expenditures of the North Atlantic Pact nations.

If these are not sufficient stimulant to their morale, it can hardly be created by exhibits of a few American divisions in Europe.

What these Continental European nations need is resolution to pull out of their disunities. That is not a question of morale, it is a question of high and determined statesmanship.

GENERAL EISENHOWER'S 50-DIVISION ARMY TWO YEARS HENCE

At the present time it is difficult to see the European sources for even 40 battleworthy divisions for General Eisenhower's army two years hence. If we assume there are to be 10 American divisions, his force would still be only 50 divisions.

As I understand the testimony given to you, no higher military success could be expected from General Eisenhower's army than some delay in a Communist invasion.

Our infantry officers contend that Europe can be defended with "adequate" ground forces, but nowhere do they define "adequate." Certainly no one mentioned 50 divisions as "adequate."

The concept of "delaying action" appears to be a sort of Dunkirk strategy. And this lurking Dunkirk idea appears also in the argument put forward to your committees that the four American divisions to be sent to Europe could the more successfully "get out" of Germany our 2 occupation divisions.

As to the deterrent effect of General Eisenhower's army, General Collins was apparently of the opinion that such an army would be so small that it would not attract Stalin's attention. We are, therefore, between two poles—so small as not to attract attention or so large as to attract the lightning. That decision is Stalin's—not ours.

Much of the argument here has been based on Europe's "doing its part." Suppose it does not do an adequate part for reasons of its own—what then? Do we withdraw our 4 divisions or our 10 divisions, or do we propose to supplement the deficiency with great American armies?

I venture the assertion that Continental Europe cannot be defended with less than 100 to 125 battleworthy divisions. In my own view, with less forces than that number from European sources, there is the utmost jeopardy of involving the United States in a full-sized land war in Europe against these overwhelming odds.

It seems to me that there is only one real salvation for Europe at the present moment. That is, to build up the air and naval power of the United States and Britain so as to overwhelm Russia in case of attack.

All this brings me to other large considerations:

First. Any war with the Communists will be world-wide. I have not been impressed with the idea that we can hold a war with Russia to the European theatre. We may be involved in a Communist invasion of Japan, or of the Middle East in search for oil, and an air attack on the United States. We must be mobile in a world sense and not wholly tied to the Western Europe theatre.

We cannot stop a sudden Communist avalanche over the continent of Europe with any present contemplated land armies. The only way I see to handle such a global situation is an air force of such range that we can reach our targets from air bases more remote than the Continental Pact countries, even from the United States, together with naval power.

Second. The problem of our economic strength arises at once. I do not believe we can make the adequate long-distance bomber defense, which our air officers urge, and at the same time create large ground armies. The proposal of a 100-division army also requires an air force increased to where it can surely destroy Communist war potential. To these costs must be added large war and naval protections for the United States. We must maintain Federal and local governments. All of which would require an annual governmental expenditure of somewhere in excess of $150 billion per annum—perhaps in excess of 160 billion. Such an economic burden is unthinkable if we intend to maintain free men in the United States. Certainly there should be no hasty decisions in these matters.

All the testimony of the Air Force officers was to the effect that the Air must be the Number One priority. Within our economic strength, we can make no great army and at the same time make such an adequate air force that there will be no mistake about where we stand and what we can do.

You have in the testimony of the infantry and air officers an implied conflict of view as to organizing large ground forces versus air forces. The sending of American ground armies to Europe at this time is based on many intangibles and is a step into the dangerous unknown. Developing of overwhelming air and naval forces would be an acceptance of known experience and the confident consequence of our air men based upon more tangibles.

These decisions must be based upon political and economic consequences as well as military considerations. I think the committees will agree that these factors must be determined by the civilian side of our Government of which the Congress is so vital a part.

Moreover, these decisions with which we are confronted are the more necessary from the Congress because of the gigantic shift in the Administration's policies since the North Atlantic Pact was ratified on the promise of no American ground armies in Europe over to the adoption now of such a course. The decision today is not merely a decision to send 4 divisions in addition to our 2 occupation divisions in Germany. It is a decision that will most likely lead to "Operation Land War in Europe."

Therefore, I believe the Congress should make two determinations: First, are we going to have, in addition to naval forces, such an unquestioned effective air force as lies within our economic strength to provide, or are we to have less air and less army forces with less certainty of results?

And, second, are we going to embark on Operation Land War in Europe?

The Congress surely still has some Constitutional authority in these matters.

Remarks Before the Annual Dinner of American Newspaper Publishers Association, New York City [April 26, 1951]

YOUR Chairman has charged that I touched off something the press calls The Great Debate. If that is true, you ought to be grateful to me. Your front pages would have been less exciting and your editors without inspiration to such turgid language.

But Joseph Stalin should get no satisfaction from our practice of free speech. He should study how Kaiser Wilhelm, Hitler, Mussolini, and Tojo mistook our family discussions. He would observe that this Republic has a fashion of closing ranks at the appropriate moment with a solidarity and a punch that is final.

On Behalf of
"Crusade for America"

Nation-wide Television Broadcast from New York City
[September 23, 1951]

I AM happy to take part here. The purpose of this presentation scarcely needs restatement. Those who appear on this stage represent every segment of American thought and American political organization—except the Communists and fellow travelers. Being a people of many varieties we do not often see such unity as this on an idea in America.

Our people have discarded the illusion that this is one world. Out of bitter experience they have learned it is two worlds. It is divided by opposing concepts of life. One is good; the other is evil.

The 800,000,000 peoples under Communist domination are being entirely misled as to the whole base of Western civilization. By their iron curtains they try to stop all knowledge of the real life and ideals of other nations. In their ignorance they are being indoctrinated for war by misrepresentation that we of the Western World are preparing to destroy them.

The purpose of this association is to penetrate this wall with the arm of truth, of faith, and of hope. We want these subjected, enslaved peoples to know of our good will. We want them to know of the evil men who dominate them.

This is not an activity of the American Government. It is a voluntary, organized effort of the American people them-

33

selves to extend the light of hope and faith into the other world of darkness. I urge your support.

If this work could wholly succeed, it would bring peace to the earth.

It may not do that much but every mite is some help to a distraught world.

The Year Since the Great Debate

Nation-wide Broadcast from New York City
[January 27, 1952]

THE Sabbath Day is an appropriate day to discuss our problems of peace. Unfortunately on this Sabbath Day, despite our full good will to mankind, peace rests upon defense from Communist aggression. And that is defense of our religious faiths.

One year ago we engaged in a great debate on our foreign and military policies.

At that time we were repeatedly told that United States policies were based upon what was called "a calculated risk" which meant risk of war or economic degeneration. With that as a basis of national policies, a changing world demands constant recalculation of risk and reconsideration of alternatives.

The risks are so great that with our experience over the past year, the Congress should now again recalculate.

I do not propose on this occasion to review how we got into these dangerous cold and hot wars, but to start from where we are now.

To indicate the necessity for recalculation of risks, I will make a short appraisal of the situations in the world.

WHAT HAS HAPPENED IN EUROPE

A year ago, when I addressed the American people, the North Atlantic Pact had been in operation for over a year. Up to that time, despite huge subsidies and sacrifices by the American people, the nations of Europe, except Britain, had done

35

little in mutual defense. And in this address, unless otherwise stated, I do not include Britain in the term "Continental" or "Western Europe."

During the course of the debate a year ago we were told that a European defense army of upward of 40 ground divisions would be created under General Eisenhower by the end of 1952, with 20 more divisions by the end of 1954.

We were told 4 more American divisions were to be shipped to Europe in addition to the 2 we already had there.

What has happened?

The rearming of Western Europe is mainly dependent upon the French and the Germans. A year ago, in urging that we send our divisions, General Eisenhower stated to the Congress that the French promised 15 battleworthy divisions presumably by the end of 1952 and more by the end of 1953. A few days ago, the French Defense Minister indicated that they contemplated only 10 divisions for the European army of which none was complete and half of them were only 50 percent recruited.

The settlement by which Western Germany is to be given a certain degree of independence and is to contribute 12 divisions has not yet gone beyond the paper stage. No battleworthy German divisions are in sight—certainly not before 1953.

The British have announced that their 4 divisions now on the continent will not be a part of the European army but that they "will co-operate." Britannia would be a friend but would not marry Mr. Europe. That is a form of independence.

In sum, the only substantial additions to Western European ground armies during the two years past have been the American divisions we have sent over.

Aside from American and British divisions it would be difficult to find 10 battleworthy divisions in the Western European army today. And it would appear that even the 60-division army is two or three years away.

This proposed 60-division army compares with over 200 equipped divisions which these same Western European nations placed in the field within sixty days after the outbreak of each World War. And their manpower and productivity are greater today.

In that debate a year ago, we were told that the Communist armies comprised 300 divisions, 20,000 planes, and 30,000 tanks. No one contended that 60 European divisions, even if created, could do more than temporarily halt an invasion. Our side in that debate replied that this was not a calculated risk but that it was a calculated Dunkirk.

I may say at once that all the American people are interested in the growth of unity in Continental Europe and their preparation of adequate ground armies for their defense. We earnestly hope that General Eisenhower will succeed in his difficult task.

There has been some progress during the past year in allaying age-old discords and dissensions. But they are obviously not yet cured.

Among forces which obstruct progressive Western European statesmen are the potent Socialist and Communist parties. These parties also have widely spread the belief that our subsidies and our urging are for the purpose of using Europe for American cannon fodder. Yet the Western European nations are contributing less than 10 percent of the total military expenditures of the North Atlantic Pact nations.

Another cause of Western European inertia is its attitude as to the risk of Communist invasion. That attitude is profoundly different from the attitude of Washington.

There is in Europe today no such public alarm as has been fanned up in the United States. None of those nations has declared emergencies or taken measures comparable with ours. They do not propagandize war fears or war psychosis such as we get out of Washington. Not one European country conducts such exercises in protection from bombs as we have had in New York.

I recently made an inquiry from European sources as to why they calculate this risk of invasion as so much less than does Washington.

The sum of this inquiry was that there was little public belief that there was risk of a Russian invasion in the near future. Their reasons for this belief were:

First. They said that the Russian ground armies could have overrun Western Europe in a two-months' campaign any time in the past five years and can no doubt do it during several years to come. That they have not done so seems proof to these observers that the Kremlin realizes several difficulties in making a Red world out of the West.

Second. They said that the Communists hesitate to stir up a war in the West because they can see no final military victory. That the Russians know they cannot invade the United States with armies, however much they might possibly trouble us with bombs. Therefore, they said the Russians have no taste for a war where they cannot effectively destroy their enemy.

Third. They stated that the Kremlin realizes that invasion of Western Europe would add a dozen nationalities to the centrifugal forces and oppositions which already trouble them from the thirty-odd races they dominate. They said the proof of these internal oppositions was the fact that the Communists have sent 15 million politically objectionable persons to slave camps. In addition, nationalism is not dead in those nations, as witness Yugoslavia.

Fourth. They said the Kremlin knows that the industrial potential they would secure by invading Western Europe is mostly an illusion. The reason they gave is that if Western Europe were blockaded by the Americans or British, and Russian transport into Europe were paralyzed by bombing, Europe would be without oil, 30 percent short of other fuel, 25 percent short in food, and without nonferrous and hardening metals. They stated that under such a blockade, Western European industrial production would diminish rapidly and ultimately fail.

Fifth. They said the Kremlin has at last learned that its conspiracies of boring from within have failed to secure more than a minor percentage of men's minds in the Western World. Its left-arm activities have there raised implacable walls to such ideological victories.

Sixth. They said the opportunities for the Kremlin are in Asia and that its face is turned East.

Seventh. They said Stalin has every reason to be satisfied with the progress of economic confusion in the United States and in Western Europe.

Eighth. Finally, they said the Communists know that, if they invade Western Europe, their own war potential will be destroyed by an atomic war from the air and a blockade from the sea, even if they succeed on land.

I cannot say whether these eight assumptions are correct or not. But they do contribute to Western Europe's lack of hysterics and their calculation of low risk and, therefore, their lack of hurry to arm.

In any event this whole European situation requires that the United States recalculate our own risks and reconsider the possible alternatives.

WHAT HAS HAPPENED IN ASIA AND THE MIDDLE EAST

In South Asia and the Middle East we are witnessing vast readjustments of political power. Behind the slogan "Asia for the Asiatics" lie two centuries of the white man's exploitation. These forces have lighted a prairie fire of revolution against the West. They are removing the "white man's burden."

America had no part in this exploitation. Yet too often we find that many of these nations vote against the United States in the United Nations.

During the past year in Korea, the United Nations vetoed General MacArthur's policies of destroying the Chinese air sanctuary in Manchuria and the employment of Chiang Kai-shek's armies to save American lives. Accordingly we denied ourselves victory.

A negotiation was begun six months ago for a cease-fire. The American people welcomed its promise to stop the loss of blood and lives of their sons. But three things have come of it. Far from cease-fire over 20,000 Americans have been wounded, and nearly 5,000 have been killed since the negotiations began.

Yet in this negotiation we have retreated from the original purpose of unity and independence for Korea to an appeasement idea of a division of Korea about where it was before. Finally, during these negotiations the Chinese have built up a great air force. What the outcome may be, we do not know. But I will presently suggest some lessons we now ought to learn from this experience.

WHAT HAS HAPPENED IN THE UNITED STATES

The outstanding phenomenon in the United States is the dangerous overstraining of our economy by our gigantic expenditures.

The American people have not yet felt the full impact of the gigantic increase in Government spending and taxes. Yet we already suffer from the blight of inflation and confiscatory taxes.

INFLATION

We are actually in a war economy without any world-wide shooting. We are diverting more and more civilian production to war materials. We are placing a greater portion of our manpower under arms. All this creates scarcity in civilian goods and increases spending power; both of which fan the flames of inflation.

We are constantly told that measures are being taken by the Government to "prevent" inflation. This ignores the fact that we are in the middle of inflationary operations at this very minute. Even since the end of the Second World War the purchasing power of our money, measured in wholesale prices, has decreased 40 percent.

Controls of the type we have imposed on wages and prices cannot in the long run prevent inflation. The experience of six great commercial nations in two wars has proved that controls are, at best, a retarding device.

Under the demands of Washington we are confronted with a probable Federal deficit of $30 to $40 billions for immediate rearmament. We already have government obligations and currency of $280 billion. And private credit is dangerously over-expanded. In the brief period since the war, it has swelled by $130 billion.

The Government will need to cover part of its deficit by selling its bonds or notes, some part of which must be sold to the banks. That is direct inflation of credit and results in an addition to the currency in the form of bank check money.

The two pressures—scarcities and expanding credit or paper money—are the irresistible forces of inflation. They are already being expressed in gray markets and a sporadic spiral of higher wages and then higher prices.

Our standard of living will be reduced in millions of families. Lifetime savings will be taken from millions of other families. Rising prices are coming through the kitchen while taxes are invading our homes through the front door.

TAXES

These huge taxes are also overstraining our economy. Moreover they have probably reached the point of diminishing return. That is indicated by the fact that the various taxes on the top bracket incomes can possibly exceed 100 percent. If all remaining untaxed income above the level of the salary and expense allowance of a United States Senator were confiscated, it would bring only about $2 billions annually to the Federal Treasury. That would last less than ten days. And that assumes that these taxpayers would continue to work for nothing, which they will not do.

It is the average family who pays the bulk of taxes, both income and hidden. Among them are corporation taxes. These are ultimately passed on to their customers or the corporation would quickly go bankrupt.

Families with income of from $3,000 to $4,000 a year will pay in total taxes an average of over $900 per year. The double effect of inflation and taxes is indicated by the fact that a family with $3,000 net annual income ten years ago must now earn over $6,000 to maintain the same standard of living.

And this spending and taxes is not a quickie program soon over. When our great military forces are assembled, they must continue to be paid for. Due to constant new inventions in weapons, the new devices must continuously replace the old. That will cost more billions.

A man can carry a load of 300 pounds across the room, but he will break his back if he carries it around the block.

Communism is an evil thing. It is contrary to the spiritual, moral, and material aspirations of man. These very reasons give rise to my conviction that it will decay and die of its own poisons. But that may be many years away and, in the meantime, we must be prepared for a long journey.

There are men who welcome these inflation and tax pressures because these forces drive to socialize the income of our people. That is the inevitable end, even if it were not the avowed purpose. If this form of creeping socialism continues, we may be permitted to hold the paper title to property, while bureaucracy spends our income. Along this road the erosion of our productive capital and the destruction of incentives to economic progress are inevitable.

SOME ALTERNATIVE CALCULATIONS OF RISK THAT MIGHT BE CONSIDERED BY THE CONGRESS

In view of this past year's experience, and these rising pressures, the Congress should again re-examine our situation.

I believe there are methods more effective to check the Communist menace in the long run and at the same time to lessen our domestic dangers.

As a basis for test I may repeat the essentials of the proposals some of us made a year ago which were supported by many military and economic authorities:

First. That the first national purpose of this republic must be the defense of this final Gibraltar of freedom—that is the Western Hemisphere.

Second. That the only way to save Europe from destruction it to avoid the third world war. The real and effective deterrent which we can, within our resources, contribute to that end is in co-operation with the British to expand our already strong air forces and navies up to a striking force. The Communists know that such a striking force could destroy their military potential if they started an invasion and it could punish any such aggression. And this applies to aggression against other non-Communist countries as well as Western Europe.

In Korea, however correct the original decisions to use ground armies may have been, our experience during the past year has certainly demonstrated that we should have relied upon air and sea forces to punish that aggression. We could have avoided most of the sacrifice of 20,000 American boys and the injury of 80,000 others. The long-run injury to the South Koreans would have been less devastating.

Third. That the only way we can hold the initiative in this cold war is not to scatter our ground armies all around the 25,000 miles of Communist borders but to concentrate on such a highly mobile striking force by air and sea.

Three weeks ago General Wedemeyer, one of our greatest military strategists, stated we should not dissipate our ground armies over the world and should put our emphasis upon a striking force of air and sea power.

Fourth. That we should furnish such munitions as we can afford to other nations who show a determined will to defend themselves.

Fifth. That maintaining the economic strength of the United States and preventing its socialization does not permit our building up great ground armies in addition to overwhelming air and sea forces and supply of munitions to other nations. If our economy should collapse, Stalin's victory would be complete. We cannot take that risk.

Sixth. That true friendship with Western European nations requires they be told certain things in no uncertain terms. They should realize the limit of our economic aid is this deterrent air and sea power and munitions. That, protected by this shield, we expect them on the basis of their performance in previous wars, and now with the aid of munitions from us to realize that ground armies are Europe's own problem. We should state that we expect them to provide ground protection to our airfields within their boundaries. We should state that not only will we send no more ground troops, but that we expect they will rapidly relieve us of that burden except to protect our airfields outside the NATO countries.

And they should be told that their delays leave our 250,000 American garrison in Europe in a most exposed position.

Seventh. Our relations to the United Nations Charter should be revised. It must not be allowed to dominate the internal sovereignty of our Government. Our courts have already made decisions that the Charter overrides our domestic laws.

IN CONCLUSION

Recalculation of our policies along these lines would greatly reduce our economic risks. By restricting our ground armies and ultimately reducing them to the force necessary to protect our homeland and our essential air bases outside of European NATO countries, together with a reduction or postponement of 30 percent in our Federal civil expenditures, we could assure our economic strength. We could return thousands of young men to their shops, their farms, and their colleges. We could apply real brakes upon this drift to inflation; we might stop the plunge into socialism; we could avoid increase in taxes. But above all, we could better halt the spread of Communist imperialism.

It has been said that in these evil times peace can be preserved only through strength. That is true. But the center and final reserve of strength of the free world lies in the North American continent. Nothing must be permitted to weaken this bastion. We should recalculate our risks.

I pray that we shall have peace and preservation of our American way of life. I hold firmly to the belief that a third world war is neither necessary nor inevitable.

And in this summary of our position and our prospects I have used only facts and the terms of sober reason. But because I have avoided words appropriate to a deep emotion, this statement may not convey the extent of my anxiety for the future of my country and the world. But I must admit that on this Sabbath Day that anxiety is even greater than one year ago.

Nevertheless I am firm in my confidence and my belief that an informed American people can and will solve these menacing problems.

God bless you all.

Endorsement of Mr. Hoover's
Address of January 27, 1952

Statement to the Press
[February 7, 1952]

THE country should know that men of great experience and high rank from the Army, Navy, Air Force, and diplomatic service have endorsed the proposals of my address of January 27. They have authorized me to quote their statements.

Among the experienced army and air officers, I attach statements from Lieutenant General Albert C. Wedemeyer, Lieutenant General Leslie R. Groves, Lieutenant General Harold L. George, Major General Hugh Knerr, General Brice P. Disque. Among experienced naval officers, Admiral William V. Pratt, Admiral William H. Standley, Admiral H. E. Yarnell, and Congressman and former Naval Captain James E. Van Zandt, an officer in both wars.

Of men from the diplomatic service, I attach messages from:

Former Under Secretaries of State Henry P. Fletcher and William R. Castle; former Ambassadors Hugh Gibson, Spruille Braden, Joseph P. Kennedy, and Arthur Bliss Lane. I append also a message from Mr. Jesse Jones.

The statements which follow are given verbatim.

FORMER ARMY AND AIR OFFICERS

Lieutenant General
ALBERT C. WEDEMEYER:

"I completely concur with Ex-President Hoover's searching analysis of the world situation. He recognizes the importance of conserving our manhood while exploiting to the fullest degree our technological and industrial superiority. Translated into military forces this means air power supplemented by sea power and minimum ground forces."

Lieutenant General
LESLIE R. GROVES:

"I hope that Mr. Hoover's words will not be ignored as they were a year ago just because they make unpleasant reading. As he points out the great danger of our position is overextension in international commitments, both economic and military. It will take courage to revise our present policies, to admit our mistakes, and even to accept minor, and we hope temporary, defeats.

"As Mr. Hoover suggests, our military policy should be based on air and sea where our great technical capabilities can be put to best advantage rather than on the ground where the number of bayonets is of prime importance."

Lieutenant General
HAROLD L. GEORGE:

"That talk contains the basic elements around which should be developed our national and military policy. This country must realize that the creation of a dominant air power constitutes the first military priority of the United States. A powerful American Air Force, in being, constitutes the greatest possible power to preserve peace in this unsettled world. It does not seem to me that even this great Nation can afford to spend vast billions of dollars indiscriminately over a period of years to create a great army, a great navy, a great air force, and also provide the arms and equipment for the military forces of other nations without economic bankruptcy. A strong economy is vitally essential for this country's long term battle against Communism. Unless our economic structure is kept strong and healthy, we cannot for long maintain the military strength essential for our survival."

Major General
HUGH KNERR:

"Congratulations on your sound military views so clearly presented in your Sunday TV and radio broadcast. You have opened the doors and windows to a breath of fresh air with your realistic, common-sense plan for insuring the continuation of American ideals in this conflict with Communist dogma and in-human action. In line with your powerful speech I am convinced:

"First. The industrial power of the United States is the only enemy that Russia fears. Therefore, we should make certain that nothing undermines this potential to stop anything that Russia may want to start.

"Second. Russia has no cause to fear land armies of any other powers. Therefore, it would not seem logical to devote any more of our industrial power to the creation of land power.

"Third. In the present cold war with Russia, we are being treated to a typical example of the oriental method of wearing down his opponent psychologically to the point where the opponent will give up piecemeal the very weapons which the oriental fears. In Korea, we clearly see this method at work. No decision is ever made by the oriental on any basis other than power. If he believes he holds the upper hand, he will use every cunning device at his disposal to cause his enemy to give up in exasperation.

"Fourth. The people of the United States are apparently unable to realize that the principles of fair play have absolutely no place in the totalitarian picture. In their view, the end always justifies the means. Therefore, we should adopt a realistic attitude in order to make certain that we can insure a continuation of the principles of fair play by fighting fire with fire.

"Fifth. Sea power is an essential adjunct of air power. However, we cannot devote an unbalanced amount of our industrial resources to forms of sea power that can be readily sunk. Rather, our naval power should be limited to those forms that are essential to keeping open sea lines of communication. And an excess of water-borne aviation is vulnerable to the rapidly growing Russian submarine menace. We need a good balance between the tactical naval power and offensive land-based air power.

"Sixth. Finally, the United States possesses all of the aces in this game that we are playing, but for some reason persists in discarding them and playing with deuces. As your speech so ably puts it, our aces are air power and sea power. We currently possess the capacity to destroy Russia's source of land power, and they know it. However, we are eroding away our superiority through an unwillingness to face reality. We set a deadline and when the deadline arrives, we back away from it to another deadline. We have the air power and sea-borne power to back up our demands for a decision right now. The procrastination that has been taking place on the plea that we are not ready is disproved by the simple fact that Russia has not already attacked us.

"I sincerely hope that your masterly presentation will be used as a guide for our Congress and the National Defense establishment."

General
BRICE P. DISQUE:

". . . As an old soldier of over fifty years experience in many parts of the world, in the regular Army and civil life, including three wars, I urge you to consider our former President's broadcast of last Sunday as the most significant statement that has been made since he spoke about a year ago.

"A re-examination of our foreign policy is an immediate and transcendent necessity. It must result in the recapture by the Congress of your constitutional duty and powers over war and spending if our nation is to survive. As a soldier, I assure you without hesitation that no regular army officer of my acquaintance and for whom I have respect will question Mr. Hoover's reasoning with respect to the military content of his proposals."

NAVAL OFFICERS

Admiral
WILLIAM V. PRATT
(Former Chief of Naval Operations)

"I agree with every word you said."

Admiral
WILLIAM H. STANDLEY
(Former Chief of Naval Operations and Ambassador to Russia):

"Again I am in entire accord with views expressed in your broadcast last Sunday. Factually your statements cannot be denied and I am in hearty agreement with the picture of the future as portrayed by you. Since my return from duty in Russia, and from knowledge of actual conditions there, I have persistently contended that a shooting war with Russia is very improbable for the reason that from an economic standpoint Russia is unable to carry on an aggressive war. Furthermore in my opinion the Russian people will not support an aggressive war, and lastly, since VJ Day a more potent reason why Russia does not want an aggressive war, flows from the fact that Stalin knows the policies the U.S. is pursuing will wreck our capitalistic system just as surely and possibly more quickly than would a shooting war, so why should Moscow bring on a shooting war? I believe you are right, Sir, when you predict that 'an informed American people can save America' and I hope they can be informed in time. It is later than they think."

Admiral
HARRY E. YARNELL:

"I endorse Mr. Herbert Hoover's speech of Sunday 100 percent. If our leaders would only follow Mr. Hoover's advice, we would soon be out of this mess we are now in."

Congressman
JAMES E. VAN ZANDT
(Former Captain in the Navy and Former Commander in Chief,
Veterans of Foreign Wars):

"President Hoover's program of an overwhelming powerful striking force of air and sea power is something which we
can afford to build and which will be the best possible war deterrent. This force, together with aid for Europe in the form of
munitions, can be created well within the limits of our budget.
Mr. Hoover's speech yesterday is a blueprint for the guidance of
the Congress and should win the support of all Republicans and
anti-Administration Democrats."

(Congressman Van Zandt pointed out that the address of
January 27 did not propose immediate withdrawal of troops
from Europe as some of the press implied.)

FORMER DIPLOMATIC SERVICE

HENRY P. FLETCHER
(Former Under Secretary of State and Ambassador to Chile,
Mexico, Belgium, and Italy):

"Please allow me to congratulate you on your broadcast
statement on Sunday afternoon last on our foreign policy. I am
in entire agreement with you that it should be re-examined and
reassessed in view of the changed and changing world situation.
Under the guise of containment or Communism we seem to be
drifting into a new Holy Alliance to suppress the aspirations of
subject peoples who have heretofore looked upon the United
States as champions of liberty. Our foreign policy is leading us
to the verge of financial bankruptcy but also toward the bankruptcy of our democratic ideals.

"I sincerely hope that your address will be pondered and
appraised by our people, the Congress and the Administration
on the high plane and in the same patriotic spirit which inspired
it. You have only asked us to stop, look, and listen before we
are overrun by events beyond our control."

WILLIAM R. CASTLE

(Former Director of European Division, Department of State, Under Secretary of State, Ambassador to Japan):

"I fully endorse your proposals. Your presentation squarely and honestly faces the problems we have to solve. Unless our aid is given more wisely and only to those willing to help themselves, we shall lose the cold war—and our own security. Your proposals can bring no satisfaction to the Kremlin."

HUGH GIBSON

(Former Ambassador to Belgium, Poland, Switzerland, and Brazil and delegate to numerous International Conferences):

"Heartily endorse your Sunday address and hope our people will follow your wise counsel as to measures necessary to safeguard our national welfare."

SPRUILLE BRADEN

(Former Assistant Secretary of State and Ambassador to Argentina, Colombia, and Cuba):

"As an American citizen I am grateful for the wisdom and patriotism of your CBS address yesterday. I pray that our people take it to heart and insist that our policies be guided by it."

JOSEPH P. KENNEDY

(Former Ambassador to Great Britain):

"You have done many noble things for your country, but your talk today must be classed as the greatest. Your very voice indicated the depth of your feeling. Not only as your friend but as a father I am grateful for your words. God bless you."

ARTHUR BLISS LANE

(Minister to Estonia and Latvia and Ambassador to Colombia and Poland):

"Heartiest congratulations on your splendid address. Our present foreign policy based on 'a calculated risk' and on the

Teheran, Yalta, and Potsdam agreements must be realistically and ethically rebuilt if we are to regain our prestige abroad and effectively defend our own national security."

JESSE JONES
(Former Secretary of Commerce and Chairman of the R.F.C.):

"I believe you spoke the thoughts and feelings of a great majority of the American people."

FROM THE PEOPLE

I have also received a flood of messages from citizens in all parts of the country. Perhaps the most heartwarming are the hand-written letters from a great multitude of American homes.

Address at the Republican National Convention, Chicago, Illinois

[*July 8, 1952*]

THIS is the fifth time I have had the high honor of addressing the Conventions of the Republican Party. From the inexorable course of nature, this is likely to be the last time I shall attend your conventions.

THE ISSUE OF FREE MEN

In our country one dominant issue overshadows all others. That is, the freedom of men. And that today includes our relations to the rest of the world.

At each of those four-year intervals I have pointed out the inch-by-inch destruction of the ramparts of free men in the United States.

This issue far transcends in importance the transitory questions of national life. It is a matter of life itself.

Throughout the centuries of history freedom has been the constant quest of men. For this the best and bravest on earth have fought and died.

The tablets of free men, lost in the Dark Ages, were again handed down to the American people. Those tablets bore not only the words of the Declaration of Independence and the Constitution but they expressed the very spirit of free men.

Do you not believe the words have been distorted and their spirit violated?

53

LET US LOOK AT THE RECORD

The genius of our Founding Fathers which preserved this Republic longer than any Republic in history was the concept of the limitation of powers within our government. One of their strong purposes was to protect free men by restriction of Presidential power.

For twenty years we have seen constant attrition of those Constitutional safeguards of free men.

I do not need recall to you the "Rubber Stamp Congress"; the packed Supreme Court; war without approval of Congress; and a score of dire secret international commitments without consent of the Senate.

And now comes, after one hundred and seventy years, a new discovery in Presidential power. That is an "inherent" power to seize anything, anytime. All Republican Presidents were densely ignorant of those inherent powers.

Over these twenty years we have seen pressure groups fostered and appeased by Presidents until they intimidate and paralyze the life of the nation. No man has been elected by the people to have such powers. If freedom is to live, we can no more have economic tyranny than we can have political tyranny. Representative government has not been maintained in the mastery of its own house.

Our social order does not rest upon Constitutional safeguards alone. This Republic was founded on a pledge of sacred honor. Yet we have writhed under shocking disclosures of intellectual dishonesty and unpunished corruption in high places—greater in aggregate than all such sins in our history put together.

The grandeur of a people comes from their moral and spiritual character. Today that grandeur is corroded by this intellectual dishonesty and corruption among public officials. The drip, drip, drip from dishonor in high places plays a part in the increasing of crime among the people.

These acts do not make for free men.

OTHER ASSASSINATIONS OF FREE MEN

And there have been other assassins of freedom.

Within eight years since victory, we will have seen tax-and-tax—spend-and-spend reach a fantastic total greater than in all the previous one hundred and seventy years of our Republic.

Behind this plush curtain of tax and spend, three sinister spooks or ghosts are mixing poison for the American people. They are the shades of Mussolini, with his bureaucratic fascism; of Karl Marx, and his socialism; and of Lord Keynes, with his perpetual government spending, deficits, and inflation. And we added a new ideology of our own. That is government give-away programs.

I will in a few moments measure for you the blight of inflation from this mixture that has poured into every American home.

By way of the bureaucracy part of the mixture, within twenty years we have seen it grow from under 600,000 Federal officials under Republican Administration to over 2,300,000 officials today—with the addition of almost a thousand of government agencies. In fascist fashion, they dictate and give orders and favors to our citizens. Still worse, they do have a real inherent power. Their inherent power is that of all bureaucracy to lay its paralyzing hand more and more heavily upon free men. They rush headlong into its fantasies of the millennium and send the bills to the Treasury.

If you want to see pure fascism mixed with give-away programs, take a look into the Brannan Plan.

If you want to see pure socialism mixed with give-away programs, take a look at socialized medicine and socialized electrical power.

These things do not make for free men.

Man was created somewhat lower than the angels, but to him the Creator gave the right to plan his own life, to dare his own adventure, to earn his own reward so long as he does no harm to his fellows.

Either we shall have a society based upon ordered liberty

and the creative energy of free men or we shall have a dictated society.

I have said before now that there are immutable principles which neither the rigors of depression, nor the tricks of inherent powers, nor lost statesmanship, nor wars, nor New Dealers, nor militarists can change. These immutable principles came into the universe along with the shooting stars of which worlds are made, and they have always been and ever will be true. Such are the presence of God, the laws of gravitation, and the ceaseless struggle of mankind to be free.

Shall we keep that faith? Must we condemn unborn generations to fight again and to die for the right to be free?

THESE FOREIGN POLICIES

For nearly forty years I have had need to deal with international relations. I would be less than frank if on this, my last address to you, I did not speak from my heart and from that hard experience. And I can relieve all candidates of embarrassment by stating in their behalf at once that these are my views alone.

And if I seem to stress our foreign policies, I do so because within them lies the future of freedom of men and women in America, and because in the first World War I witnessed the Communists give rebirth to slavery on earth. One Democratic and three Republican Presidents refused to recognize their government and thus admit their official agents into our household.

Over those years I have known of a long roll of good men and women in many foreign lands, with whom I worked in intimacy to save their starving peoples, who died in Communist dungeons or dangled at the end of a hangman's rope.

For years I have protested that the lost statesmanship of dealing with them would drag the world into great calamities. However, there is no satisfaction in having been proved right by disasters to the American people.

Until twenty years ago our dedication to free men was admired and aspired to by all mankind. The undertakings of our government were trusted throughout the whole earth. Today, that respect and trust have been blemished by a hundred actions.

Twelve years ago we were led into a great war crusade on the promise of freedom to men and to nations under the banner of the Four Freedoms and the Atlantic Charter. Then at Teheran, Yalta, and Potsdam we sacrificed the freedom of 650 millions of human beings on the altar of appeasement to Communism. The souls of one-quarter of mankind have been seared by the violation of that American promise. The ghosts of the Four Freedoms and the Atlantic Charter now wander amid the clanking chains of a thousand slave camps.

Where have we arrived after this war crusade for freedom? I need not remind you that we lost the peace despite the valor and the sacrifice of our manhood on a hundred battlefields. Our bewildered statesmanship has brought no return from the sacrifices and the tears of millions of mothers and wives. There is less freedom in the world today than at any time for a whole century. Have our foreign policies over those years been a success? They certainly did not make free men.

THE COMMUNISTS

Our opponents frequently remind me that this is all in the past. The past is the father of right now. And we have to deal with the menace they created.

Nurtured by policies participated in by our government and by Communists in the highest echelons of our Washington Administration, the Kremlin now cracks its whip over a horde of 800 million people. They are now armed with 300 divisions, 30,000 tanks, and 20,000 war planes. American and British traitors have given them the atomic bomb.

Our need today is a cold and objective look at where we have got to, both abroad and within the United States, under the Truman-Acheson foreign and military policies dealing with the Communists.

Time tonight only permits me to appraise where we have got to on three major fronts. They are Korea, Western Europe, and the United States. And I shall add some constructive alternatives.

KOREA

The situation in Korea was born at Yalta, and nourished by American support of so-called "agrarian liberals" in China.

We joined with more than two score of non-Communist members of the United Nations to defeat this Communist aggression. But we find ourselves furnishing 90 percent of the military forces sent there and taking 90 percent of the losses.

America's price so far is 120,000 dead, wounded, and sick, with 300,000 of our youth still fighting.

General MacArthur well said that in war there is no substitute for victory. Instead of victory, the Administration substituted appeasement on the 38th Parallel, just where we started from. After twelve months of negotiation, the Communists so far do not seem to want to be appeased. In the meantime they have so increased their forces that the military initiative is now in their hands. The end is not yet.

But can anyone say these policies in Korea have been a great success?

CONTINENTAL EUROPE

We may also take a cold look at the second major area of the Truman-Acheson policies. That is—Western Europe.

Beginning six years ago with an unrepayable loan of over $3 billions to Britain, the Administration has poured $35 billions into Europe trying to build up their will power, their military strength, and furnishing them an American ground army.

For six years we have listened to a multitude of plans, agreements, pronouncements, and promises of great European armies. What is the net result of these efforts?

Three years ago, with the signing of the North Atlantic Pact, we were again told that great ground armies would at last spring up on that continent. And to pass that treaty, a pledge was given to the Senate by the Administration that we would not contribute more ground troops to Europe. Then we shipped them 200,000 more American boys.

Three years after the Atlantic Pact, in February of this year, there was another conference at Lisbon. It was impressively announced that by the end of this year there would be, exclusive of American and British divisions, an army of about 15 battleworthy and 25 reserve divisions in Europe.

The *London Times*, commenting on the Lisbon agreement, published an editorial entitled, "A Phantom Army." The *Times* pointed out that even this small army could not possibly be ready in 1952.

Six weeks ago we witnessed the signing of a step toward freedom of Western Germany. That was a good deed. A few days later we saw the signing of the European Defense Community treaty by six Continental nations. That will be an advance in European unity provided it is ratified by six distracted parliaments. But it was announced in the *New York Times* of May 28 that, by a secret agreement, these six nations would by 1954 or 1955, create 55 divisions of which 15 would be reserve divisions.

Aside from American and British divisions, this European army seems determined to keep its phantom quality.

Can anyone say that this size army even three years hence is any real deterrent in a ground war to the already six times greater forces of the Communist horde? Or that it could even avert a Dunkirk of the six American divisions we have placed there?

Compare this promised fifty-odd division army three years hence with the 160 effective divisions these same six Western European nations—comprising 160 million people—put in the field within 60 days in both World War I and World War II. Today their manpower and productive capacity is greater than in either of those wars. The potential is there, but we must by now realize that the will is lacking.

The only other explanation of their attitude is that these six nations of Western Europe have no stirring belief in present danger. We have heard no clamor from these countries to spend their lives, their fortunes, or their sacred honor to defend their liberties. They have proclaimed no such emergencies, carried on no such propaganda of peril, nor stimulated such war psychoses as have emanated from Washington, D.C.

Can anyone honestly say that these policies of making great ground armies in Western Europe have been a great success?

THE EFFECT OF THESE POLICIES
ON FREEDOM IN THE UNITED STATES

Now let us take a cold look at the economic and social effect of these Administration policies on the United States. It is no news to you that the federal and local governments are spending about 35 percent of the national income. That is more than any nation can bear.

I have long had great sympathy for the humble decimal point. He has to jump three zeros every little while. He had to make three jumps to punctuate our present deficit.

We do not need to look far to find the blazing proof in our midst that we cannot carry this economic burden.

If you think these policies are not producing an inflation which is wrecking American lives, just recall but a few things. Already after this six years of these Washington policies the American worker must have an annual income of $4,500 today to live as well as he did on $3,000 six years ago. If this does not convince you, look about you at the necessary round of wage increases going on today which means you can buy less with your money tomorrow.

Look around and you will see millions who have earned pensions or saved to protect their old age being reduced to the tragedy of want.

Look still further and you will find not only inflation but that the intolerable taxes stifle initiative and are driving millions of our people to become more and more dependent upon the Government.

Look again and you will find this tax-and-spend used as a vehicle to mix collectivism into American life.

You can look even more deeply. No government can spend such sums of money and not corrupt the spenders. And no government can levy such taxes without breeding a horde of tax dodgers and bribers.

Do you want to go on with this spending, inflation, and corruption?

If free men are to survive in America, we must reduce spending and taxes. It is true we can make some cuts in spending by stopping waste, corruption, and private privilege. But the total of all such reductions would not even reduce the prospective budget deficit by one-half. To say nothing of stopping inflation or reducing taxes.

It is not enough just to say we will balance the budget and reduce taxes. Or to say we will do it some years hence. We must face the grim reality of how and where to do it now.

The reality is that we cannot ever balance the budget and reduce taxes except by cutting into this military and foreign spending.

To find this how and where, and still do our part in the world, we must take a new look into these military policies.

The Administration and the Pentagon have been building up four gigantic military programs. First, they insist upon huge ground armies; second, naval forces; third, air forces; and fourth, munitions and cash subsidies to other nations. And now they propose to add huge numbers to these armies by compulsory universal military service. All this step-by-step building of great ground armies is the road to militarism. That is at its base a threat to all freedoms. That has brought ruin to freedom ever since Rome. That wrecked Germany and Japan.

Moreover, the military strength of America does not lie today in great ground armies.

How many mistakes do we have to make before we learn that our genius lies in the invention, production, and operation of great weapons? Our future is in these great weapons, not in bayonets. And we can furnish these great weapons to nations who have the will to defend themselves.

Lest you think the Pentagon is not determined on bayonets, I may mention their bulletin of February 1 of this year, which I quote.

"The individual rifleman is the most effective and most essential weapon against the enemy. All other services exist to support the infantry soldier."

THE ALTERNATIVE

All Americans wish to see civilization preserved in Western Europe.

But we must recognize the lack of will in preparedness which might have been a deterrent to Communist aggression. Therefore, we must determine what real deterrent America can furnish within our economic and manpower capacities.

The effective deterrent which American resources can contribute is not bayonets against overwhelming land forces, but the expansion of air power and navies to make up a great striking force, which could destroy the Communist military potential if it started any aggression anywhere. And this striking force naturally includes strategic bases with a stretch of water in front of them over which Communist armies cannot pass our Navy.

It is asserted today that our air force is now inferior to that of Russia. Yet simply as an example we could add one-half more to our air strength and maintain it at less cost than we can recruit, train, arm, and maintain 10 divisions of ground troops. And those planes, so essential to our own safety, would be a far better defense of Europe.

The American people will start no wars. But the sure defense of New York, London, and Paris is the fear of counterattack on Moscow by air. The Kremlin will not be much frightened over an American ground war against their overwhelming forces. In that area of menace the military initiative is on the Communist side today.

Sometime ago when, as a mere civilian, I proposed this alternative program of less armies and an overwhelming striking force at less cost, a yell went up, "Here comes the armchair strategist." But promptly this proposal was supported by seven of our most distinguished retired Army, Navy, and Air officers. It was supported by six of our most seasoned diplomats.

Such a program would restore the advantage of military initiative to us.

It would extend our effectiveness to aid all menaced countries.

It would assure American youth that their lives will not be widely interrupted and that they will not be sent into the overwhelming Communist quicksands.

It would enable us to stop this creeping Fascism and Socialism.

It would balance our budget and start to cut our taxes.

It would avoid our bankruptcy which is Stalin's greatest hope.

It has been said that in these evil times peace can be preserved only through strength. That is true. But the center and final reserve of strength of the free world lies now in the Western Hemisphere. I am not ashamed to say that our first duty is to defend the United States. For if we fall, the freedom of men falls in the whole world.

What I propose is an entire reconsideration of these policies based on the realities which have today developed both in the United States and abroad.

I do not propose that we retreat into our shell like a turtle. I do propose the deadly reprisal strategy of a rattlesnake.

The way out from the perils, begotten from these twelve years of lost statesmanship, is not easy. Certainly sane policies cannot be made amid college yells of "isolationist" or "internationalist," nor by smears and slanted news which are the ugly instruments of those who would dictate.

OTHER TASKS BEFORE US

The Republican Party must not blink the other many difficulties of the times and the other tasks before us. Our Party welcomes change in the social and economic order when it will produce a more fair, a more free and more satisfying civilization. But change which destroys the safeguards of free men and women will be only an apple of Sodom. Again I may say I have great sympathy for those who honestly seek for short cuts to solve our complex problems. But the structure of betterment can only be built brick by brick by men and women free in spirit and mind. The bricks must come from the mold of religious faith, of justice, of integrity, of fidelity to the spirit of the Constitution. Any other mold is distorted; any other bricks are without straw.

THIS ELECTION

This election may well be the last chance for the survival of freedom in America.

In a time of confusion and crisis the action of a Republican Convention ninety years ago saved this nation for free men.

The Whig Party temporized, compromised upon the issue of freedom for the Negro. That party disappeared. It deserved to disappear. Shall the Republican Party receive or deserve any better fate if it compromises upon the issue of freedom for all men, white as well as black?

If you make free men your issue, you can again revive the call which your and my ancestors issued ninety years ago when this party was born to make all men free.

Also there was a Convention in 1776. Their Declaration stirred the world with its ringing appeal for free men, its righteous recital of transgressions and its pledge of Life, Fortune, and sacred Honor.

America needs today a new Declaration that will raise the hearts of our people to their spiritual purpose and their eyes into the sunlight of freedom.

Its first sentence should read:

"The Republican Party is determined to restore free men in the United States."

That Declaration really needs nothing more to revive again hope in a frustrated people.

That is your great issue.

Yours is the task to stop this retreat; to lead the attack and recapture the citadels of liberty in the United States. Thus can America be preserved. Thus can it hold the lamp of free men aloft to a confused world. Thus can we wipe out coercion and corruption. Thus can the peace, plenty, and security be re-established and expanded. Thus can the opportunity, and the spiritual future of your children be guaranteed. And thus you will win the gratitude of posterity, and the blessing of Almighty God.

In my opening remarks I stated that from the inexorable course of nature, this is most likely the last time I will have the honor of attending your Conventions. Therefore, in clos-ing, I wish to express my deep gratitude to this great party you represent, for the many honors you have bestowed upon me. If I have won some measure of your affections, it is a high award. But the greatest glory that can come to man is to be given the opportunity to fight for free men. And I shall continue the fight for those principles which made the United States the greatest gift of God to freedom. I pray to Him to strengthen your hands and give you courage.

On the Occasion of the Return of Freedom to Finland

A "Voice of America" Broadcast
[December 6, 1952]

I AM glad of the opportunity to join in wishing the Finnish people many returns of this day which marked the return of freedom to Finland after one hundred years.

I perhaps have some right to join in this occasion. I was one of those close to Finland at the birth of her independence in 1918. At that date I was administering the Reconstruction and Relief of Europe on behalf of the American and Associated Governments. We arranged on that day the first finance of Finland for her foreign trade and the first ships of food for the relief of her terrible famine. Beyond that, one of my treasures is a letter from the Foreign Minister of Finland, expressing Finland's gratitude to me for securing the recognition of her independence by the Allies in April 1919.

During this time I came to realize those sterling qualities which make a great nation. Nations are not great because of the number of their people, nor their area, nor their wealth— Finland truly is a little nation in these measures but she has made a great place in the world by the spirit of courage and accomplishment of her people.

It has been my privilege to witness this greatness over the years. I visited Finland twenty years after her independence and witnessed the amazing progress of a free people. Ten years later, at the request of the Prime Minister, I headed the fund for relief of her suffering women and children from the wicked Communist invasion.

No finer statement of character of a people can be made than to repeat Finland's immortal declaration at that time. She said, "We would rather die on our feet than die on our knees."

Almost eight years later again I visited Finland in the course of my duties directing the relief of the great famine after the second World War. I then witnessed a nation struggling with a Carthaginian peace. In that she has also succeeded.

No nation which does not possess true greatness could have overcome these terrible experiences.

Statement Supporting the Petition Against the Admission of Communist China to the United Nations

[*January 1954*]

FORMER President Herbert Hoover today reaffirmed his opposition to the admission of Communist China to the United Nations in a strongly worded statement issued by the Committee for One Million, currently conducting a nation-wide petition campaign on this issue.

He stated:

"One of the greatest dangers the cause of freedom faces today is uncertainty in the minds of both governments and peoples abroad as to the position of the United States in relation to Communist China. The nations in the Far East are in constant danger of their aggression. In the meantime they work and conspire to break down the morale of these free peoples of Asia; they endeavor to create disunity and spread lies about the stand of the United States. The Communist propaganda mill has misinterpreted, taken out of context, and distorted many statements by our public men.

"In November, Secretary of State Dulles discussed the Communist regime in China. The reports of the conference misquoted Secretary Dulles to the effect that he was in favor of recognition of the Peking regime. This misinterpretation was picked up by the press throughout the world and particularly by the Communist propaganda machine. It was spread widely throughout Asia and did great injury to the morale of our allies in that area of the world which is fighting Communism. Secretary Dulles issued a denial which received little notice abroad. As recently as last week, a direct quotation was attributed to me which said I advocated a trade 'agreement' with Communist China by the United States. In spite of my denial, this alleged quotation received widespread distribution in the Far East. I have opposed recognition of Communist China by the United States and its admission into the United Nations from the day the Communists conquered China four years ago.

"Any and every effort that we as Americans can make to prove to our friends overseas just where we, as a nation, stand, is of enormous value.

"This petition campaign is now being conducted throughout the nation by the Committee for One Million, headed by Warren R. Austin, formerly Ambassador of the United States to the United Nations. The aim of the Committee is to gather upward of one million signatures. It would support these ideas if our citizens would join in this petition. The headquarters of the Committee is at 36 West 44th Street, New York City. Members of the Steering Committee are:

> Charles Edison (former Governor of New Jersey),
> Joseph C. Grew (former Under Secretary of State),
> Walter H. Judd (Representative, R-Minn.),
> John W. McCormack (Representative, D-Mass.),
> H. Alexander Smith (Senator, R-New Jersey),
> John J. Sparkman (Senator, D-Ala.)."

On Foreign Policies

*Portion of a Nationally Broadcast Address Given Before
the Merchandise Mart Hall of Fame, Chicago, Illinois**
[June 24, 1954]

GETTING ALONG WITH OTHER FREE NATIONS

B UT the American people are in far greater trouble than
teen-age delinquency or reforms in our Federal establishment.

I do not need to describe the center of world conspiracy from
which our international dangers arise. And our difficulties are
not limited to the Communists. They arise also from a lack of
unity among the free nations in dealing with these difficulties.

I have no intention of speaking upon specific foreign policies.
Our disunities with the Communists are easy enough to appreciate, but our relations with free nations require more understanding. To discuss these problems objectively will not make the
cold war any hotter. And it may illustrate that this is a time for
patience and forbearance.

First. We must realize that there are wide differences in
racial inheritances, economic and political objectives in each of
the free nations. They come down from centuries. Also among
them are age-old dislikes, and fears.

Second. It must be realized that military alliances or peacetime collective action can endure only as·long as there are common objectives and purposes among the participants.

* The first part of this address, "Some National Problems," will be found
in the next section.

70

Third. Our people must realize that the interests, objectives, and policies of nations constantly shift with this rapidly changing scene. The last nine years offer abundant proof of the rapidity of shifting national policies. In this short period, the policies of the United States have shifted, as witness our reversal of attitudes toward Russia, Germany, and Japan.

Fourth. We must realize that the atomic bomb and the steady growth of Communist military strength have contributed to shift the policies of some of the free nations.

Fifth. We must realize that the Communist members of the United Nations have paralyzed our hoped-for protection from military aggression through that organization; and that the United Nations is weakened in this major purpose by lack of full unity among the free nations.

Sixth. Our people should realize that many of the free nations of the world, in despair of protection by the United Nations from major aggression, have been forced into a multitude of military alliances. There are also groups present today determined to maintain their neutrality in any major conflict.

Seventh. We must realize that some of our military allies are faltering in the march. That hesitation again arises from shifting of interests and objectives with the changing scene in the world.

Eighth. Our people should realize that with these alliances, groupings, and shiftings, the whole concept of preservation of peace by collective action against an aggressor through the United Nations has gone by the board—at least for the present. We are now in the presence of age-old balances of power, power politics and ancient forms of diplomacy.

Ninth. Our people must realize that in dealing with these gigantic problems of today we must have patience, tolerance, and understanding of these differences of interests and objectives of the free nations.

Tenth. Through this terrible labyrinth our Government must pilot our foreign policies. We cannot expect miracles. Free men must hold to the right to disagree with any policy of the Government. But especially in foreign affairs support should be the watchword, until issues of deep conscience arise. And moderation is a good watchword even then.

Someone said the world is at the crossroads. My belief is that it is a clover-leaf junction.

Eleventh. In appraising the forces in the world, we should not conclude that the United Nations should be abolished. It furnishes a place with electronic equipment where nations may discharge their batteries of the evil things which they think about each other in five languages all at once.

But seriously, this institution has proved of value in pacific settlement of disputes among secondary nations. It has contributed to the spread of scientific knowledge, to philanthropic and public-health measures.

These activities form a tenuous road to more unity of free nations and we should cling to any hope they may provide.

Twelfth. Above all, we cannot abandon the ideal that someday, somehow, unity for peace can be built in the world. Nor can we abandon the hope that some time the free nations who believe in God will mobilize against Red atheism and human slavery.

If inside or outside of the United Nations the free nations could unite, they have many potent moral, spiritual, and even economic weapons at their disposal besides military alliances.

Thirteenth. In these shifting shapes in the world, we must realize the vitality of a great spiritual force which we call "nationalism."

The fuzzy-minded intellectuals have sought to brand nationalism as a sin against mankind. They seem to think that infamy is attached to the word "nationalist."

But that force in the world cannot be obscured by denunciation of it as greed or selfishness—as it sometimes is. The spirit of nationalism springs from the deepest of human emotions. It rises from the yearning of men to be free of foreign domination, to govern themselves. It springs from a thousand rills of race, of history, of sacrifice and pride in national achievement.

Every nation has laid its dead upon the altar of its country. These died with their national flag before their eyes and their national hymns upon their lips. The pride of race has swelled from their suffering and sacrifice.

In our own country does not the word America stir something deeper within us than mere geography? Does not the suffering and the sacrifice of our forbears who fought for our independence flash in our minds with every mention of that word? Was it not our independence which gave the most expansive release to the creative spirit of mankind in all history? Was it not the release of intellectual and spiritual freedom on this continent that gave the moral strength and the self-reliance which penetrated our plains and forests?

Nationalism does not mean isolationism from the common interests of nations. We have ourselves proved that. Just as we have valued our own independence, we have fought for the independence of other peoples.

And equally do these emotions flow wide and deep in all free nations. Within them and their religious faith is their spiritual strength. It sustains their resolution against aggression and domination.

"Nationalism" cannot be abandoned if civilization is to last among free men. And we can have some hope that slumbering nationalism in the satellite countries will awaken to throw off the Moscow yoke as it has in Yugoslavia.

Fourteenth. And from all this, our people must realize that our own right arm plus some deterrents unhealthy to the aggressors are our major reliance for our defense. And these strengths are no weak reliance. With the magnificent officers and men in our defense establishments, with our genius and our productivity, we can defend ourselves.

The Protection of Freedom

*Address at the Reception Tendered by West Branch, Iowa,
on the Speaker's 80th Birthday*
[August 10, 1954]

THE Legislature and the Governor of Iowa did me the great honor of inviting me to a reception by my native State on this my 80th birthday.

It is more than difficult adequately to express my appreciation for such evidence of affection.

I am glad to come to West Branch. My grandparents and my parents came here in a covered wagon. In this community they toiled and worshipped God. They lie buried on your hillside. The most formative years of my boyhood were spent here. My roots are in this soil.

This cottage where I was born is physical proof of the unbounded opportunity of American life.

My first paid job was in this community picking potato bugs at one cent a hundred. I was not inspired by altruism to relieve the world of a pest. Such altruism as was attached to that labor was to secure firecrackers with which to commemorate properly the Declaration of Independence. But Iowa is a progressive State. Its mothers, anxious to avoid repairs to small boys, secured a law abolishing that kind of tribute to the Founding Fathers. Moreover, by insecticides, the slave wage of only a cent a hundred has been overcome.

Iowa has made fabulous progress since I left here. I can prove it by statistics—and all speeches must have statistics because nobody can defy a statistic.

74

Since that time, the people of Iowa have multiplied the wealth of the State nine times over. That statistic is weakened by the decrease in purchasing power of money. In the meantime with the blessing of "the tall corn" you have sent to market enough hogs to cover the Chicago Stock Yards 5,045 feet deep. You can vary that statistic as you like.

Also, you have sent forth a host of men and women who have distinguished themselves in every State in the Union and every foreign country. Their quality is proved by the fact that I have never seen Iowa attributed as the origin of any of our leading bank robbers, gangsters, or Communists.

A VARIED LIFE

Eighty years is a long time for a man to live. Mine has been a life of work in many lands under many kinds of governments, both good and bad. I have been honored by my countrymen in many public offices and with many opportunities to serve outside the Government. I have watched the two great world wars with their holocausts of death, destruction, and famine. I have taken some part in remedy of their terrible aftermaths. I have participated in the search for a healing peace.

I have witnessed the legacy of war in doubting minds, brutality, crime, and debased morals. Moreover, I have witnessed on the ground in twenty nations the workings of the philosophy of that anti-Christ, Karl Marx.

THE PROBLEMS OF FREEDOM AND PROGRESS

After these long years and from all these experiences, there rises constantly in my mind the forces which make for progress and those which may corrode away the safeguards of freedom in America. I want to say something about these forces but I shall endeavor to do so, not in the tones of Jeremiah but in the spirit of Saint Paul.

New forces from science and new ideas, both good and bad, constantly arise in the world. We welcome changes which advance the welfare of our people. Our system always needs repairs.

Also we have to clean up the vast wreckage and disorders of two devastating tornadoes of wars which have swept over mankind during the past forty years.

And above all, we have need to remedy constant corruption of the safeguards of free men.

The remedies in America are not revolution. They are, except for peace and war, mostly jobs of marginal repairs around a sound philosophy and a stout heart.

THE SAFEGUARDS OF FREE MEN

Our Founding Fathers did not invent the priceless boon of individual freedom and respect for the dignity of men. That great gift to mankind sprang from the Creator and not from governments.

The Founding Fathers, with superb genius, welded together the safeguards of these freedoms.

They were mostly concerned with the dangers of political tyranny. With the coming of the industrial age our people welded in new safeguards. We could no more have economic tyranny than political tyranny.

And with these safeguards our people were at one time closer to the goals of human welfare than any other civilization in all history.

POWER OF FEDERAL AND LOCAL GOVERNMENT

The progress of freedom is a never-ending struggle to prevent the abuse of power, whether by individuals, by groups, or by government or nations.

Our Founding Fathers created unique restraints on power by the Bill of Rights and a structure of built-in checks and balances. Among these new concepts was a division of power between the Federal and State Governments and between the three branches of government. I do not need to tell you that. But what I have to tell you is that these separations of power became seriously confused, corroded, and weakened during the twenty years before this Administration.

These confusions have included Executive encroachment on the Legislative and Judicial branches. There has been judicial encroachment on the States' rights. There has been Congressional encroachment on the Executive. The Federal Government has grasped many of the vital functions of State and local government.

Some of the corrosions of our division of power are the aftermaths of our wars. Some of them come from the various infections of Socialism. I will tell you more of that later.

Some of the corrosions come from the discovery that it is easy for the Federal Government to light the magic power of Federal credit. But the flame that warms can also consume the safeguards of free men.

Some of these encroachments come from a long era of beguilement by pressure groups and local government for subsidies from the Federal Government.

One of the end results of all this is the growth of a huge centralized Federal bureaucracy. It has expanded in twenty years from 600,000 to 2,300,000. Some increase is necessary. Most of them are fine men and women. But innate in bureaucracy are three implacable spirits. They are self-perpetuation, expansion of their empires, and demand for more power. Bureaucracy rushes headlong into the visions of the millennium and sends the bill to the Treasury.

Today we have more Federal employees in nearly every state than all the local officials, including constables. They penetrate every part of local government. They produce great waste of the taxpayers' money. They create a vested interest or a vested habit for some pressure group. They interfere in politics and too often are infected with corruption.

Their magics invade personal freedom of every citizen, every moment of every hour.

The remedy is to restore the checks and balances of power, to reinvigorate State and local governments, and to deflate the bureaucratic empires.

Many of these confusions of power are today under vigorous investigation in which I have some part.

My countrymen, all these corrosions of the checks and balances of power call for constant battle from you, the people. They must be wiped out if you would stay fully free.

POWER IN OUR FOREIGN RELATIONS

In our foreign relations there are great dangers and also vital safeguards to free men. During the last war we witnessed a special encroachment of the Executive upon the Legislative Branch. This has been through a new type of commitment of the United States to other nations. I am not going to argue legalisms, for they do not go to the center of the issue. The real issue is whether the President, through declaration or implication or by appeasement or by acquiescence, or by joint statements with foreign officials, can commit the American people to foreign nations without the specific consent of the elected representatives of the people.

There has been a grievous list of such commitments. They include international agreements which shackle our economy by limiting a free market. But more terrible were such executive agreements as our recognition of Soviet Russia which opened the headgates for a torrent of traitors. Our tacit alliance with Soviet Russia spread Communism over the earth. Our acquiescence in the annexation by Russia of the Baltic States at Moscow and the partition of Poland at Teheran extinguished the liberties of tens of millions of people. Worse still was the appeasement and surrender at Yalta of ten nations to slavery. And there was the secret agreement with respect to China which set in train the Communization of Mongolia, North Korea, and all of China.

These unrestrained Presidential actions have resulted in a shrinking of human freedom over the whole world. From these actions came the jeopardies of the Cold War. As a by-product these actions have shrunk our freedoms by crushing taxes, huge defense costs, inflation, and compulsory military service.

We must make such misuse of power forever impossible.

And let me say, I have no fears of this evil from President Eisenhower, but he will not always be President.

OUR PRESENT FOREIGN SITUATION

Our dangers from the Communist source of gigantic evil in the world are unending. All of the peace agencies we have created and all of the repeated conferences we have held have failed to find even a whisper of real peace.

Amid these malign forces, our haunting anxiety and our paramount necessity is the defense of our country.

It is not my purpose to define the foreign policies of our government.

Sooner or later a new line of action will become imperative.

I have disagreed with, and protested against, the most dangerous of our foreign political policies during the whole of the twenty years prior to the last Presidential election. I opposed and protested every step in the policies which led us into the second World War.

Especially in June 1941, when Britain was safe from a German invasion due to Hitler's diversion to attack on Stalin, I urged that the gargantuan jest of all history would be our giving aid to the Soviet Government. I urged we should allow those two dictators to exhaust each other. I stated that the result of our assistance would be to spread Communism over the whole world. I urged that if we stood aside the time would come when we could bring lasting peace to the world.

I have no regrets. The consequences have proved that I was right.

THE COMMUNISTS

Today the Socialist virus and poison gas generated by Karl Marx and Friedrich Engels have spread into every nation on the earth. Their dogma is absolute materialism which defies truth and religious faith. Their poisons are of many sorts. The preservation of the safeguards of liberty makes it imperative that we give heed to their every variety.

The bloody virus type, radiating from Communist Russia, is today rotting the souls of two-fifths of all mankind, which it has enslaved.

From the day Lenin rose to power in Moscow, the Communists have carried on an underground conspiracy against every
other nation. The rank and file of our people are immune from
this infection. The recruiting grounds for their agents are from
our minority of fuzzy-minded intellectuals and labor leaders.
Over a thousand such Communist agents have already been
rooted out of responsible positions in our Government and other
spots of influence.

Many of these spies and traitors when exposed sought sanctuary for their infamies in the Fifth Amendment. Such a plea
of immunity is an implication of guilt. Surely these people
should not have the right to vote or to hold office, for thereby
they use these privileges of free men against the safeguards of
freedom.

Despite the clamor over ferreting out these persons, you
must not be led into the mistake that Moscow has closed down
its recruiting offices for American agents. Or that continued
action of the F.B.I. and Congressional committees is not equally
imperative.

I have little fear that these Communist agents can destroy
the Republic if we continue to ferret them out. Our greater concern should be the other varieties of Karl Marx virus.

THE SOCIALISTS

Among them are the Socialists. They assert they would
proceed only by Constitutional means.

The Socialists prowl on many fronts. They promote the
centralized Federal Government, with its huge bureaucracy.
They drive to absorb the income of the people by unnecessary
government spending and exorbitant taxes. They have pushed
our government deep into enterprises which compete with the
rights of free men. These enterprises are endowed with exemp-
tion from control of state and local governments. Congressional
committees have listed hundreds of these Federal activities. But
only a drop of typhoid in a barrel of drinking water sickens a
whole village.

Every step of these programs, somewhere, somehow, stultifies the freedom, the incentives, the courage, and the creative impulses of our people.

Beyond all this, there is proof in the world that the end result of Socialism can be bloody Communism. In the Iron Curtain States, it was the Socialist intellectuals who weakened the freedom of men by destroying free enterprise. Thus they furnished the boarding ladders by which the Communists captured the Ship of State.

THE WELFARE STATE

One of the postwar cousins of Socialism is the so-called "Welfare State." This poison gas is generated by the same sort of fuzzy-minded intellectuals. Its slogan is "Planned Economy." The phrase itself was borrowed from totalitarian governments. The end of it would at least be a government wherein whatever is not forbidden would be compulsory.

One of the annoyances of this cult is its false assumption that our nation has never been heedful of the welfare of our people. That we are our brother's keeper was rooted in religious faith long before these fuzzy-minded men were born. Since the foundation of the Republic, we have recognized and practiced both private and government responsibility for the unfortunate and the aged; for the education of our youth and the health of our people.

Moreover, this cult has a host of gimmicks for giving away the people's money. Among their idea is that government should guarantee every citizen security from the cradle to the grave.

But it is solely the initiative and the labor of the physically able in the prime of life that can support the aged, the young, the sick—and the bureaucracy. And this active earning group requires the pressures of competition, the rewards of enterprise and new adventure to keep it on the job. Even if security from the cradle to the grave could eliminate the risks of life, it would be a dead hand on the creative spirit of our people. Also, the judgment of the Lord to Adam about sweat has not been repealed.

When we flirt with the Delilah of security for our productive group, we had better watch out, lest in our blindness we pull down the pillars of the temple of free men.

The British under a Socialist government tried it. Its result was a level of poverty which British Socialists sought to obscure with the term "austerity." Britain is now in retreat from it.

THE COMMON MAN

Among the delusions offered us by fuzzy-minded people is that imaginary creature, the Common Man. It is dinned into us that this is the Century of the Common Man. The whole idea is another cousin of the Soviet proletariat. The Uncommon Man is to be whittled down to size. It is the negation of individual dignity and a slogan of mediocrity and uniformity.

The Common Man dogma may be of use as a vote-getting apparatus. It supposedly proves the humility of demagogues.

The greatest strides of human progress have come from Uncommon Men and Women. You have perhaps heard of George Washington, Abraham Lincoln, or Thomas Edison. They were humble in origin, but that was not their greatness.

The humor of it is that when we get sick, we want an uncommon doctor. When we go to war, we yearn for an uncommon general or admiral. When we choose the president of a university, we want an uncommon educator.

The imperative need of this nation at all times is the leadership of the Uncommon Men or Women. We need men and women who cannot be intimidated, who are not concerned with applause meters, nor those who sell tomorrow for cheers today.

Such leaders are not to be made like queen bees. They must rise by their own merits. America recognizes no frozen social stratifications which prevent this free rise of every individual. They rise by merit from our shops and farms. They rise from the thirty-five million boys and girls in our schools and colleges. That they have the determination to rise is the glorious promise of leadership among free men.

A nation is strong or weak, it thrives or perishes upon what it believes to be true. If our youth is rightly instructed in the faith of our fathers; in the traditions of our country; in the dignity of each individual man, then our power will be stronger than any weapon of destruction that man can devise.

THIS WHOLE SOCIALIST GAMUT

And now as to this whole gamut of Socialist infections, I say to you, the neighbors of my childhood, the sons and daughters of my native State, God has blessed us with another wonderful word—heritage. The great documents of that heritage are not from Karl Marx. They are the Bible, the Declaration of Independence, and the Constitution of the United States. Within them alone can the safeguards of freedom survive. Safeguard the true spirit of these guarantees for your children, that they may not become the prisoners of a Hydra-headed Socialism.

If anyone rises to say that all this is reactionary, you may class him as either fuzzy-minded or an ignorant enemy of free men.

THE NEW FRONTIERS

Amid this recitation of our problems, I would not have you think that there are not great fields of promise for the future if we can keep out of war.

The last few years have seen advances in science and technology which amount almost to revolution in our life and world relations. If we maintain free minds, free spirits, and direct our steps aright, still other new horizons and new frontiers are open to us. New inventions and new applications of old knowledge will come to us daily.

These new frontiers give us other blessings. Not only do they expand our living but also they open new opportunities and new areas of adventure and enterprise. They open new vistas of beauty. They unfold the wonders of the atom and the heavens. Daily they prove the reality of an all-wise Supreme Giver of Law.

CONCLUSION

There are voices in our country who daily sound alarms that our civilization is on the way out. Concentrated on the difficulties of our times, they see an early and dour end for us. But civilization does not decline and fall while the people still possess dynamic creative faculties, devotion to religious faith and to liberty. The American people still possess these qualities. We are not at the bedside of a nation in death agony.

Eighty years is a long time for a man to live. As the shadows lengthen over my years, my confidence, my hopes, and dreams for my countrymen are undimmed. This confidence is that with advancing knowledge, toil will grow less exacting; that fear, hatred, pain, and tears may subside; that the regenerating sun of creative ability and religious devotion will refresh each morning the strength and progress of my country.

Some Hopes for Peace

Address at the German and International Press Associations
Luncheon, Bonn, Germany
[November 24, 1954]

I T IS indeed a great honor for me to be an invited guest of the Chancellor and the German people.

I have visited Germany many times over forty years. My last visit was nearly eight years ago. In the eight years since then West Germany has risen from the ashes of war; the shackles of stifling and destructive economic policies have been stricken off; famine has been overcome; productivity has been re-established. And, finally, sovereignty and full membership in the family of nations has been acknowledged as Germany's right.

I have rejoiced in each of these steps to the restoration of a great people. And these accomplishments are the vivid proof of the genius and virility of the German people.

When I learned that you wished me to make some sort of an address, I inquired as to what subject within my province might be of interest to you. Your officials suggested that I appraise the Hopes of Peace as seen through some American eyes.

There never was a time when the Western world was more anxious for peace. All our peoples have had their fill of war. The daily prayer of all free men is for a lasting peace.

In this nine and a half years since the guns were silenced, the disordered world with all its aftermaths has made some progress toward stability and peace. And from this progress there is hope.

You will remember the Biblical legend of the Four Horsemen of the Apocalypse, the names of whom were War, Death,
Famine, and Pestilence. War and Death have abated. Through
aroused compassion, Famine and Pestilence were overcome at
that time.

But out of these gigantic tumults has come another Horse-
man to ravish the world with Fear, Hate, and a passion to
destroy Western Civilization. The ancient prophet was unac-
quainted with him, but his name is Communism.

The tensions of military conflict with Russia seem to have
abated in these recent months and from this abatement, I believe
we can have at least a gleam of hope. Moscow has made many
declarations of peace-loving intent. They speak of "peaceful
co-existence."

It may be that they want more time to consolidate their
gains. They may want more time to promote their infiltration
of conspiracies in free nations. It may be that the growth of our
deterrents against military aggression has influenced their minds.

It may be that internal forces are working within to restrain
them. Every deep-seated social or political revolution has generated within itself a dynamism of military aggression or a crusading spirit to spread their new ideas. That was the case of the
Mohammedan Revolution, the French Revolution, the American Revolution, as well as the Russian Revolution. Incidentally,
in the American case, we had a vacant continent to invade, but
we have been nonetheless crusaders to spread our concepts of
freedom.

With time, the original leaders of these revolutions die off
and some revolutions have the bad habit of devouring their
young. At least their successors are less violent. They become
more concerned with their dangers and improvements at home.
From all this it may be that the Communist protestations are
genuine. All of which possibly warrants a faint hope.

But from our many years' experience with the Communists,
we should learn more about what peaceful co-existence means
—and we must await works rather than words. The Western
world has many times enumerated some of these works to which

the Communists might contribute. They could join in the completely free unification of Germany; they could sign the peace with Austria. They could cease their germ warfare of conspiracies directed to overthrowing free governments.

With such steps, we might at least advance out of the thunder and lightning of this cold war into the dawn of a cold peace.

THE DEFENSE OF WESTERN CIVILIZATION

But all this is too much to expect, and we should not be lulled into the abandonment of our means of defense. The only hope for our safety is the building up of arms and of a united front among free nations which *will deter* Communist aggression against us. The Western World has no intention of military aggression against the Communists. The sole purpose of our alliances and our armament is to have such powerful deterrents as to convince them of the futility of starting war.

In this role of deterrents, the present proposed agreements looking to the arming of Germany and Europe have a very large part. Without the consummation of those agreements, the security of Western Civilization in Europe becomes dependent on the malevolent will of the Communists.

NEUTRALISM

The coming of the fission bomb and guided missiles has contributed to the deterrents. But one of its discouraging effects has been that for fear of its use upon them by the Communists, some nations engage in the futile hope to escape its ravages by neutrality in a great conflict.

Neutralism is no answer to the security of free nations in case of a major conflict. And moreover, it gives comfort only to the spirit of aggression from the Communists.

The only hope of at least relief from military aggression by the Communists is if each one of the powerful nations associate itself in the real building of arms for mutual defense. That is the most powerful of deterrents.

AMERICAN PARTICIPATION IN THE DEFENSE OF EUROPE

Our American people have joined in the defense of Western Europe. It is an illusion of some European statesmen that we have joined and spent huge efforts for the selfish purpose of defending ourselves. I and most of my countrymen have held that this is untrue. We can defend ourselves at much less cost in manpower and money, and build effective deterrents against Communist attack upon us. The fundamental reason for our participation is to preserve Western civilization in Europe and the freedom of nations in the world.

The strength of the West in effective defense is not a goal in itself but only a precondition and guarantee of freedom for unlimited development of our cultural and spiritual life.

Nor is there an atom of truth in the assertion that American action is animated by imperialistic ambitions. The world should know from our many actions in the past there is no imperialism in our blood.

Our people have met many discouragements and frustrations in these efforts. We have greatly reduced our resources with which we could increase the comfort and living of our own people. Europe must realize that many of my countrymen had lost confidence in these projects of European defense.

But the statesmanship of Chancellor Adenauer and your Parliament, through joining Germany in the effective defense of Europe, has done much to restore confidence and hope in the American people. We await similar action by other nations, but our patience is not inexhaustible.

THE UNITED NATIONS

At one time we builded great hopes on the organization of the United Nations.

When that temple was built to guard the flame of peace, the world concerned itself with the architecture of the superstructure, but neglected its foundation. When Communists were taken into that structure, the foundation of its major purpose which was to stop military aggression was destroyed.

But it has some values as a forum whereby with electronic

equipment we can denounce the ways of the Communists in five languages all at once. It does perform useful services in mediating minor conflicts, in public health, in some economic and philanthropic fields. It might also be a place where free nations can promote their unity. But the inability of the United Nations to prevent military aggression has given rise to defensive alliances intended for the protection of the free world.

THE RISE OF PEACEFUL NATIONALISM

One of the real foundations of peace is the rise of what is sometimes derisively called "nationalism." There are those who with the organization of the United Nations had further dreams of some sort of World Government where the independence of nations would be curtailed or abolished. They denounce nationalism as a sin against peace and progress and as a wicked force.

But the spirit of nationalism in its true sense springs from the deepest of human emotions. It springs from a thousand rills of inspiring national history, its heroes, its common language, its culture, and its national achievements. It rises from the yearning of men to be free of foreign dominations, to govern themselves.

Nationalism rises from our national sacrifices. Every nation has laid its dead upon the altar of its country. These died with their national flag before their eyes and their national hymns upon their lips. National pride has swelled from their suffering and sacrifice.

And equally do these emotions flow wide and deep in all free nations. Within them and their religious faith is their spiritual strength. It sustains their resolution to defend themselves against aggression and domination.

Nationalism does not mean isolation from unity of action among nations. Rather does internal spiritual strength make common action for defense more secure and more potent.

And we can have some hope that slumbering nationalism in the Iron Curtain nations will awaken to throw off the Moscow yoke as it has in Yugoslavia.

I have rejoiced at the rise in Germany of a peaceful and constructive national spirit. It has brought great steps in her independence and her strength. From her full freedom alone can come the common defense and her full contribution to all mankind.

THE UNIFICATION OF GERMANY

I can well claim that advocacy of German unification is no afterthought of mine for this occasion.

Twelve years ago, just after America entered the war, some of our leaders in a spirit of revenge and as a requirement of peace began to demand dismemberment of Germany. At that time, I said:

"The Germans, like all virile races, are cohesive. The history of Europe's wars might be written around her dismemberments and the explosions from her movements to unity. . . .

". . . There can be no lasting peace . . . with a dismembered Germany.

"Nations cannot be held in chains.

". . . No people can be punished and at the same time leave any hope of lasting peace. . . . Victory with vengeance is ultimate defeat in the modern world. . . .

"We can have peace or we can have revenge, but we cannot have both."

In my country we hold that unification must be the purpose of free nations. We hold that the work of unification must have their full co-operation. We hold that unification by the hand of Russia alone is not likely to be on terms which preserve Germany's association with Western Civilization or which can assure the defense of Germany from Communist domination.

The German peoples have before now been the bastion of Western Civilization which deterred its destructions by the Asiatic hordes.

My prayer is that Germany may be given the unity and full freedom which will restore her to that mission in the world.

CONCLUSION

I am not here to offer certain solutions to these dreadful aftermaths of war from which we still suffer, but to indicate the good will of my countrymen.

We must realize that in dealing with these gigantic problems the statesmen of free nations cannot perform miracles. But that they can, by vision, patience, tolerance, moderation, and understanding abate the dangerous forces which breed aggression, fear, and hate, and they can increase good will among men. Nor can we abandon the hope that some time the free nations who believe in God will mobilize in unity against Red atheism and human slavery.

In Germany, the rebuilding of prosperity and independence from the demoralization of defeat has of necessity been by the patient laying of stone upon stone.

My countrymen believe that the reconstruction of West Germany, the revival of its economic life and the respect it has won among nations is due to the great statesmanship of your Chancellor, and to the great people he is privileged to lead.

The Service of Universities to Freedom

Address Given upon Receipt of Honorary Degree from the Eberhard Karl University at Tübingen
[November 25, 1954]

YOU have conferred a great honor upon me by a degree from this, one of the oldest of the world's great universities.

I have many affections for universities. I have only one earned degree, but this event today constitutes my eighty-first unearned one. However, I may plead that I served for over forty years on University and College Boards of Trustees, mostly collecting money to pay professors. Perhaps, thereby, I have earned some academic attention.

On this occasion I could not fail to acknowledge the obligations which our much younger American universities owe to their older German brothers. The structure of our faculties and our methods of instruction were established largely on the pattern of your universities.

Over the years literally thousands of German-educated professors have taught in our institutions. Over twenty percent of the races poured into the American Melting Pot are of Germanic origin. The very names of many American leaders in every branch of our national life are witness to the value of this inheritance.

There is no better example of this fruitful interchange of intellectual life than the case of Friedrich List. His name especially comes to my mind because I have received the distinguished honor of being made an honorary citizen of Reutlingen, the city of his birth. List was indeed one of the great economists during the first half of the 19th century. As a member of your faculty, his pioneering ideas on economic freedom brought him trouble and exile. He naturally migrated to America where he took part in molding American life. Becoming an American citizen he was appointed American Consul at Stuttgart. Over his remaining twenty years he was a frequent visitor to this university. Nor did he cease in his contributions to an understanding of the basis of the successful economic life of nations.

I have been in Germany many times, but one occasion was on a scholastic adventure. Some years before the first World War, together with Mrs. Hoover, we undertook to translate from the Latin the first comprehensive book published on my branch of the engineering profession. That was a work entitled *De Re Metallica*, by Georgius Agricola—being a huge folio of 600 pages with many intelligent illustrations. It was published almost exactly 400 years ago. The author's real name was Georg Bauer, a doctor living among the mines of Saxony and Bohemia. He also held some public offices, among them Burgomeister of Chemnitz. Agricola had a tendril of memory with this university. Although he was a staunch Catholic, he was a lifelong friend of Melanchthon, a lecturer here, who aided in securing the publication of his book.

Previous translators had failed at any adequate translation because Agricola wrote in a language which had ceased to grow on the technical side a thousand years before his time. He therefore invented or adapted a maze of Latin terms for materials and technical processes unknown to the Romans. As a part of disentangling these puzzles, Mrs. Hoover and I visited the scene of his work. She also probed the literature in German libraries on these subjects which began to appear some years after Agricola. Ultimately, with these aids, we disentangled some hundreds of terms that he had added to the Latin language.

It might interest you to know that this book by a long-since

forgotten German scholar had some responsibilities for the torrent of gold and silver with which the Spanish Conquistadors
of Peru and Mexico flooded the world in the 15th and 16th
centuries. It seems highly probable that the processes used in
working the mines were taken from Agricola's book. No other
text existed at that time, and the particular processes which they
needed were not used in Spain. And as a further tribute to this
scholar, he was the first to illuminate correctly the principles of
many metallurgical processes which we still use today. However, we have improved the machinery.

I have been interested in your library and its ancient setting.
Again I can establish a certain comity of action. I began during
the first World War to make use of my many opportunities to
collect what has become millions of items about this forty years'
tumult of wars, peace, and revolutions. In this library at my
university we have certain collections of German history of the
first World War that were given to me by the Ebert regime,
which I do not believe are available in Germany. Again after
the second World War with the aid of our American officials
and certain Nazis who wanted to be rid of their documents, we
formed an extensive collection on the rise and fall of the Hitler
regime, which might otherwise have been lost. Some of the first
World War documents we agreed would not be disclosed for a
term of years not yet expired. Sometime this library may be of
use to your students of your own history.

An added burden has fallen upon our universities. The
Communists, by infiltration, propaganda, and conspiracy are
seeking to corrupt the truth, the morals, the religion, and in
fact to destroy the freedoms of Western Civilization. They use
our freedoms to destroy freedom itself, but they do not compre-
hend the spiritual, moral, and educational force which will defeat them.

I may be rightly accused of carrying coal to the Ruhr, but
I might touch upon other of the immense mutual responsibilities of our universities in free nations.

Aside from the primary duty of instruction of the young,
our universities have great mutual responsibilities in the gener-

ating of ideas bearing upon our great problems of scientific, social, and economic development.

It is by the free shuttle of ideas between our universities that we weave the great tapestries of knowledge. Our academic traditions have developed a system that is peculiarly effective in spotting outstanding intellects and putting them to work in a climate that fosters creative, original thinking.

From the mutual building by our university faculties and laboratories devoted to abstract science have come most of the great discoveries of natural law. The application of these discoveries through invention and production has been the task of the engineers and technicians whom we train. Applied science dries up quickly unless we maintain the sources of discovery in pure science. From these dual activities of the scientists and the technicians, a great stream of blessings in health, comfort, and good living has flowed to all our peoples.

It may be that at one time scientific discovery and invention were the product of a poverty-driven genius in a garret. Even if that were so, it is no longer the case. The discovery of natural law does not come as a sudden concept. It comes mostly slowly —step by step—through the action and reaction among our university scientific faculties and their laboratories.

For instance, the parents of our radio communications of today were not the broadcasters. Its parents were Maxwell from one university, who by mathematics formulated the hypothesis of electrical wave motion. It was Hertz of another university who experimentally confirmed Maxwell's deductions and carried them further to the demonstration that these waves could traverse the atmosphere. Then university-trained technicians from a score of institutions gave the world mounting inventions which finally handed this great tool to the broadcasters.

I could illustrate this mutuality also of Faraday in one university, who discovered that energy could be transformed into electricity through induction. It was a German, a Britisher, and an American who, by applied sciences, fathered the whole system of transmitting power. It is said that Gladstone, on a visit to Faraday, after witnessing Faraday's "contraption," said: "Has this thing any practical value?" To which Faraday replied: "Sir, someday you will collect taxes from it."

It was Sir William Perkin who, as a student of the Royal College in London, first synthesized colors from coal tar. The chemists of both German universities and industrial laboratories made his original discovery the basis for an entire new spectrum of color.

It was Pasteur from another university who discovered that the Perkin aniline dyes could be used to differentiate living cells one from another. Von Bering in still another university developed the first antitoxin, and with this accrued knowledge Koch and Ehrlich were able, in their university laboratories, to develop the principles which led to modern biochemistry and chemotherapy.

We have another mutual duty. For it is our universities which must train the men for leadership in our professions and as executives of great economic institutions. It is they who must guide them away from incompetence and in their social responsibilities. It becomes the mutual obligation of our universities to inculcate in these future administrators morals, rectitude, and their responsibilities to the public.

But our universities have a still greater purpose. From them must come the expansion of the human spirit; with its ever-widening penetration into the unknown; and finally, as Huxley says, "the inculcation of veracity of thought."

But again I return to the fundamental of all—that is freedom itself. The discoveries of natural law can flourish only in an atmosphere of free minds and free spirits. And inventions and production flourish only in a climate of reward for effort.

And finally, as a tribute to the influence of German universities, I may mention that my own university bears on its seal the words, *Die Luft der Freiheit weht.*

It has been indeed the universities of the world which have molded and defended the freedoms of mankind. That has been your greatest mission over 400 years and it is our greatest mutual mission today.

Again, may I express my appreciation for the honor of this occasion.

Resistance to Communism

Address Before the Municipal Senate,
Berlin, Germany
[November 26, 1954]

THIS city of Berlin is on the front line of the cold war. You are combat soldiers in that war. Should it, which God forbid, ever become a hot war, you would be the first to face the enemy. Thus you more than others have the right to feel a sense of relief that the tensions of imminent war have sensibly decreased during these recent months. We can only speculate upon the outcome of this change in Moscow's protestations.

Whatever the outcome, we must remember that the Communists still confront us with three problems.

The first is their declared amoral basis of relations between nations. That must cause us to hesitate to accept their assurances of good will toward men without more particulars. St. James said: "Even so faith, if it hath not works, is dead."

The second is that ever since the war they have held to increasing armament. And that, even in the period when other nations had demobilized. That does not seem to spell simple defense measures. We have been compelled to resume arming to the teeth in order to deter their possible aggression.

The third is their militant promotion of the Communist faith. They incessantly seek by propaganda, infiltration, and conspiracy within free nations to destroy the very foundations of civilization.

For 6,000 years, since recorded time, every civilized race has believed in a Supreme Being. They have realized that the laws which control the orderly movement of the stars were not

97

economic materialism. For the first time in this long corridor of human history, a group of men with the resources of a powerful nation and all the modern techniques of communication are seeking to inflict Red atheism on the world.

Let there be no mistake. Lenin declared that "religion is the opiate of a people." And his malign announcements have been ratified before his tomb every year with fanatic zeal. And their agents at work every day in every free country provide ample confirmation. Their crusade would destroy men's belief in God. It would destroy the moral foundations of mankind. It rots the souls of men.

And the dreadful degenerations of thirty years of war have fertilized the soil of even free nations for the growth of these malign ideas.

Those dangers cannot be met by suppressing our own freedoms. Our governments can take care of tangible conspiracies to overthrow them by violence. But the organized infiltration of Communist ideas into disturbed and weak minds can be met only by moral and spiritual resistance.

The first bastion of that resistance is religious faith, whether it be Mohammedan, Jewish, or Christian.

Nothing is more true than George Washington's statement: "National morality cannot exist in the absence of religious principle." And that strong bulwark of resistance to Communism requires incessant strengthening of the moral foundations in our people.

The Sermon on the Mount established the transcendent concept of compassion and good will among men.

There was profound confirmation of the validity of religious faith when compassion defeated the scourges of famine and pestilence which were inevitable after these two great world wars, even to the extent of famine relief to the Communists.

A further stronghold of resistance is the unquenchable aspiration of the human heart for personal freedom and respect for the dignity of the individual man. The free nations hold that the right to this dignity and personal freedom comes from the Creator and not from governments—especially Communist governments.

But freedom does not come like manna from Heaven; it must be cultivated from rocky soil with infinite patience and great human toil. To assure the resistance of nations to Communism, our governments must find solution to many social ills which prepare the soil for its evil growth.

I have faith that the yearning for freedom is not dead even behind the Iron Curtain, for their peoples have tasted the invigorating waters of free men in years gone by.

I do not need to discuss the values of freedom with the people of Berlin. You live cheek by jowl on the boundary behind which you daily witness the naked poverty, the inhuman toil, the terror, the repressions of mind and spirit which the Communists inflict upon your own compatriots.

INCREASING PRODUCTIVITY

One of the greatest resistances to Communism has been the increase in productivity in the Western World. And among the discouraging events in the world, it is a heartening encouragement.

Since the war there have been revolutionary strides in scientific discovery and invention.

These improvements have almost wholly come from the countries where men's minds and spirits are free. It is only in those countries that men have the incentives to strive and receive rewards for their efforts.

To these astonishing scientific discoveries and inventions Germany has contributed a full part.

We of the free world have developed new materials in artificial fibres and plastics.

We have invented thousands of new labor-saving devices and better tools which relieve sweat from the backs of mankind.

We have by new designs immensely increased the power of our older aviation engines. We have invented the turbo jet and turbo engines. We have made huge advances in electronics. All of them have created an enormous expansion of transportation by air.

We have so improved the automobile as to bring it more nearly within reach of every family in the Western nations.

In agriculture, we have improved the quality of animals and plant life. We have improved the farmers' tools and his fertilizers.

We have enormously improved our fuel-produced electric power and its distribution. And now comes the possibility of the greatest source of power yet discovered by man. That is the fission of the atom. In its benevolent aspects we are already building atomic power plants, we are improving the health of men with its by-products. And President Eisenhower has proposed the sharing of these benevolent uses by all nations.

The discoveries in new drugs and antibiotics have brought relief from a multitude of diseases. They have lengthened the span of life and reduced pressures on our doctors and hospitals.

The sum of all this, and many other improvements, amounts to industrial revolution in only one decade of time.

Without this increase in productivity my country would have been unable to carry the burden of aid to other countries. And in Germany these improvements in productivity and the invigoration of private initiative under economic freedom have enabled you to carry the almost overwhelming burdens of the refugees and ruined industry.

Nor have you neglected the solution of stupendous social problems and the building of moral and spiritual bulwarks of resistance to Communist corruption.

With all this promise of increasing productivity, if the world could have peace, we would find a new Golden Age.

But meanwhile you, the leaders of Berlin, have a great responsibility toward the free world. And may I add, the nations of Western Europe have a great responsibility toward you. You face an enemy who lives just across the street. You have seen your duty and have performed it well. Thanks to the spirit and courage of men like your late great Mayor Reuter, you can, like the men of ancient Athens, hold your heads high and say:

"I am a Berliner."

Can We Ever Have Peace With the Russians?

This Week Magazine
[February 6, 1955]

[In reply to the question: "Mr. Hoover, recently you said that the tensions of imminent war have substantially decreased during recent months. Do you think the day will ever come when we can trust the Russians, and so live at peace with them?"]

WELL, "ever" is a long time. It is not, of course, impossible that the day could come when this Communist revolution devours itself or disintegrates or reforms its conduct. But before we start to relax it is important for us to recall certain *facts* and set certain *tests*. I would sum them up as follows:

Fact 1 is that in the past thirty-four years, Soviet Russia has signed a maze of solemn nonaggression treaties and peace covenants with other countries and then, by count, it has broken thirty-eight of them.

Fact 2 is that in fifteen years Soviet Russia, by direct or indirect conquest or conspiracy, has brought into the Communist group fifteen once free countries, so that the Communist bloc now represents five times the land area of the United States and nearly one third of the total population of the earth. It has gigantic arms and a passion for expansion.

Fact 3 is the purposes of Soviet leaders as repeatedly stated by themselves. Lenin, at various times, wrote:

"We have to use any ruse, dodges, tricks, cunning, unlawful method, concealment and veiling of the truth."

"The basic rule is to exploit conflicting interests of the capi-
talist states and systems."

"As long as capitalism . . . remains we cannot live in
peace."

Stalin supported all of Lenin's ideas and added others. I
give two samples:

"Sincere diplomacy is no more possible than dry water or
wooden iron."

"One must be a revolutionary, not a reformist."

Nor is all this just revolutionary bombast. Every year the
Soviet leaders swear allegiance to those ideas at Lenin's tomb.
The books of Lenin's writings are required reading in Soviet
schools. Together with Stalin's writings they are sold today in
every Communist bookshop of the world, including the United
States.

Fact 4. For 6,000 years, since recorded time, every civilized
race has believed in a Supreme Being. They have realized that
the laws which control the orderly movement of the stars were
not economic materialism. But Lenin dismissed religion as "the
opiate of the people."

For the first time in human history, a group of men with the
resources of a powerful nation and all the modern techniques
of communication are seeking to inflict atheism on the world.

CHANGE OF HEART?

Now for some tests that might serve to indicate a change of
heart of the Soviet. First we must seek the answers to these
questions:

1. Have the Soviets ceased their conspiracies to overthrow
free governments and modified their military aggressive policies?

2. Have we any reason to accept the full sincerity of "peaceful co-existence" and assurances of goodwill?

Up to now, the Soviets' immoral basis of relations between
nations must cause us to hesitate to accept their assurances of
goodwill without more particulars. Every morning's headlines

are confirmation of more conspiracies in every free country. As St. James said: "Even so faith, if it hath not works, is dead."

FOUR TESTS

But if they are sincere, the Soviets have great opportunities to demonstrate their good faith, not with words, but with works. Specifically, here are four tests they could meet right now:

Test 1. Sign the treaty giving freedom to Austria.

Test 2. Join in the unification of a truly free Germany.

Test 3. Permit free elections in satellite countries.

Test 4. Stop Red conspiracies in free nations.

All of which would indicate something better than "peaceful co-existence." With such "peaceful co-operation" they would help extend goodwill on earth—at least for a while.

PART II

ADDRESSES AND COMMENT
ON DOMESTIC ISSUES

On the Situation in the Mineral Agencies

Press Statement at Pioche, Nevada
[August 4, 1951]

AN admirable action has been taken in Washington consolidating the multitude of mineral agencies having to do with the armament program. And the appointment of Mr. Lawson to head the consolidated administration is an admirable choice. The confusion and red tape hitherto usual to these agencies has seriously damaged the whole nonferrous production.

However, the difficulties in the nonferrous segment are far deeper than the strangulation by red tape. We are in the midst of a famine in American production of these metals. That famine was born from government policies of the past twelve years. The first of the shackles on the industry has been tax policies which totally fail to recognize that this industry, above all industries, is born from venture capital. And venture capital or the profit from it has been largely extinguished. Mines are of short life and ore reserves are inevitably of decreasing metal content. The depreciation, development, and depletion allowances are wholly inadequate for this type of industry. The capital from profits is starved.

The lowering of tariff has built up foreign industry at the expense of the Americans. The assumption has been that our country would thus get cheaper metal from abroad. Now the government puts a price ceiling on American metal below the foreign prices. The consequence is that foreign-produced metals do not come to the United States. Now as the result of war demands on sparse American production we have thousands of industries starved and we will have many people out of employment.

The present ceiling price of these metals except tungsten and manganese is not high enough to cover expenses and proper development of the lower-grade mines and does not stimulate new mines. However it is never worth saying, "I told you so."

Sometime it may be hoped that the Congress and the administrators will listen to the Senators and Congressmen from the Western States. All this has been stated to them many times. The last and most able presentation was made by Senator Dworshak.

On the Two-Party System

Remarks at Salt Lake City, Utah
[August 1, 1951]

HERE in Utah you have Governor Lee, who has set a mark for the country of personal integrity, great vision, and no compromise with evil.

The record of the Republican Party in this State under his courageous leadership is setting a standard for the nation. If the country had forty-eight Governors his equal, they alone could save this country.

The very basis of Representative Government is a two-party system. It is one of the essential checks and balances against inefficiency, dishonesty, and tyranny.

A dozen nations in Europe collapsed into collectivism because the opposition decayed. One-party government is the end of Representative Government.

An organized, effective opposition which insists upon disclosure of the facts and submits them to the anvil of debate is the one safety Representative Government has.

Moreover, the people must have alternative programs of action upon which they may decide at the ballot box.

Beyond this, any party in power accumulates barnacles and deadwood which can only be rid by a change in administration.

I am not going into the details of how the present situation in Washington stands these tests. You can do that. You must need do at an accelerated pace for the next eighteen months.

Your job is to oppose, to expose, to propose. There is no place for me-too-ism if the American way of life is to be saved.

And it is youth that has the vigor, the character, the idealism to carry this cause. And in keeping up the battle you are doing a great national service.

Concerning Honor in Public Life

Nation-wide Broadcast Address at the
Iowa Centennial Celebration, Des Moines, Iowa
[August 30, 1951]

I AM indebted to the Governor, the Legislature, and the people of my native State for a most distinguished honor at this celebration of Iowa's Centennial.

In view of our serious national situation I would like on this occasion to review a few things for you to think about. They are mainly related to honor in public life. Let me say at once that honor is not the exclusive property of any political party.

I may start with the idea that all things in government which bear the prefix "new" are not necessarily new. They may not all of them even be good. Truly every generation discovers the world all new again and knows it can improve it. It is a good thing that each generation does—or our race would shrink in vitality and grow senile.

Each generation also wants to find out for itself that the stove is hot. A renewal of that sort of information is valuable.

But we have overworked this word "new" in trying to get out of this age of misery from our thirty-seven years of hot and cold wars, with intervals of hot and cold peace.

In this period we have either been cured or made over "new" about fourteen times. We have had the New Order, the New Freedom, the New Day, the New Era, the New Outlook, the New Epoch, the New Economy, the New Dawn, the New Deal, the New Religion, the New Liberalism, the New War, and several New Foreign Policies. None of these were really "new" discoveries.

And the New Testament is too often omitted. After each "new" we have a relapse and take another pill, labeled "new."

Some of these somethings "new" have value. Too many have been false signposts on the road of national progress. Some point to will-o'-wisps of security not to be had on this earth. Some lead the nation over the precipice of inflation and socialism. Some just lead to the land of make-believe. Certainly some of them are tainted with untruth and a diluted intellectual honesty.

The word "new" applies better to physical things than to human forces. Indeed when the sun rises in the morning we hail it as a new day. We cheer the passing of the night. But it is a false analogy in the march of civilization.

Most of our chores for the new day were assigned the night before. Our abilities to perform them were formed not only last year but over centuries or even geologic time. If the new day has no link with yesterday we would be without know-how and morals today. The loss of that link can bring chaos to the whole economic, the moral, and the spiritual world.

AN ADJOURNMENT FOR A WHILE

As an aside, I suggest at least we adjourn trying to make America over into some other shape until we get out of this cold or hot war. Our present crisis is dangerous enough to require one concentrated undeviating purpose in Washington.

Many of our so-called social and economic gains will go by the board, anyway, if this hot and cold war keeps up. After all, the great social gains of the last century were a mixture of liberty, compassion, unlimited meat, automobiles, and washing machines. These are at least getting scarcer.

There will be plenty of time to exercise our muscles on "new" experiments after these violent changes in international temperature are survived. And these programs of making America over add an especially destructive "new"—that is, New Taxes.

Think about it.

LET US USE THE WORD "OLD" ONCE IN A WHILE

The practical thing we can do if we really want to make the world over again is to try out the word "old" for a while. There are some "old" things that made this country.

There is the Old Virtue of religious faith.

There are the Old Virtues of integrity and the whole truth.

There is the Old Virtue of incorruptible service and honor in public office.

There are the Old Virtues of economy in government, of self-reliance, thrift, and individual liberty.

There are the Old Virtues of patriotism, real love of country, and willingness to sacrifice for it.

These "old" ideas are very inexpensive. They even would help win hot and cold wars.

I realize that such suggestions will raise that cuss word "reactionary." But some of these "old" things are slipping badly in American life. And if they slip too far, the lights will go out of America, even if we win these cold and hot wars.

Think about it.

THE FLIGHT FROM HONOR

We might explore some of the things that have happened to the "old" virtues of integrity, truth, and honor in public life. During the recent past we have had a flood of exposures by Congressional committees, by State Legislatures, by Grand Juries in scores of cities, and the press.

A few days more than one hundred seventy-five years ago, the 56 members of the Continental Congress of the United States unanimously declared a program of action and certain principles of American life. The concluding words of the Declaration are a pledge of "our sacred Honor."

I sometimes wonder what the 56 Founding Fathers, from their invisible presence in our Congressional Halls, would say about the procession of men in responsible positions who have come before its committees of this day. What would they have thought of the "sacred Honor" of the five percenters, mink coats, deep freezers, and free hotel bills? Or favoritism in Government loans and Government contracts? Or failures to prosecute evil-doers who spread cancerous rackets and gambling rings with their train of bribed officials?

But I am less concerned at stealing public money than with the far more destructive forms of dishonor. What would the Founding Fathers have thought of those who coquette with traitorship? Or of secret and disastrous commitments of our nation which were denied at the time? Or high officials under oath contradicting each other as to facts? Or the failure to keep promises to the people? Our civilization moves forward on promises that are kept.

We thus have a cancerous growth of intellectual dishonesty in public life which is mostly beyond the law. One of its chief instruments is corrupt propaganda. There has been such propaganda by foreign governments and our own designed to get us into war. Then we have the propaganda to keep up our pep. Then the habit continues in peace time. And some pressure groups have learned this trick to get something they ought not to have.

The mildest form of corrupt propaganda is a process of persuasive part-truths. At times it even rises to the high moral levels of selling snake oil.

But the malignant form of propaganda spreads deadly poisons. Its process is to create suspicion, hate, and fear. Its purpose is less to persuade than to conceal truth and to crush opposition.

The machinery of propaganda is made of standardized gadgets by which you can detect it.

One of these standard gadgets is slogans. They freeze the real process of thought.

If you will examine the two-score loud slogans created during this last third of a century, you will find most of them, like the apples of Sodom, have turned to bitter ashes in our national mouth. Most of them became ripe in a year or two, some lasted a little longer. Some very new ones are already turning mouldy.

One of these gadgets is to create fear by describing the horrors of invasion of the United States by foreign armies. This one always arises to its maximum decibel when pressuring legislation and elections. While aircraft can come our way no armies on earth can land on our shores.

Another gadget is to give new meaning to old, simple, and well-understood expressions until the integrity of our language is polluted. The term "liberalism" has turned pink inside. The term "welfare" never before meant the "welfare state" with its red or pink colors. The Chinese Communists were not "agrarian liberals." From that perversion of truth alone, we suffered a gigantic defeat of free men in China.

You can test malignant propaganda from another of its gadgets. That is the smear. This gadget has wide potency. When Mr. X presents an inconvenient fact or argument, the propagandists can simplify matters by pointing out that he was once a banker or was fined for speeding. With this gadget you can get your opponent either way in the international field by just suggesting he is an appeaser, or a warmonger, or an isolationist. On the issue of government spending, he can be flattened out by calling him an inflationist or he is against the underdog. If he comments on either side of ideological matters, you can defeat him going or coming by calling him a Fascist, or a reactionary, or a fellow-traveler, or just a red herring.

There is still another of these propaganda gadgets. That is to squelch debate by cries for "Unity!" Unity! The implication is that the citizen is disloyal to his country if he disagrees with the powers that be.

I suggest that these are not operations of rugged intellectual honesty. They are attempts to coerce men into the intellectual concentration camp named fear. These gadgets have been very handy tools for making America over into these fourteen new varieties and getting us into hot and cold wars.

Think about it.

UNVEILING TRUTH BY DEBATE

It is difficult enough to debate against the gadgets of propaganda. But there is something worse. That is the concealment of truth and commitments. I am not here discussing our foreign policies. But may I ask you a question?

Does anybody believe that the propaganda-promoted foreign policies over the past dozen years have always been right? Or that there has always been a disclosure of the whole truth?

For example, certain secret commitments were entered into at Teheran and Yalta which sold the freedom of half a billion people down the river. They were not disclosed to the Congress or to the American people. Does anyone believe that, had they been submitted to the American people for debate and to the Congress for decision, they would ever have been approved? That is where we lost the peace and wandered into the land of hot and cold wars.

Debate founded on the full disclosure of the whole truth and free of these gadgets is the stuff that can save free men.

Think about it.

OUR SACRED HONOR

I would like to explore this "old" virtue of truth, integrity, and honor in public life a little further.

Congress can well widen the laws so as to clutch the "new" kinds of bribes and benefits they have discovered. But Congress cannot reach intellectual dishonors.

Part truth, concealment of public commitments, propaganda and its gadgets, and failure to enforce the laws are but part of them. And there are group pressures "to get theirs" which smell from both the decay of integrity and the rotting of patriotism. And some persons arrive at the morals with a divining rod that measures morals in terms of votes.

The Congress, from its own inquiries, is confronted with the fact that sacred Honor cannot always be tested by legality or enforced by law. In its frustration, the Congress is groping for some sort of code of ethics, which with a prefix "new" might protect the citizen from his own officials.

Might I suggest that there are already some old and tested codes of ethics? There are the Ten Commandments, the Sermon on the Mount, and the rules of the game which we learned at our Mother's knee.

Can a nation live if these are not the guides of public life? Think it over.

OUR RIGHT TO COMPLAIN

The American people have a right to bitter complaint over these disclosures of dishonor in high places. The duty of public men in this Republic is to lead in standards of integrity—both in mind and money.

Dishonor in public life has a double poison. When people are dishonorable in private business, they injure only those with whom they deal or their own chances in the next world. But when there is a lack of honor in Government, the morals of the whole people are poisoned.

The drip of such poisons may have nothing to do with dishonor in some college athletics or the occasional policemen on the beat. But the rules of the game have been loosened somewhere.

Some folks seem to think these are necessary evils in a free government. Or that it is smart politics. Those are deadly sleeping pills. No public man can be just a little crooked. There is no such thing as a no-man's-land between honesty and dishonesty. Our strength is not in politics, prices, production, or price controls. Our strength lies in spiritual concepts. It lies in public sensitiveness to evil.

Much as the Congress has my good wishes, something stronger than a new code of ethics is needed by America. The issue is decency in public life against indecency.

Our greatest danger is not from invasion by foreign armies. Our dangers are that we may commit suicide from within by complaisance with evil. Or by public tolerance of scandalous behavior. Or by cynical acceptance of dishonor. These evils have defeated nations many times in human history.

The redemption of mankind by America will depend upon our ability to cope with these evils right here at home.

Think about it.

CONCLUSION

But I do not wish to leave you, the neighbors of my child-hood, with any implication of pessimism. I speak to you of some of our weaknesses, not because of frustration or despair, but to urge remedy. The fact that we are vigorously washing our dirty linen in the open is a sign that moral stamina still survives.

Without bitterness in our hearts, we are raising our eyes to the Creator of man who assured us that in American soil we can find the moral and spiritual forces which make free men and women. In His guidance, we shall find the fortitude to correct our errors, to straighten our courses, to resurrect the spirit that made our America so free and bountiful a nation.

For reassurance in the future I need only to turn my thoughts to my grandparents who came to this State in the covered wagon. Here they and my parents toiled that their children might have greater opportunities than had been theirs. Here they worshipped God. Here they lived out their lives in the faith and hope of Americans. They lie buried on an Iowa hillside.

Therefore, here in this State where I was nurtured, I cannot but feel a strength that comes up from the deep roots in the very soil on which we stand. That strength is in character and truth and decent living. And it will triumph.

It will triumph because I know America is turning its face away from the maudlin left "isms" and the spread of untruth of the past two decades. We sense the frauds on men's minds and morals. Moral indignation is on the march again.

The Inflation Threat

The Journal-American, New York City
[January 8, 1952]

THE current expenditures, taxes, and economic controls may be necessary in this cold and hot war, but the American people should rest under no belief that the economic and social consequences will be good to take. It should be frankly faced and not covered up with soft phrases and economic illusions.

There are two major economic forces now current: inflation and confiscatory taxation. They affect, and will further affect the standard of living of millions of families. Their visible evidence is the high prices which enter by the back door and taxes which enter by the front door of every cottage.

We are in a war economy except for world-wide shooting. In this situation, we are diverting civilian production to war materials. We are placing a greater portion of our manpower under arms or armament. All this creates scarcity in civilian goods and labor with consequent rising prices and rising wages.

We are constantly told that measures are being taken by the government to "prevent" inflation. All of which ignores the fact that we are in the middle of a roaring inflation. Since the end of the second world war alone the purchasing power of our money, measured in wholesale prices, has decreased 40 percent. And the wholesale prices will in the end express themselves in consumers' prices.

Under the demands of the Pentagon we are confronted with a probable Federal deficit of $30 to $40 billion before this major rearmament period is over. We already have vastly overexpanded government obligations by $280 billion and private credit is greatly extended as well.

The financing of the Federal deficit will produce more inflation. The government will need to cover part of the amount by selling its bonds or notes, some part of which will need to be raised from the banks. That is direct inflation of credit and results in bank check money.

The two pressures—scarcities of commodities and expanding credit or paper money—are the irresistible forces of further inflation. All of which is being expressed today in black markets and a continuous spiral of higher wages and then higher prices.

Controls of the type we have in force on wages and prices can do little more than retard inflation. The experience of six great commercial nations in two years has proved that it is, at best, a retarding device.

Huge taxes are already overstraining our economy. Sufficient additional levies cannot be made to meet the inevitable deficit because taxes are already at the point of diminishing return. That is indicated by the fact that incomes in the top bracket will be paying Federal, State, and local taxes of over 100 percent.

At a lower level, if all incomes above that of a United States Senator's salary and expense allowance were confiscated, it would bring only about $2 billions annually to the Federal Treasury. And that assumes that these taxpayers would continue to work for nothing which they will not.

Corporation taxes in the long run are passed on to their consumers or they would go bankrupt. They thus become part of the multitude of hidden taxes.

Therefore, any increase in present taxes must fall on the still lower brackets. Under the present rates persons in the $3,000 to $4,000 brackets will pay an average of about $900 per year per family in Federal, State, and local direct and indirect taxes. The double effect of inflation and taxes is indicated by the fact that a family of $3,000 net annual income ten years ago must now earn over $6,000 to have the same standard of living.

There are men in Washington who welcome these pressures because they are driving down the road of socialism. That road leads to socializing the income of our people. That is the inevitable end, even if it is not the avowed purpose. In this form of creeping socialism we may be permitted to hold the paper title to property, while bureaucracy spends our income. No less an authority than Lenin once recommended inflation as the certain road to socialism.

Rearmament is not a quickie program. It is a continuous process, due to continual new inventions in weapons and the rapid deterioration in these instruments of precision. A man can carry a load of 300 pounds across the room, but he cannot carry it around the block or he will break his back. We must prepare for a long journey.

Communism is an evil thing. It is contrary to the spiritual, moral, and material aspirations of man. It can live only in a slave state. These very reasons give rise to my conviction that it will decay and die of its own poisons. But that will be many years away and in the meantime we should adjust our expenditures to maintain our economic stability.

The Constructive Character of the Republican Party

Nation-wide Radio and Television Broadcast,
New York City
[October 18, 1952]

MY FELLOW Americans:

I have tonight come out of what I had hoped was final retirement from political activities. I have done so at General Eisenhower's request. I have done so because I believe General Eisenhower and the Republican ticket should be elected. I am convinced that the fate of our country in these confused and perilous times hangs upon a change in the Administration in Washington.

A major safeguard of American freedom is two virile political parties. A great political party, despite secondary internal differences, is welded together by certain common loyalties and beliefs, certain principles, and certain ideals of government.

When we elect a President, we are not electing a single person. We are electing a group of party members to take over the direction of the Government.

My major purpose tonight is to address the 40 percent—about 40 million—of our eligible voters who have come of age since there was a Republican Administration. You 40 million must choose the course, select the management of the United States in the immediate years ahead. With you rests the destiny of our country.

You 40 million new voters have known little of the Republican Party's background of principles and of its forward-looking constructive accomplishments.

Incessantly for the past twenty years, and including this campaign, the American people have been deluged by misrepresentations and false slogans aimed at the principles, the ideals, and the record of the Republican Party. Such statements do not befit the sense of fair play, of honor, or of statesmanship in our national life or in either party.

No political party is perfect and I have no desire to minimize the service of the Democratic Party under such leaders as Jefferson, Cleveland, and Wilson. They as did Republican leaders believed in that true Liberalism which made this country great.

THE MAJOR MISREPRESENTATIONS

The major misrepresentations and falsehoods now current today appear in seven categories.

1. That the Republican Party is the party of privilege and the tool of Wall Street or "big business."

2. That the Great Depression was caused by Republicans and they did nothing about it.

3. That the Republican Party is a reactionary party opposed to change and reforms so necessary in a progressive national life, or is not "forward-looking."

4. That the Republican Party neglected and is opposed to the conservation and development of natural resources.

5. That the Republican Administrations were corrupt.

6. That the Republican Party is incompetent to preserve peace.

7. That the growth of communism in the United States was caused by the Republican years of the Depression.

The proper reply to these misrepresentations is not counter-smear, but presentation of the facts to thinking people.

1. WHAT ABOUT PRIVILEGE, WALL STREET, BIG BUSINESS?

The Republican Party is now almost one hundred years old. Its dominant principle has always been the freedom of men.

Twenty-five years after Lincoln's emancipation of the slaves there was a second great revolutionary act by Republicans to free men from oppression. The gigantic economic development of our country had led to new forms of oppression of free men. These were abuses by big business, monopolies, and restraints of trade.

By the Republican Sherman Act of 1890 these doings were prohibited. It produced far deeper consequences than mere negation. It produced an economic revolution. Our whole economic system was transformed from the unrestrained laissez-faire, dog-eat-dog concepts which we had inherited from Europe. By this Act our economy was first geared to standards of conduct which preserve freedom. We call it regulation. I may say at once such regulation is not to be confused with regimentation.

By the standards in the Sherman Act we assured competition in the United States. Under competition American business has been forced to earn its profits by constantly improving its plants, by lowering its costs of production. Europe continued the system of trade monopolies, cartels, and combinations, whose profits were thus partly made from control of prices and distribution. European business lost much of the pressure for improvement of plant and method. Under the impulses of competition, American industry leads the world. Much European economy has so lost efficiency that Socialism has become their fatal answer.

"Big business" did not rejoice over the Sherman Act. Many of them have never become reconciled to it. They induced the New Dealers in 1933, to, in effect, repeal the Antitrust laws by an imitation of Mussolini's Corporate State through creating the N.R.A. Only the Supreme Court saved our competitive economy from fascism. A Democratic President denounced this action of the Court as "reactionary."

Nor was the Sherman Antitrust law a solitary action in

safeguarding free men from economic oppression. The Republican Party continued to put restraints on oppressive business up to its last moments in office in 1933. To prove that, I must recite a long list of Federal laws passed under Republican Presidents.

It was Republicans who, by successive laws from 1903 to 1910, gave the Interstate Commerce Commission its full authority to control railway rates. In 1910 came the control of the telephone and telegraph rates.

In 1906 Republicans passed the Pure Food and Drug Acts.

Returning to office after being out for eight years, Republicans, in 1922, regulated the grain exchanges. In 1924 they secured regulation of the Federal fisheries. In 1926 came the regulation of aviation. In 1927 came the regulation of radio. In 1930 the Tariff Commission (a statistical agency) was transformed into a bipartisan body for the regulation of the tariff, in order to take the tariff out of politics.

And in 1930 came the creation of a real Federal Power Commission.

In 1932 we reformed the Bankruptcy Laws so as to prevent the flood of fraud on creditors.

I may sum up that of the eighteen major acts erecting standards of conduct for business, twelve were of Republican origin and four originated under Cleveland and Wilson.

Does this Republican record look like the tool of "big business" or privilege? It is the very essence of preserving men free from oppression.

The New Dealers have preferred creeping socialism to the establishment of proper standards of conduct among free men.

2. THE MISREPRESENTATION THAT THE REPUBLICANS CREATED THE GREAT DEPRESSION AND THEN DID NOTHING ABOUT IT

The misrepresentation that Republicans created the Great Depression, which came ten years after the first World War, is still oratory in this campaign. That nonsense has been exploded a thousand times by a multitude of economists, historians, and statesmen.

The Great Depression started elsewhere in the world before it struck the United States. Its major violence came from the inevitable bankruptcy of Europe as the aftermath of the first World War.

In this economic hurricane, the economy of one foreign country after another crumbled, panics and political revolutions took place in a score of foreign nations. In effect all but two nations in the world abandoned the gold standard. Trying to protect themselves these foreign nations imposed restrictions on their exchange and imports. They suspended payments on their obligations. Our farm and other exports to Europe practically ceased. Unemployment spread over the whole earth. Our gold standard was jeopardized. The impact of these forces spread constant fear and near panic in the United States. Our weak banking and credit system was toppling all around us.

To solve these emergencies and ameliorate the successive shocks the Republican Administration created unprecedented agencies and took unprecedented actions.

RELIEF TO THE UNEMPLOYED

We organized direct relief to those in distress and indirect relief to the unemployed by huge public works. We did so with never a charge of corruption. No one went hungry or cold if our system of committees knew of it. We temporarily stopped immigration to prevent loss of jobs by our workers. We sustained wages, we reduced employer-employee friction to the lowest levels in recent times.

AIDS TO FARMERS

In 1923 Republicans had already created the Federal Intermediate Credit Banks to finance the marketing of farm products. In 1929 Republicans created the Federal Farm Board with a capital of half a billion dollars, which supported farm prices in the Depression. Out of it came the present Bank for Farm Co-operatives. Republicans expanded the Farm Loan

Board and created the Agricultural Credit Banks to finance farmers' production. The Democrats abolished this one.

AIDS TO BUSINESS

We created the Reconstruction Finance Corporation with three billion dollars capital. We created the Home Loan Banks. We expanded the Federal Reserve Credit System. We accomplished these measures against the opposition or delays of a Democratic House of Representatives.

Far from "bailing out" the rich, as one orator says, 90 percent of the loans under Republican Administrations went to saving Building and Loan Associations, Savings Banks, insurance companies, small country banks, and Farmers' Loan Associations. These were not the institutions of the rich. They represented the small savings of the people.

We incessantly urged reform of our obsolete banking laws so as to protect depositors. But a Democratic Congress refused.

We prevented panic in the United States until after the election of the New Deal. We secured the country from being forced off the gold standard and kept the American dollar ringing true on every counter in the entire world.

CO-OPERATION WITH FOREIGN NATIONS

To protect foreign economy from complete collapse in the Depression, we created a moratorium on world governmental debts and brought about the Standstill Agreements. To restore the demoralized world monetary standards and to decrease trade barriers we originated the World Economic Conference. That conference was convened in London after we left office. But it was assassinated in its youth by a Democratic President. In his memoirs the then Democratic Secretary of State implies this action sowed the seeds of the second World War.

Too many young voters have been led to believe the New Deal enacted all this multitude of measures.

Most outstanding economists are agreed that Republican measures brought beginnings of the recovery in July 1932. But our recovery then in motion was reversed by a wholly unnecessary panic of bank depositors. That was created by refusal of the incoming New Deal to co-operate with us in foreign and domestic remedial measures for the whole four months after the election. It was also due to public panic over the New Deal proposals to tinker with the value of our money and thus bring inflation. And now the New Dealers date all their doleful statistics from the bottom of this setback, which they themselves created.

They might mention that they have continued to tinker with money, credit, debt, and inflation until an income of $3,000 per annum in 1932 would buy more than an income of $8,000 today. Your annual Federal taxes in 1932 averaged under $100. Today they are over $1,300 per family.

A dozen other nations, with free economies, within three years after the New Deal election, marched out of the Depression to higher levels of employment and production than those of the boom year of 1928.

There were about 11,000,000 unemployed at the time of Roosevelt's election in November 1932. But the New Deal violated their every election promise and attempted to mix fascism and socialism into the American system. From their actions America continued to wallow every winter in 10 to 11 million unemployed. Eight years of this New Deal unemployment only found remedy in jobs from the second World War.

If you want more proof of these misrepresentations, I have published a whole book on the subject.

3. REACTIONARY AND OPPOSED TO CHANGE

A daily misrepresentation in this campaign is that the Republican Party is reactionary, opposed to change, and without courage to take action needed in a progressive country.

It would seem that what I have recounted as to Republican action on business oppression and action during the world-wide depression would be sufficient answer. But just in case you want some more evidence I will give you a few of many samples of Republican attitudes to reform and change in the fields of labor, children, farmers, veterans, and homes.

LABOR

As to labor, in 1903, Republicans created the Department of Labor and Commerce. Returning to office after the Wilson Administration, we secured in 1923 the abolition of the twelve-hour day in industry. A Republican administration was the first officially to establish collective bargaining when we established the Railway Mediation board in 1926. The act limiting the use of Federal Court injunctions in labor disputes was signed by a Republican President. Was this reactionary?

CHILDREN

As to the protection to children, in 1912, Republicans established the Children's Bureau in the Federal Government. Following our return to office after World War I, Republicans in 1924 submitted a Constitutional Amendment prohibiting child labor. The Amendment failed because enough State Legislatures, predominantly Democratic, refused to ratify it. In 1931 a Republican Administration proposed subsidies for Rural Child Welfare, which were passed by the House of Representatives but killed by a filibuster of a Democratic Senator. Were these actions reactionary?

FARMERS

I have already given evidence of our interest in the farmers' well-being. I may point out further that for ninety-six years Republicans supported tariff protection for the farmers. Republicans in 1862 created the Agricultural Commission which subsequently became the Department of Agriculture. Republicans expanded the Department from 1902 to 1932 by creating six of its most important Bureaus. In 1932 we proposed the retirement of marginal lands from production to remedy the farmers' chronic surplus production. It was turned down by a Democratic Congress. Was this reactionary?

HOUSING AND HOMES

As to housing and homes, after the dislocations of the first World War the Republicans in 1922 established the first Bureau of Housing in the Federal Government. By co-operative

measures with the people, we secured construction of more new
homes during the decade of the Twenties than the whole eight
years of the New Deal. A Republican Administration in 1932
established the Home Loan Banks and the same year initiated
the first Federal aid to slum clearance. Was this reactionary?

VETERANS

As to veterans, in 1868, Republicans established pensions for
veterans disabled in the Civil War and for their widows and or-
phans. They did so in 1908 for Spanish-American War veterans.
They did so for World War I veterans. In 1924, Republicans
enacted the Veterans' Bonus Bill. In 1932, Republicans established the Veterans' Administration as a major agency of the
Government. In 1930, Republicans provided disability allowances and hospitalization to all indigent veterans, irrespective
of the origins of the illness. In 1933, the New Deal repealed
this service and deprived 300,000 veterans of this aid. From
1921 to 1933, Republicans built 46 hospitals with 25,260 beds
for veterans. A study by The Brookings Institution says:

. . . The eight years ending with March 4, 1933 saw the greatest
expansion and liberalization in legislation relating to Veterans ever
known in this country or probably in any other country.

FEDERAL ADMINISTRATION

And we may look at the organization of the Federal Government itself. In addition to establishing the Departments of
Labor and Commerce, Republicans established the Patent Office, the Weather Bureau, and the Postal Savings Banks.

To take civil employees out of politics, Republicans in 1883
established the bipartisan Civil Service Commission. The act
provided that all new employees with a few exceptions were to
be admitted on merit by open competitive examinations and
proof as to character. This meant equal rights to all irrespective
of politics, religion, or race.

By 1932 all but 19 percent of the 580,000 Federal employees had entered government service through the non-

partisan merit gate of the Civil Service Commission. But during the succeeding eight years of the New Deal, twenty-four acts were passed exempting groups from Civil Service requirements. The Democratic County chairmen did most of the appointing. One might also note that, in 1937, a Democratic Administration attempted to abolish the Commission and was defeated in Congress. By 1952 the bureaucracy has swelled to over 2,500,000 persons of whom I doubt one-half ever originally passed the full competitive Civil Service Commission examinations before their employment.

In 1921, Republicans established for the first time a Federal Budget and a General Accounting Office for control and audit of accounts.

If all these evidences of reform and "forward look" to meet the change in national life are not enough, I will give you some more from the record.

In 1930 and 1932 a Republican Administration reformed the Federal Criminal procedures so as to abolish much of the trick delays in criminal trials.

We reformed the whole Federal prison system, with separate prisons for hardened criminals and special prisons for women. We established a system of probation and parole. We passed the Federal anti-kidnaping laws.

In 1926 and 1930 we established the FBI.

4. CONSERVATION AND DEVELOPMENT OF NATURAL RESOURCES

The statement is made that Republicans would stifle governmental aid to conservation and development of natural resources.

Republicans originated practically the whole idea and every bureau of Federal conservation of natural resources.

In 1891, Republicans established the first National Forests and, in 1905, the Forest Service.

The National Forests comprised 161 million acres in 1932. They have been increased by only 12 percent in the last twenty years.

In 1872, Republicans established the first National Park.

Of the 28 major National Parks, 23 were founded by Republicans.

In 1924, Republicans established the Oil Conservation Board and, in 1929, all oil beneath the free public lands was withdrawn from private entry. That same year a Republican administration initiated the great interstate compact for conservation of oil which has since come into being among twenty-one states.

In 1902, Republicans established and vigorously carried out Federal reclamation of arid lands. Of the 62 reclamation projects today, 41 were created by Republicans. And these included the first gigantic multiple-purpose dam on the Colorado River and we nearly finished it. Furthermore we approved and were engaged in the engineering plans for the great Grand Coulee Dam and Central Valley of California developments.

In 1930, laws were recommended for the conservation of the public ranges in the west.

OTHER GREAT PUBLIC IMPROVEMENTS

As to purported Republican opposition to public improvements generally, I may mention that a Republican Administration in 1905 undertook and built the Panama Canal. Seven administrations of Republicans constantly expanded the development of our rivers, harbors, and canals. In 1929 we established the concept of an integrated waterway system connecting great cities 1,600 miles east and west and 1,500 miles north and south. We largely completed it. Without this system we could not have handled our traffic in World War II.

From 1927 to 1932 we rebuilt the flood control on the lower Mississippi and Sacramento rivers. We did so good a job that there have been no flood disasters on these rivers since.

The Republicans vigorously supported the States in constructing interstate roads. By 1932 about 129,000 miles of surfaced roads had been built. In 1932 a Republican Administration, through the RFC, established the policy of Federal loans for self-liquidating public works then financially unfeasible by private capital or State funds. The San Francisco

Bay Bridge and the Colorado River water supply to the Los Angeles area were examples. And those loans made by Republican Administrations have all been repaid to the Federal Government.

In 1928, Republicans undertook the public building program which has so beautified Washington and many other cities.

In fact, in the single four years from 1929 to 1933, Republicans built more useful public works than in the entire previous thirty years.

Taking all this into account it would seem that phrase "Republicans do nothing" is somewhat overdone in this campaign.

5. CORRUPTION

During the last fifty-two years Republicans and Democrats equally divided the time in office. The Republicans had just one bad episode of corruption. That was during the Harding Administration. Democrats do not fail to recall it even in the present campaign.

Without examining whether corruption can be absolved by pointing an accusing finger at older sins, I suggest a wide difference between the conduct of Republican and Democratic administrations in their two fields of wickedness. There were nine men involved in the Harding episode. The other members of the Administration were aghast. They determined to pursue these men implacably. Before we had finished with them, two of them had committed suicide, one died while awaiting trial, four landed in prison, and one escaped by a twice-hung jury.

Can the perpetrators of the present mess in Washington point to any such vigorous house cleaning?

In the past twenty years of Democratic Administration, there have been over 300 cases of Congressional or administrative condemnation or public exposure of every variety of transgression of national honor. It appears that except for cases forced by Congressional Committees, so far less than twenty-five persons have landed in jail. Washington nowadays seems neither aghast nor implacable.

6. REPUBLICANS AND PEACE

The misrepresentation that the Republican Party is an isolationist Party is false on the record.

Republicans in 1899 established the Open Door policy in China and in 1922 brought about the Nine-Power Treaty for its protection. In 1928, Republicans initiated the Kellogg-Briand Pact against aggression. From 1921 to 1932, Republican Administrations entered into over sixty conciliation and arbitration treaties with different nations. For 12 years—from 1921 to 1933—Republican Presidents ceaselessly urged our joining the World Court. The New Deal dropped it.

In 1922, Republican Administrations brought about partial limitation in size of the major navies of the world and, in 1930, completed that job. The ending of naval competition over the following decade contributed to peace and saved billions of taxpayers' money.

In our Western Hemisphere relations, beginning in 1890 and by 1910, Republican Secretaries of State had established the Pan-American Union. Returning again to Washington after Wilson, a Republican Administration in 1929 established the Good Neighbor Policy.

I have already related our international co-operation to alleviate the Depression.

As to ability to keep peace I may mention that during twelve years of the last Republican Administrations, nations embracing nearly 2 billion of the world's population, as a result of American policies, held the United States in high esteem and warm friendship. I doubt if there are twenty-five percent of those 2 billions remaining our friends today.

All this is scarcely an isolationist record.

Our critics are correct that most Republicans opposed our joining with Stalin in the second World War. We believed these monsters, Stalin and Hitler, should exhaust each other. We said repeatedly that by joining with Stalin in the war we would spread communism over the earth. If this was isolationism, I am proud of it.

7. COMMUNISM

A few days ago it was said that the growth of communism in the United States was caused by the "Republican Depression."

In the 15 years after the Communist Revolution in Russia until the end of Republican Administrations the Communist Party had grown to a meager 13,000 members. During this time we had refused to give respectability to this slave state by having any relations with it. In the ten years after the New Deal recognition of Communist Russia, the Communist Party in the United States grew to over 80,000 members.

Their front organizations cast over 500,000 votes.

Republicans tolerated no communists in the Federal Government. I must leave the recital of the New Deal record to you.

IN CONCLUSION

I could go on endlessly with this record of constructive courageous action. I have surely said enough to refute the myriad of falsehoods and misrepresentations in this campaign.

This is not ancient stuff. It is pertinent to this moment as these daily misrepresentations indicate the character of the party seeking by such means to retain their hold on Washington. Second, it is pertinent to reassure new voters from the record that the party behind such great men as General Eisenhower and Senator Nixon is a constructive party of probity, courage, ideals, and vision, worthy to be entrusted with the administration of our country.

Message of Congratulation

Telegram to General Dwight D. Eisenhower
[November 4, 1952]

New York City
November 4, 1952

General Dwight D. Eisenhower
Hotel Commodore
New York, New York

You are to be congratulated upon a great victory not alone for yourself but for our country. I am sure the whole American people pray for your success in the most difficult task which confronts you.

HERBERT HOOVER

On General Eisenhower's Election

Statement to the Press
[November 5, 1952]

THE American people have ordered a change in the administration of our Government. But the hour of victory for our cause is no time for either recrimination or exaltation. The problems before us are more difficult than were even debated in this campaign. The majority of our people are giving their faith of solution of our problems into the hands of General Eisenhower and his friends. I am sure the whole American people pray the Almighty for his success in the great task now before him.

What's Happened to the Two-Party System?

This Week Magazine
[December 28, 1952]

EVENTS of this presidential year indicate that there are a host of reforms needed in our democratic process. Number one, in my opinion, is the restoration of a real two-party system.

Obviously, our form of representative government can function only with two major political parties who differ in attitudes and measures. Otherwise the ballot box cannot even reprimand the political bosses.

I am not going to deliver a lecture on the history of the rifts between and within our two parties, so you can relax. The dominant elements in both of our major parties for 150 years held to that interpretation of Liberalism which meant more and not less liberty for the individual. Now comes the claim that such an interpretation is "reactionary." In fact, our major parties have become confused ever since the ghosts of Benito Mussolini, Karl Marx, Lord Keynes, and our own give-away ideologists began to meddle in our national life. Under their influence, the definition of "Liberalism" is certainly badly befuddled. Today, ideological differences smash around like a loose cannon on the decks of both our political parties.

However, the new ideological split has been defined instinctively by the common tongue of all nations where free speech still has a part in their proceedings. That unrefined definition is now "right wing" and "left wing." That is, except for candidates. They say they are in the middle of the road. However, they differ on where the middle is.

If there were a Man in the Moon, who knew the essentials of representative government and its need of a two-party system, and if he had been observing events on this planet during the past noisy presidential year, he would probably have some pointed things to say to us.

He would say to the Republican Party, "There is no room for you on the 'left'; you must be the party of the 'right,' or you will split into feeble fragments and disappear."

He would say to the Democratic Party with equal force, "Your die is cast. You are the party of the 'left' or you will likewise split into futile fragments."

He would say to the minority of Republicans on the "left" and to the splinter Democrats of the "right," "You are not in your proper spiritual homes."

And the Man in the Moon would continue his remarks to the effect that unless you resolve your positions on the right and on the left, you will see the democratic process wrecked on the rocks of conspiring futile fractions; your two political parties will be on the road to a place where the people can have no authority in the ballot box or in the government. And he would point out that the governments of fifteen nations in Europe cracked up because of the multitude of fractional political parties. In each case, after a long period of stalemates, compromises, and negative actions, they were able to agree only on give-away programs. At last the people—bankrupt, frustrated, overwhelmed, and confused—actively welcomed the Man on Horseback—with a hidden ideology in his pocket.

If our country is to avoid this fate, we must restore an active, honest, clear-cut two-party system.

Federal Socialization of
Electric Power

Nation-wide Broadcast Address at the Diamond Jubilee
of the Case Institute of Technology, Cleveland, Ohio
[April 11, 1953]

THIS is a celebration of the founding of a great institution dedicated to scientific research and the training of engineers and scientists. You seek to sharpen their abilities and initiative for a climate of free men. It is an appropriate time for discussion of some of the forces in our Federal government which have been destructive of such a climate.

In the field of Federal electric power we have an example of twenty years of creeping socialism with a demonstration of its results.

Three years ago the Commission on Organization of the Executive Branch of the Government, under my chairmanship, made an investigation into the Federal activities in electric power. As the Commission was not dealing with public policies, its recommendations were confined to administrative reforms. Even these have not been carried out. The highly critical reports of our staff of accountants and engineers amply illuminated the results of this socialist invasion.

And at once let me state that the present Administration is not responsible for this situation; they inherited it on January 20, 1953.

WHAT IS THE AMERICAN WAY OF LIFE?

Before I go into more detail I wish to say something as to what the American way of free men really is.

The socialists, with their ideas imported from Europe, totally misconstrue the unique structure of American life. They envisage it in terms of European societies.

Ours is a system of free men and free enterprise in which our concepts have steadily departed from those of the Old World in two directions.

We have conceived that, to have free men, we must be free from the economic tyrannies which were nurtured in Europe's laissez-faire, dog-eat-dog system of economy.

Free men can no more permit private economic power without checks and balances than governmental power without checks and balances.

The great enterprises of production and distribution can be used for economic oppression. To prevent this oppression of free men, we originated government regulation unique in the world. We regulate rates and services of natural monopolies such as the electric power utilities. We insist upon freedom from trade monopolies and the enforcement of constructive competition. We adopted this economic philosophy seventy years ago in a revolution from European concepts and practices.

And in another departure from European social structures we have developed a far greater expansion of free co-operation between men in community interest. Its extent is without parallel in any other country. It gained force from the necessities of a pioneer people where co-operative action was vital to their existence. Today I dare say we have a million nongovernmental organizations for co-operative action in our country. They include thousands of health, educational, sports, musical, social, business, farmer, and labor organizations. They have been created without the aid of bureaucrats. In some aspects we could add to these our insurance and savings banks and our corporations in general.

And we hold 10,000 annual conventions of them and survive unending speeches and banquets.

This co-operative system is self-government of the people outside of government. It is the most powerful development among free men that has taken place in all the world.

The Old World, however, went on with its lack of effective economic safeguards for free men and its dearth of co-operation in the American sense. One result was the rise of socialism as a protest.

I emphasize this unique structure of our American economic and social life because it is into this system, far divorced from the Old World, that our fuzzy-minded socialists are striving to inject ideas foreign to our concept of life.

And they have made progress with these adulterants. They intrude into many avenues of American life. And they threaten a new oppression of free men greater than the old dog-eat-dog economy.

Tonight I shall appraise the aspects of creeping socialism in the electric power industry by the *Federal Government only*. Rightly or wrongly the State and municipal governments do engage in electric enterprises. But at least their activities respond to the will and scrutiny of local government.

Nor do I include the Rural Electrification Administration in this discussion although it receives great government subsidies. It has worthy purpose, but that operation is so small a percent of the electric power in the country that it cannot eat up the industry.

PRIVATE ENTERPRISE IN ELECTRICITY

In the electric field there are certain transcendent facts.

First. Under the initiative of free men we developed the technology and use of electricity far beyond any other country.

Second. Stemming from private enterprise, we have created a per capita supply of electrical power for our people three times that of the combined Western European nations and eleven times the average of the whole foreign world.

Third. Private enterprise could keep in pace with demand,

and could have more advantageously distributed the power from Federal water conservation projects.

Fourth. With our advancing technology and individual initiative, the average price of household electric power is sold today by our private enterprise utilities at one-third of the price of thirty years ago—and that is while most other commodities and wages have increased by 50 percent to 100 percent. There is no such parallel in any other commodity.

Despite these results from a free economy, these concepts of free men were abandoned twenty years ago when the Federal Government entered into the socialization of electric power in a big way.

THE METHOD OF SOCIALIZATION

The device by which our Federal bureaucracy started to socialize this industry was through the electric power from our multiple-purpose water conservation dams. We needed these dams. And we need more of them. They were built to serve navigation, flood control, irrigation, and domestic water supplies and to provide electric energy. However, the central question here is not the creation of this electric power but using it to promote socialism. The first step toward socialization was taken when the Federal Government undertook itself to generate and distribute this electric power from multiple-purpose dams. And now the Federal Government has taken further socialistic leaps by building steam and hydro plants solely for the generation of electric power.

Up to twenty years ago we avoided socialism by selling the energy at the dams to private utilities and irrigation districts. The Government received a return without incurring operating expenses.

Let no one misinterpret my views on water conservation. I have been for thirty years an ardent exponent of multiple-purpose dams. I can claim some credit for the first gigantic multiple-purpose dam in the United States. That one is in the Colorado River.

But again on the Colorado we avoided socialism by stipulating that before construction began the energy should be leased to the private utilities and municipalities. And we contracted to sell it at a rate which provided for interest on the Government investment and the complete repayment of the investment within a period of fifty years. The consumers over these seventeen years since have found no cause for complaint from that arrangement.

Do not think these Federal electric enterprises are small business.

Twenty years ago the total generating capacity of electric power from Federal dams was about 300,000 horsepower. It was about two-thirds of one percent of the total electric generating capacity at that time.

As some people are confused by the technical terms "kilowatts" and "kilowatt hours," I have translated them into horsepower.

By the middle of 1953, the Federal Government will have a generating capacity of about 15,000,000 horsepower. That is about 12 percent of the utility generating capacity for sale to the public. Federal power is already being sent into twenty-seven states.

But far beyond this, there are Federal generating plants in construction or authorized by the Congress, making a total of over 200 plants which will bring the total up to about 37,000,-000 horsepower. If completed the Federal Government would be furnishing somewhere from 20 percent to 25 percent of the electric utility capacity of the nation. The cost in capital outlay to the taxpayer will be about $10 to $11 billions, plus some great deficits in promised interest and other returns.

But that is not all. Further projects have been recommended to Congress. And still more are contemplated in Government reports. If they were all undertaken, it would bring the total to about 90,000,000 horsepower.

This bureaucracy now employs 33,000 persons and is increasing every day. And if all these dreams were realized, their employees on the Federal payroll will likely exceed 200,000.

But even this is not the whole story. Lest anyone thinks this is good for us, I may point to some of the already evident consequences of socialized electric power.

EXPANSION BY DURESS

Under the irresistible nature of bureaucracy and the backing of the socialists every one of these Federal enterprises becomes a center of encroachments upon or coercion and absorption of the private industry. For instance, by the threat of WPA gifts and low interest rates on loans to municipalities, private enterprises were absorbed at less than their worth.

Great duplicate transmission lines have been built and more are contemplated.

Some of these Government enterprises are given the power of eminent domain by which they could seize transmission lines and substations of competitors and, if the owner refuses their price, he can pay lawyers for years to fight for compensation in the courts. Free enterprise never had such a privilege.

Some part of the heavy taxes on private utilities goes to build up and support their Federal competitors.

Private enterprises have been prevented from undertaking certain hydroelectric developments in favor of the Government agencies.

These manipulations and powers threaten and weaken the ability of many private concerns to finance their needed expansions.

Indeed some of them with these guns pointed at them have already thrown up their hands.

Socialization in other directions has been injected into these projects. For instance, the provision that water will not be supplied to farms of over 160 acres in some of the California Central Valley operations. Apparently all others are Kulaks. Also, some of these Federal power enterprises, with cheap Federal capital and subsidized power, are engaged in manufacturing business in competition with private enterprise.

FREEDOM FROM TAXES

These Federal enterprises and their distribution allies pay no taxes to the Federal Government and comparatively little to the local governments. In the last fiscal year the private enterprise utilities paid over $750,000,000 taxes to the Federal Government and nearly $470,000,000 to the State and local governments. The actual Federal electric enterprises paid less than $5,000,000 toward State and local taxes.

Obviously there is here a huge burden thrust onto every taxpayer throughout the nation. It will be much greater if the 37,000,000 horsepower program is completed.

Nor is this all of the burdens thrust upon the nation-wide taxpayer as I will show you in a few moments.

UNKEPT REPRESENTATIONS TO THE CONGRESS

In many cases the cost of constructing these projects has been woefully underestimated. For instance, the Colorado–Big Thompson project was originally estimated at about $44,000,-000, but is costing over $160,000,000. The Hungry Horse project originally estimated at $39,000,000 will cost over $109,-000,000. Work has been started on the Oahe project. It was originally estimated to cost about $72,000,000. It is now estimated that it will cost $293,000,000.

Some of the increased cost has been due to rising prices but such an excuse by no means explains the degree of underestimate. Some of this underestimation is possibly due to presenting the Congress with a modest project and then hugely edging it up.

Another variety of underestimation is shown in the case of the Cumberland River development where the proposals were justified to the Congress on a valuation of the power which was subsequently sold for less than one-half that amount. Whether these are devices to persuade and commit the Congress or just incompetence, I do not know.

In any event such methods would break any business except government.

UNKEPT PROMISES AS TO RETURNS

The original New Deal promises assured Congress that these enterprises would pay 3 percent interest and pay back, that is, amortize the Federal investment over fifty years. This formula has either been abandoned, sadly ignored, or juggled.

First. The cost of a multiple-purpose water project must be divided among its several functions, such as navigation, flood control, irrigation, community water supply, and hydroelectric power. The interest and amortization of the Federal electric power investment can be decreased by assigning more capital cost to flood control and navigation. The reports of the Federal Comptroller General have protested that such favors have been done.

Some of the Federal enterprises do not include interest on their capital cost during construction, which, again, decreases the payment of interest and amortization on the Federal taxpayers' capital invested. All of which thereby decreases the claimed costs.

But these practices again subsidize the rates to a minority of consumers at the expense of the nation-wide taxpayers.

Second. Taking these enterprises as a whole, comparatively little interest and amortization have been paid to the Federal Treasury on the Government investment over all the past years. There is a huge accumulation of this deficiency which should be repaid. Some of these Federal enterprises do not take into account interest and amortization in their costs and thus lower the rates they make their consumers. Some of them do not even enter such a charge in their books.

Some of them do not include the pensions to their employees which, under Civil Service, are partly loaded on the taxpayer.

Further, a question could also be raised as to the method providing for the costs of depreciation and provision for obsolescence.

Third. Our Federal Reorganization Commission employed Haskins and Sells, one of the leading accounting firms in the United States, to investigate the finances and accounting practices of a large part of these Federal electric power activities. They

applied the yardstick of 3 percent interest and amortization in
fifty years to the acknowledged Federal investment in power
in many of these Federal enterprises. They found many of
them would never be able to make the return which was at one
time promised to the Congress.

STILL FURTHER BURDENS AND LOSSES TO THE
NATION-WIDE TAXPAYERS

And there are more burdens thrust on the taxpayer from
this program of socialized power. He has to furnish by taxes
the huge capital being invested. Also, as these Federal enterprises have not paid the promised interest, the taxpayer has had
to pay it on government bonds. And the nation-wide taxpayer
will have to stand all the deficits from mistakes and underesti-
mates.

Under these present methods and practices, this burden and
losses to the nation-wide taxpayer are not small change. They
will run into billions.

And from another angle, if the price of power from the
Federal enterprises were placed at a level which would include
tax equivalents and all the other nonincluded costs, their rates
generally would be equal to, and in some cases higher than, the
rates of neighboring private utilities.

THE OPERATING BALANCE SHEET

We can appraise what all this means in actual figures. I
have received from the Federal Budget Bureau a statement of
the gross receipts and gross operating expenses of these Federal
enterprises taken as a whole for the fiscal year 1952, and the
estimates for the year ending June 30 of this year. This statement shows an apparent surplus over operating expenses of
about $100,000,000 for each of these years. Here, however,
come in several great "buts."

If the omitted interest, the omitted amortization and the
refunding of the accumulated deficiency of these items, and
other costs I have mentioned were included, this so-called "surplus" would turn into a deficit.

And I do not include in this deficit any equivalent for taxes —another large sum.

Also, I am advised that the operating receipts for 1952 could have been $75,000,000 greater had this power been sold at the market price.

ACCOUNTING

Our Reorganization Commission accountants condemned many of the Federal power financial and accounting methods and estimates. They found the true construction and operating costs to be obscured. They proposed many reforms which have not been adopted. The Comptroller General of the United States, as late as sixty-six days ago, commented on accounting deficiencies.

The Federal power enterprises do not even keep their accounts or present their statements in the intelligible manner which the Government requires of private enterprise. They do, however, emit a host of propaganda figures in press releases.

I recommend to anyone interested in bureaucratic action to see whether he can add up the sums, past and present, involved in Federal electric enterprises from among the 4,000,000 words and sums in the Federal budget.

OTHER EFFECTS ON CITIZENS

All this affects the citizen in many ways aside from the injustice of huge losses and tax burdens which result in subsidized power to favored groups and communities.

There is a constitutional question involved in these enterprises which must concern the citizen. No one can even attempt to defend many of these activities except on the Welfare Clause in the Constitution. Under that interpretation, the Federal Government could take over about everything except elections and the churches.

And there is a further important question to the citizen. There is here being erected a sort of Federal regional control in which State governments have some nominal representation but without authority. The people in these regions may get power at the expense of the nation-wide taxpayer, but they are surrendering the control of their resources and energies to a Federal bureaucracy.

However, I do not believe in criticism without remedies.

Over twenty years ago I recommended to Congress the transformation of an ex officio Commission into a full Federal Power Commission with regulations which had teeth in them. The purpose was to control the oppressive empires then growing in the private electric utilities. The transformation was made but without the teeth. My successors set up the Securities Exchange Commission to do this de-empiring. Now, however, it is the Federal Government itself that urgently needs the same de-empiring.

The first steps should be:

1. The Congress should cease to make appropriations for more steam plants or hydroelectric plants solely for power. If they are justified, private enterprise will build them and pay taxes on them.

2. The Congress should follow the precedent of the Colorado project and make no more appropriations for new multiple-purpose projects unless the electric power is first leased on terms, the standards of which I will describe in a moment.

3. The Congress should, jointly with the President, set up a temporary Commission on reorganization of this whole Federal venture with resources to employ technical assistance.

a) This Commission should investigate and recommend proper methods of accounting and a revision of the division of Federal investment in these projects between electric power and other purposes, and recommend proper practices for the future.

b) The Commission should report on the actual cost of, and the prospective returns from, each of these major enterprises.

c) The Commission should formulate the methods and standard terms for leasing generating plants, transmission lines, and the electric energy to private enterprise or to municipalities or to the States or to regional authorities that may be set and

managed by the States. These standard terms should provide
for payment of interest and amortization of the Federal investment, the refunding of arrears in these items, and also some contribution in lieu of taxes. The latter would not need apply in
cases of private enterprises as they pay their own taxes.

d) The Commission should develop methods by which non-
Federal agencies can share co-operatively in the cost of future
capital outlays on the electrical part of multiple-purpose dams.

WORKING OUT THESE POLICIES

Some of these projects could be disposed of so as to return
these standard terms to the Federal Government. Others, due
to excessive cost, may need concessions, and the Federal Government would need cut its losses.

Others of them, pending disposal, will need continue to be
operated by the Federal Government. In these cases the Commission should recommend what rates they should charge their
customers so as to make the standard returns. They should recommend methods to compel such payments to the Federal
Treasury instead of their diversion to other purposes. Such action would test the value of these enterprises and, in some cases,
indicate what losses may need be cut.

The objective of the whole proceeding should be to get the
Federal Government out of the business of generating and distributing power as soon as possible.

In any event, the consumer at all times can be protected by
regulation of rates by the State or Federal authorities.

THE RESULTS

It is my belief that, if these proposals be carried out, the
ultimate result would be a substantial return to the Treasury
without consequential operating expense or bureaucracy.

Moreover, the agencies to whom these projects were leased
would undertake or co-operate in their own expansions.

It is my belief that if these things be done, the Federal Government ultimately could reduce its annual investment in power
enterprises by at least $600,000,000 per annum.

This program would begin the end of Federal bureaucratic regional control of the States and their people.

Above all, we would rescue free men from this variety of creeping socialism. The American people have fought off socialized medicine, but here is a hole in the dike of free men that is bringing a flood.

There are those who shy away from the use of the term "socialism," or the name of Karl Marx, in connection with what is going on in the power field. But, excepting those who *desire* socialization, they are blind to the facts. Socialism has become the world's nightmare. It is not the American dream.

The intellectuals who advocate these Federal activities carry a banner on which they falsely inscribe the word "liberalism." There is one thing I can say beyond any measure of doubt. It is a false liberalism that expresses itself by Federal operation of business in competition with the citizen. It is the road not to more liberty but to less liberty. True liberalism is found not in striving to spread bureaucracy, but in striving to set bounds to it. True liberalism seeks all legitimate freedom, in the confident belief that without freedom, all other blessings are vain. Liberalism is a force truly of the spirit coming from a realization that economic freedom cannot be sacrificed if political freedom is to be preserved.

Your Inheritance

Address Before "Excursion"—Ford Foundation Television Workshop, New York City
[October 18, 1953]

I HAVE been asked to talk to our young people about our Government. You have already begun to find out something about it. That is good—for government is going to be all around you for the next sixty or seventy years of your lives. And you will need to look after it.

Also, some day you will inherit all the homes and farms and stores and factories and churches and schools in the United States —and you will need look after these too. But if you have good government, you will find in all these places good jobs, great opportunities, and comfortable living. If you do not own them already, you will also inherit all the instruments to make good and bad noises by way of bands, orchestras, radios, juke boxes, and millions of bells. This is one of many spots where your generation can do some reforms.

During nearly two hundred years we have built up on this continent what we call the American System. The essence of it is that you are free to do whatever you like, choose any calling you like, and go into any enterprise you like, so long as you do not injure your neighbors and so long as you co-operate for the common good.

Our American system of life and Government differs from the Old World and from much of the New World. In my lifetime I have lived in nearly forty different foreign countries under many kinds of government. I was not a tourist. I worked in their industries, their wars, and the terrible aftermaths of those wars. I was associated with their peoples, their officials, and their statesmen, their writers, and their spiritual leaders. The differences between their systems and ours were before my eyes every day.

Every one of my scores of homecomings from those missions was a reaffirmation of the glory of America. For here was a land free of the grinding poverty of most countries. And here was a land of greater kindliness, greater frankness, which comes from our more full acceptance of the equality and the dignity of each human being.

In those foreign countries in which I worked were many different kinds of government. There were limited monarchies and despotisms. There were Socialistic governments where economic freedom is limited. There were Communist governments wherein the people were reduced to slavery. There were even many varied forms of representative governments elected by the people. All of these governments presented contrasts with our form of government.

Our Founding Fathers built for the United States a government new and different from all the governments of the Old World by three strokes of genius.

Those acts of genius were when they enacted a written Constitution; when they provided a Federation of States with a separation of powers between the Federal Government and the State governments; and when they made a division of powers within the Federal and State governments by separating the Legislative, the Judiciary, and the Executive branches. And they reinforced all this by the declared purpose to establish a government of laws where every citizen was equal before the law, and not a government of men who can tell people where they get off. By these concepts of government, new to the world, our forefathers created not only the American System of free men but of protections to freedom unique in all the world.

But above all this machinery of government, there is another concept in our system which was unique to America. From our religious faiths we have held that every individual has rights and freedoms that are given him by the Creator and not by any government. We have defined these rights in our Constitution. I hope your first lesson in Government was to read the first Ten Amendments to the Constitution together with the Thirteenth, Fourteenth, Fifteenth, and Nineteenth Amendments. Here, in black and white, are the guarantees of freedom of worship, free speech, trial by jury, equality of all races, and a dozen other rights. And from these concepts come your right to an equal opportunity and to choose your own way in life.

Our American System of government today still differs radically in other ways from even the free countries in the Old World. Those countries combine the legislative and executive branches of government by electing from the members of their legislatures a Cabinet headed by a Prime Minister. This form of government continues in power only as long as they have a majority of the members of their legislative branch. The membership of all legislatures constantly shifts and, in consequence, under this form of government, their administrations may change frequently. For instance, the French Ministry has changed eighteen times in eight years.

Because our President is elected by the people and for a fixed term, and nominates his own Cabinet, we have far greater order, stability in government, and more continuity in governmental policies.

The job of being President of our country has become much more complicated than it was in the time of George Washington. Indeed, the Presidency is more complicated than the job of the Prime Ministers even among the free nations.

The President has the duty to see that the laws are enforced and that the host of government departments are doing their job honestly and without waste or discrimination between persons. He must appoint the major officials, many of them being subject to approval by the Senate. He must attend to our foreign relations, and through them, try to make and keep peace in the world. He is Commander in Chief of the Armed Forces needed to protect our country from foreign enemies. He must also advise the Congress on the laws that are needed to meet the problems of a growing country. If he does not approve of laws passed by the Congress, he can veto such laws. He is the head of his political party and is responsible for carrying out the promises on which his party was elected. He is supposed to lay cornerstones, attend funerals, advance all good causes, make periodic speeches, and hold press conferences on public questions.

He has but little time to go fishing. But all Presidents do go fishing because they want to be alone to think at least once in a while. Except for prayer, fishing is about the only time when the people respect the privacy of the President. Moreover, if the President goes away from Washington the public and the press demand to know what for and why? But everybody accepts fishing as a proper mission.

Every one of you has a chance to be President if you think you would like that complicated job.

All free countries choose and elect their candidates for public office by political parties whose machinery is outside the government. And the political parties in all free countries present programs, make promises, and debate the failings of their opponents. But here comes another feature of the American System that has few parallels abroad. While we do not disapprove of new or fractional political parties, we believe in two major political parties. The one which wins the election has the responsibility of government and of carrying out its promises. The one which loses has the responsibility to debate and oppose policies and actions which they do not approve. We believe in two major political parties, because a basic concept of freedom is rule by the majority but with respect for the minority. If there are many political parties, as there are in most of the free countries on the continent of Europe, the choice of the Prime Minister and the Cabinet are the result of compromises between parties, and policies which lead to negative action and inability of the people to express themselves on the issues of the day. It all results in lack of continuity and instability in government. It was partly such wrangling, instability, and chaos which led the people in a dozen European States to welcome dictatorship and all freedoms were lost.

Our Government has grown like a mushroom in the twenty years since I was President. Twenty years ago we had about 350,000 men in soldiers' and sailors' uniforms. Today, to protect us from our enemies, we have about 3,500,000 men. Twenty years ago we had about 600,000 civilians working for the Federal Government. Today, as the result of social and economic experiments, our wars, and our defense needs, we have about 2,500,000 civilians working for the Federal Government. Our taxes have increased from four billions to over seventy billion dollars a year.

Out of this sudden growth of the Federal Government there has been much duplication, inefficiency, and huge waste. Five years ago I was appointed head of a nonpartisan Commission created by the unanimous consent of the Congress to try and straighten out some of these weaknesses. We made about two hundred seventy different recommendations or suggestions, of which all but about seventy have been wholly or partly carried out. And now again the Congress has unanimously re-created that Commission with even wider authority in recommending to the President and the Congress further improvements in operation and policies. Again I have been appointed to head this Commission. Its end purpose is to save Federal expenditures and thus relieve the burden of taxes. If you wish a good understanding of your Government today, you might read the reports of these Reorganization Commissions.

And at this point we arrive at another of your coming responsibilities. Government by the people depends on whether you vote in the primaries which choose the candidates of the political parties and whether you vote in the elections. You will soon be voters. And if our government is to survive, you must vote. And to vote rightly, you will need gather a lot of information about the candidates and on the programs of their political parties.

But our form of government will not endure unless there is a willingness to serve it at a sacrifice. And it will not endure unless there be absolute honor in its officials.

We hear much criticism of our Government—and it is often

justified. No government is perfect because human beings are not perfect. But let me say that, despite many disheartening things, by and large the ideals of our country are still strong. And under our unique American system, we have given more opportunities to every boy and girl than any other government. And the proof of the rightness of the American System is that we have grown to the most powerful nation with the highest standard of living on the earth. But more important than all, we, more than most nations, respect the individual rights and personal dignity of our citizens.

You are sometimes told that the older generations have made a mess of things. I have often agreed with that idea. But we must bear in mind that it was the older generations who built for you all these millions of ways of making a living, obtaining an education, and of enjoying life. Above all, they gave you the greatest heritage that can come to man—national freedom and personal liberty. And some day you will be the "older generation."

And one last word. When you go out into this complicated world to make your own way, you will find your elders anxious for your success. They will extend you more kindness and helpfulness than is the case in any other nation on earth. Do not be afraid for your future—and it is a bright future if we conduct our government rightly.

American Good Government Society Award

Nation-wide Broadcast, Washington, D.C.
[February 22, 1954]

MR. CHAIRMAN, Senator Byrd, Governor Shivers, and members of the American Good Government Society. I deeply appreciate the honor you have shown me and for many reasons. It is an honor to be associated with Governor Shivers. It is a high honor to be the successor of Senator Taft in receiving this Award. It is an honor to be introduced by Senator Byrd. I can unhesitatingly confirm the greatness of leadership which he has given to our country. But I cannot confirm what he has just said about me.

You will expect me to say something further in response to your kind reception and the honor I have received than just an acknowledgment. I have, therefore, explored a number of possible subjects upon which I could occupy your minds during my allotted twelve minutes on the radio.

As throughout our whole land, this day is dedicated in tribute to George Washington. My first impulse was to speak about the Father of our Country. I have spoken many times in the past upon the greatness of his service to all mankind. There is nothing I could say on this occasion that would add to his glory. And in your program are two others who will speak of Washington more eloquently than I can. I therefore decided to leave that subject exclusively to them.

In search for a subject that might fill in my remaining

eleven minutes on the radio, I explored the many anvils of debate that have been ringing throughout the country. I examined anvils dedicated to the Communists at home and abroad, the recognition of Red China, the Berlin Conference, and then Molotov arose in my mind.

Momentarily he seemed a good subject, as he has been in the headlines for thirty years. In fact he is the only important Communist who shows surviving durability in Russia. I thought a speech on his life and works might be appropriate—but then it seemed a depressing subject for a pleasant occasion like this, or upon Washington's Birthday.

I then explored our anvils of debate on more domestic subjects for a fitting subject to try my hand at. There is the Constitutional amendment pending in the Congress; the Commission on organization of the Government; the budget, taxes, and socialism. But none of these subjects seemed appropriate for a happy party and I must not leave you depressed.

It finally occurred to me that there was one of the current headline debates in which I could usefully spend ten minutes. That is the subject of where we are in an unemployment phase of the economic cycle. And I shall keep my remarks friendly and hopeful in this atmosphere of Washington's Birthday. In that light I will not quote the dead cats being traded in by some debaters.

Some of the differences of opinion on the economic situation are over whether or not we are in a dip, a slump, a readjustment, a recession, or a depression. Another part of this current battle of opinion is whether or not we are going into or coming out of this particular hole. By the way, the words "readjustment" and "recession" were added to the list a few years ago to make the unemployed feel better. And for your comfort I may observe that, except for foreign cyclones or war we have had one of these dips, slumps, readjustments, or recessions—whichever of the milder terms you prefer—about every five or seven years throughout our industrial maturity. That is the inevitable result of the ebb and flow of a free economic system. The rising tide of business is overspeeded by its self-generated optimism. And the inevitable readjustment results in an outgoing tide which is overspeeded by self-generated pessimism. Like some diseases, these wholly domestic tides are never fatal—except when candidates for public office are on the wrong side of the tide.

I should be regarded as an expert on these subjects. At least I was credited with having constructed, all by myself, the entire world-wide depression in which unemployment lasted at the same rate in the United States for ten years from 1931 to 1940. I even received the honor of having that depression named after me by various candidates for political office. However, out of modesty, I must again state that this was an overdone honor and that I have never claimed such gigantic political economic or intellectual power.

Yet I will admit that I am an expert on one phase of those problems. At that time I learned something about what economic dips, slumps, recessions, or depressions are made of. I got that skill from burning my fingers in the ordeal by fire.

From this expert experience I can assure you that the combustible materials are not hereabout to construct another conflagration like that of the decade of the thirties.

At that time there was the combination of two gigantic destructive explosives which added to the fire of a normal explosion from domestic overoptimism.

The first of these great explosives was a total financial collapse of all Europe in which all European banks closed; even the Bank of England ceased to meet its obligations. All but two nations abandoned the gold standard. For months we scarcely had an order for our farm products from Europe. Our security markets were drenched with the sale of foreign-held American securities from the panic-stricken foreign world. Most countries defaulted in their debts to American banks and they demanded that our banks pay their debts to them in gold.

The second group of explosives were the fifty-one different, weak, and motley banking systems in the United States that could not take the shocks. Without some combustibles like these, dips, slumps, or recessions do not develop into Great Depressions. I do not see them anywhere on the landscape at the present time.

I may venture my own analysis of the present trouble. I believe that due to scientific discovery, invention, and improvement of production methods, our present industrial plants can support the present standard of living of our people and, beyond that, can produce some surplus. It is these surpluses, plus some dehydrated optimism, that are worrying the situation today.

And, like everybody else, I have a remedy. My remedy follows the proposal of President Eisenhower—that if necessary we should reduce taxes in such fashion as to increase the buying power of all the people, so that they can absorb the surplus and thus lift the whole level of the standard of living another stage. The surest route to that end is to reduce government expenses and thus justify reduction of taxes.

That is what the Commission I head is striving for in cooperation with the Government agencies.

There is plenty of room in this situation today for this kind of action. On the occasion twenty years ago when I was battling with that progressively worse "dip-slump-readjustment-recession-depression," our government was spending only about $4 billion a year. We had no room to lift the standard of living in cuts of that $4 billion. Now we are spending about $65 billions. Somewhere in this increase of $61 billions we have an opportunity for remedy that was not open to us twenty years ago.

Thus in the absence of the gigantic combustibles and with an opportunity for remedy you can have high confidence that this is only a passing dip, a slump, a readjustment, not a great depression.

The Editors and the Federal Deficit

*Nation-wide Broadcast Address Before the American
Society of Newspaper Editors, Washington, D.C.*
[April 17, 1954]

I HAVE no doubt that everyone in this town has been tell-
ing the editors what to do next. You would not expect
me to accept your urgent invitation to speak unless I, like
all the rest of the town, say something more about how to run
your editorial job.

This whole town is full of people with some kind of a
cause for which they want your help. There are, in fact, more
than 1,200 organizations or persons licensed under the law to
pressure the Congress for some cause. Each of them employs
a public relations man—or a dozen of them—to present their
cause to editors with handouts. That makes life simple for you.
You only have to add their handouts to those you receive from
the Federal Departments to fill your columns—that is, in so
far as paid-for advertising will permit. It also helps unemployment, because you must engage a lot of bright young men to
sort out two or three thousand daily handouts.

There are four varieties of these handouts. The first are
designed to bring good to somebody. Those require a double
check. The second variety of handouts come from those who
believe they need something from the Federal Treasury. They
should be subject to violent suspicion. The third group want
their particular taxes reduced. They should have sympathy
tempered with perplexity. There is a fourth pressure group
who want to reduce government expenditures. There are only

two of these organizations in addition to Senator Byrd. Their proceedings are righteous. They are popular in the abstract.

Certainly each of you will agree as a broad generalization that all of the first three handout groups—plus the governmental ones—ought to relax. That is, except of course, for the particular cause you favor. And you will bear with me if I casually mention that if there are enough of these exceptions, the dynamics of this generalization as to mass force for reducing expenditures has about the power of goose feathers.

But I do not want to leave the impression that all civil organizations and government agencies with a cause and a handout are evil. They are an essential expression of free men. Moreover each of their organizations and each of their handouts are specifically authorized by the First Amendment to the Constitution. I said the First Amendment.

A NATIONAL PROBLEM

Be all this as it may, on this occasion I wish to discuss a grave problem which needs your urgent consideration and service. That is, the deficit in the Federal Budget. I have been assigned a job of finding methods and policies of economy and increasing revenues. I, therefore, view this town with an anxious eye.

With the exception of two years, we have diligently maintained the practice of a deficit for twenty-three years. For the fiscal year ending June 30, 1953, the deficit was $9.4 billions. We began to be more cheerful when, due to the valiant efforts of President Eisenhower, Secretary Humphrey, and the Administration generally, the Budget provided a reduction of the deficit to $3.3 billions for the fiscal year ending this June 30. We even became more cheerful when their budget proposals for next year showed a decrease of a further $400 million. It seemed we were on our way to the sunshine of a balanced budget the following year.

But the disciples of more spending, and still lower taxes, are having their way. Until Congress completes its surgical operations on the budget the position will not be precise. But it is already clear that the deficit for this year ending seventy-six days hence will be larger than the Budget estimate. For next year, instead of a $2.9 billions, it will rise to a minimum of $5 billions; and if the George Amendment passes, the deficit may rise to $7.5 billions or possibly more. This does not take into account what Congress may do by way of appropriations. But here again if the demands of pressure groups have their sweet way the situation will be even worse. Some people have expressed the horrid thought that it may reach $9 billion.

In fact, by my inquiring mind and my adding machine, I detect that the handout brigade would chain you to this tread-mill until death.

I can, however, give you a partially cheerful note. The handout philosophy at one time was "tax-and-tax, spend-and-spend." Now the tax end of the formula is "cut taxes, cut taxes," but the "spend-and-spend" end is still alive. That is a philosophic improvement, but it does not cure the deficit. There needs to be a fundamental change of ideas or there is no end of deficits.

WHERE THE EDITORS COME IN

This is the place where you come in. You are familiar with the whole gospel of balancing the budget. I don't need to tell you the elements of deficit economics, or the theology of deficit salvation, or the future damnation from this economic sin.

But I wonder if it would not help the country if you again would spell out for your readers what really happens from a Federal Government deficit. It needs to be done in such elementary terms that any grammar school youngster can get it—also many elders.

And I am going to take three minutes of your time to spell it out myself—although I know the repetition will not be front-page news like quarrels over hunting Communists.

Obviously one of three things must happen from a Federal Budget deficit. The deficit must be met by decreased government expenditures which hurt the feelings of some pressure

groups or by levying more taxes which hurts most everybody's
pocket nerves; or it must be met by the Federal Government's
borrowing the money. The borrowing alternative is where the
eternal damnation comes in.

I will deal with the tax side first. That indeed needs to be
spelled out so as to still the clamor of the people and the
pressure groups for excessive tax reductions until we get out
of the deficit treadmill.

I will not take your time to demonstrate the particular pain-
ful element in every variety of taxes. Or which of the excise
taxes on luxuries should not have been removed. Nor to tell
you about the sweet nostrums for putting the tax burden on
somebody else.

I fully sympathize with all these pressures for reduced
taxes because, in my view, our tax burden has been more than
the country can bear. Whether this abstraction is true or not,
our taxes are still stupendous, they are still overburdensome,
and they raise many questions of grave concern. One of these
questions is the moral corruption from the spreading evasion
of taxes. Another of these grave questions is that they are undermining the economic foundations of progress.

By the valiant efforts of the Congress and the Administration, the tax burdens will be reduced for the next fiscal year
by over $7 billions without the George and other Amendments.

However, in any ecstasy from this relief, do not forget we
will still be spending about $65 billions a year—and do not
forget the sin of the continued deficit.

The theology of this is that only a period of self-denial in
expenditures and no further tax cuts can wash this sin away.

GOVERNMENTAL BORROWING

Thus the tax question which stands out today is whether
bearing the pains of holding up taxes is worse than the greater
pain of the undermining of our economic health from government borrowing.

The borrowing medicine to cure the deficit is easiest of all for the taxpayers to take. But it is the deadliest of poisons that can be poured into the Nation's system of life. It is a far greater economic sin than higher taxes. For when the Federal Government borrows to make up a deficit, it must do one of three things—print currency, borrow from the banks, or borrow from investors. The latter is the least evil, but there are never enough investors about. Printing currency and borrowing from the banks have only one end—that is inflation. And let no one believe that Government borrowing from the banks is in the long run any less inflationary than printing currency. Its results are the same—it either inflates credit or the banks turn their bonds into the Federal Reserve for currency.

I will not spend your time in comment upon the illusion spread by Lord John Maynard Keynes that it does not matter how much the Federal Government may borrow, because we "owe it to ourselves." Just the same, you have to pay taxes to meet the interest on the debt. And worse, you get stabbed in the back by the inflation it can produce. You might try that philosophy on your food bills and see how the groceryman takes it.

INFLATION IS IN ACTION

Do not believe that inflation has been stopped. It will continue as long as we have a deficit. And we have not stopped the deficit. As sure as the sun sets, its continuation will produce the darkness of rising prices and wages, no matter what some cheery economists may say.

We might, in extension of these elementary remarks, take a short look at what has happened from our national experience of twenty-three years of deficit borrowing—with those two exceptions. Our Federal debt has increased to $275 billions from $19.1 billions. The interest on this amount alone is almost twice the whole cost of government of twenty-three years ago. Currency in circulation has increased from $4.5 billions to over $30 billions. Government revenues, which are mostly taxes, have increased from $3.5 billions a year to over $65 billions.

The consequence of all this is that the cost of living has increased by about 80 percent. By taxes through the front door and rising prices through the back door, a family requires an income of $3,700 a year to give the same standard of living that an income of $1,500 a year would buy twenty-three years ago. And the purchasing power of all pensions, savings bank deposits, and income from trustee securities has been reduced by more than one-half amid millions of tragedies.

These effects have been repeated ever since government discovered this barbiturate to put deficits to sleep. It has happened repeatedly over the last five hundred years. It has happened in forty nations. It is the surest road to disaster in our system of free men. It is the surest road to disaster in our defense against the Communist horde.

Now I am not unaware of the effect on the deficit of World War II, the Korean War, the Cold War. But there have been huge unnecessary expenditures and waste alongside these events. Nor am I dense to the political implications of these problems, but I am also alive to the political and living consequence of failure.

REDUCTION OF EXPENDITURES

Now I come to the real remedy for this disease of Budget Deficit. The immediate medication is no further reduction of taxes than the Administration proposals, and to systematically reduce government expenditures until the Budget Deficit is met. Then, and then alone, can inflation be stopped. You will be surprised how quickly the patient will respond to this treatment.

The Congress has not yet passed the appropriations for next year. The appropriation committees headed by such valiant soldiers of economy as Senator Styles Bridges and that old Trojan Congressman John Tabor are earnestly searching for reductions in spending. They may, I believe, have some success. But they cannot cure this immediate huge deficit.

Again this is where you come in, for theirs is a battle with pressure groups and handouts.

There are some matters of theory and practice you could

urge upon the pressure groups who want more spending and upon those who oppose its curtailment. Their projects may be meritorious but the Nation will not be destroyed if they wait awhile and give the Congress a chance to act and the taxpayer a chance to breathe.

SOME FUTURE HOPES

There are hopes for the future if the pressure groups and the people will have patience. And again here is where you come in because you are potent in advocating patience.

I recently mentioned elsewhere publicly that if the private pressure groups and the pressures of state and local governments for Federal money would quit their handouts, and would leave the Federal Government alone for two years, we could reduce expenditures between $5 and $7 billions, annually, without damaging necessary functions. My colleagues of the Commission on Organization and our "task forces" and I will be able to give you the full details in a few months. By such reductions we could come near to wiping out the deficit even with the already agreed tax reductions.

RELIEF IN MILITARY EXPENDITURES

With a little patience, there is another hope of reduction in government spending. Our major burden is for defense. But, let there be no mistake, we must have full defense. However, some of us during four years have urged a reappraisal of our methods of warfare and the weapons we make and use. We insisted that in view of scientific discovery and the character of our enemy, some of our methods of warfare and some of our weapons are now obsolete. We also urged during these years that we were spending too much trying to cure the age-old hates, fears, and disunities of Western Europe. We have contended that our genius in producing the gigantic deterrents of aggression would give a better assurance to the free world and lessen our economic burdens and deficit.

There is hope in these fields, for the new looks by the Eisenhower Administration gaze in these directions.

RELIEF THROUGH INCREASED PRODUCTIVITY

I can give you still another hope for reducing our economic burdens and deficit provided the people will have a little patience. With maintained free minds and free spirits we daily open vast new frontiers of science and invention. They expand our productivity and thus increase the government's revenues.

It was the increased productivity from the invention of the steam engine that aided Britain to carry its economic burden after the Napoleonic Wars. It was the railway development of our country that helped us carry the burdens after our Civil War. It was the advances in air transport, electric power, communications, and agriculture that helped carry our burdens after World War I.

We now have again many new inventions and new applications of older knowledge. One of them is the growing application of atomic energy and its by-products to industry. We are today in another new era of great promise in further expansion of our productivity and our government's income.

CONCLUSION

We could both cure the budget deficit and many of the pains of taxes without lessening our effectiveness in defense or in the needed functions of government if we could now have a period of self-denial and patience.

That is the end of this sermon. The text has been to balance the Budget, and afterwards to cut taxes as fast as we can further reduce expenditures. The penalties of failure are more than you may think.

But this being an educational job directed to the public and the pressure groups, it is mostly up to you. You have thousands of pulpits and millions of voices.

Some National Problems

*Portion of a Nationally Broadcast Address
Given Before the Merchandise Mart Hall of Fame,
Chicago, Illinois**
[June 24, 1954]

I WOULD be remiss if I did not at once state to this representative group of merchants that our magnificent distribution system has had a large part in building the highest standard of living for a nation ever known to mankind.

I could observe that my life has been periodically spent resisting the wiles of merchants in a frantic effort to balance my budget. In other words, I have been compelled to restrict my standard of living below your beguilements.

It is a privilege to be in company with General Wood and former Ambassador Joseph Kennedy who sponsor this occasion.

My association with General Wood began in the First World War when he was Quartermaster General and I was Food Administrator. His friendship has continued over these thirty-eight years—in bad as well as in good times.

Mr. Kennedy and I served and fought alongside on the First Congressional Commission on Organization of the Executive Branch of the Government, and he is today serving again on the present Second Commission. General Wood served on the "task forces" of the First Commission, and is serving again with the present Commission.

* The last part of this address, "On Foreign Policies," will be found in the preceding section.

The General and I have long been associated in the work of the Boys' Clubs of America. He is a Director, William E. Hall the President. I am the Chairman.

In this effort General Wood has given outstanding leadership to that organization in Chicago. And in this connection, I will tell you a secret—Mr. Kennedy has just contributed $25,-000 to this work in Boston.

REORGANIZATION OF THE GOVERNMENT

Several of you who are present are serving today on the Task Forces of the Commission on Organization of the Government. And several of you served on the Task Forces of the First Commission.

The first Commission accomplished much in decreased cost and increased efficiency in the Departments. But that First Commission was restricted in making recommendations as to policies of the Government. This time the Congress enjoined us to cover this field. The law, however, contains a special reservation that we shall not apply our activities to the Judiciary or the Congress.

The previous Commission secured the removal of road-blocks which held up internal reorganization of the Departments and agencies. Today the heads of the different agencies are each diligently placing their own houses in order. Our present Commission has therefore generally limited its activities to matters involving more than one agency with their duplications and overlaps. Just as an indication, I may mention that forty-one agencies of the Government deal with medical matters. Twelve of them deal with the weather.

We are still in the study stage in the Second Commission. Some 200 leading citizens are serving with us on 24 Task Forces or subcommittees.

I am confident that the recommendations of this Commission can show the way to balance the Federal Budget and stop this spiral of inflation. That is provided we can overcome the roadblocks and are not forced into war.

JUVENILE DELINQUENCY

One of our rising national problems is juvenile delinquency. Some discussion of it is warranted here because not only General Wood and Mr. Kennedy and I have a joint interest in the Boys' Clubs, but there are several of you who are also in this service.

Of the many agencies in the country devoted to this problem of delinquency, the Boys' Clubs have an important part. In this organization we are concerned with pavement boys—the boys in our slum areas whose only outlet after school and on Saturdays, Sundays, and holidays is the streets.

Over the whole country, we have over 380 of these Clubs in 252 communities with approximately 360,000 self-starting boys.

These Clubs are not a paper organization. They are as solid bricks and mortar as any man's club and would today cost upward of $120,000,000 to replace. In them we provide constructive joy, health, occupational, and moral guidance.

Together with his sister, the boy is our most precious American possession. The normal boy can seem to be a child of iniquity yet he makes a great nation. The whole world is new to him. Therefore, he seeks adventure, discovery, and great undertakings. He must spend much time, if he is to expand, in the land of make-believe.

This normal boy is endowed with a dynamic energy and an impelling desire to take exercise on all occasions. His primary instinct is to hunt in a pack and that multiplies his devices.

But the normal boy has a primitive instinct and takes to competition and battle. In the days before our civilization became so perfect, he matched his wits with the birds, the bees, and the fish. He cannot find battle with animal or plant life in zoos or parks. If he doesn't contend with nature, he is likely to take on contention with a policeman.

The fine qualities of loyalty to the pack can be turned to sports where the spirit of fair play is the greatest moral force outside religious faith. Sport is not so good on the pavements. For here the pack turns to the gang. And here we make gangsters and feed jails.

This Boy's Club organization has proved one of the most effective preventions of delinquency—always excepting Mother. Some years ago in a certain tough district in Chicago over 80 percent of the boys in the district were in the hands of the police during the year. A few years after the completion of a Club, the delinquency percentage dropped to 12 percent.

As to physical benefits to the boys I might mention that the national rate of 4-F's was over 30 percent in the last war. A canvass of 200,000 alumni of Boys' Clubs showed only 4½ percent. And they fought and died bravely.

Great editors, great musicians, great sculptors, and five Major League Baseball players were started in the channels of this organization. And today millions of boys from these Clubs are solid patriotic citizens of our country. Due to the indefatigable efforts of General Wood and others in this work, Chicago slums are proportionately better served by the Boys' Clubs than any other city in the country. For here there are 21 Clubs with 11,000 boy members.

On Hydroelectric Power

Statement to the Press in Answer to Mr. Adlai Stevenson's
Charges in His Eugene, Oregon, Speech
[July 12, 1954]

M R. STEVENSON, in his Eugene speech, was led into three grave misstatements of fact or implication in respect to myself.

First. As President, I did not veto the very first multiple-purpose dam for hydroelectric power. On the contrary, I have advocated multiple-purpose dams when justified for the past thirty years. Further, I had a large part in bringing about, and almost completed during my Administration, the construction of the first and largest multiple-purpose dam in our country. That was the Hoover Dam on the Colorado. During my Administration we prepared the plans and I recommended the construction of the Grand Coulee. It was later built as planned.

Second. I did veto the Norris Dam bill although I had recommended the construction of this dam. I vetoed it because the bill contained none of the adequate protections of the Federal Treasury which had been included in the Hoover Dam legislation of four or five years previously and because the bill would establish pure socialism through the Federal manufacture of fertilizers.

Third. I never said that the Government should get out of the electric power business. What I did say was that the Federal Government must continue to construct multiple-purpose hydroelectric dams but that the Federal Government should get out of the socialistic and bureaucratic empire building by way of operating the power houses and distributing power; that the Federal Government should sell its power at the bus bar to the municipalities, the States, and the private utilities; that it should sell it at rates which would return interest and amortization to the Federal Government on its investment in power and pay State and local taxes which are now mostly exempt.

The above is to correct misstatements.

I may add that whatever my ideas may be they do not dominate the Task Force on Water Resources Development under Admiral Ben Moreell or the Commission on Organization of the Executive Branch of the Government. In order that this Task Force should be objective in appointing its members, I included no one connected with private utilities although I did include one or two who are connected with public power.

PART III

ENGINEERING MATTERS

A Discussion of *De Re Metallica*

"Invitation to Learning"—Columbia Broadcasting System
[April 15, 1951]

THIS seems an incongruous performance far away from the dangers which haunt all our minds. This occasion was scheduled many months ago, but we must keep up our programs of life and living. Moreover, it may furnish a half-hour's escape from the dread things that race through our minds.

What we are doing here is to look back four hundred years at some of the things that have made modern civilization possible—even if it seems somewhat creaky at the present time. What we are discussing today is a particular segment of Renaissance literature.

The great awakening of learning had begun more than a century before the period we are discussing, but it did not really get under way until the invention of printing in 1454.

With printing the great Greek and Roman classics had become generally available in books instead of being confined to manuscripts treasured in the few great libraries.

Printing, however, brought many new branches of literature into being in addition to the old classics. One of these new branches included the books on medicine, chemistry, metallurgy, mining, and other branches of applied science.

There were some classical ancestors of this literature but it took on a new form. Men compiled folk experience—the teacher-to-pupil instruction, the father-to-son secrets—and they described the actual practice of these professions and arts. By the printing press, this knowledge was spread rapidly. It became an important part of the Renaissance in both literature and economic development. We are here to examine some part of the early literature on mining and metallurgy.

Metals were used before the dawn of written history. And as few metals occur pure in nature there had to be some metallurgy. But the first written description came much later. We have a description of a smelter in Homer's *Iliad* (xviii) during the siege of Troy (about 1200 B.C.).

The mines have always borne a relation to the prosperity of nations. For three centuries coincident with the highest development of Greek civilization, Athens received a munificent income from the silver and lead mines of Laurion. Themistocles paid for the construction and manned the victorious fleet at Salamis out of these mines. During their greatest productivity the annual revenue of the city rose to the purchasing power of about $6,000,000.

With this much introduction we can come up to the segment of early printed books on the chemical, metallurgical, and mining side.

The first of these books were apparently what we know as *Probierbüchlein*, printed in German, some of them probably before 1500. They were small books, constructed like cookbooks of recipes for assaying, chemical, metallurgical, and mining problems. Very few of them are still extant.

The first man to really systematically compile the literature and experience of the world in these subjects was Georgius Agricola, who wrote and published several books during the years from 1530 to 1556. Another writer of importance was Vannuccio Biringuccio who published a single book in 1540.

Georgius Agricola's last name was really Bauer—a farmer—but he lived all his adult life under the Latinized form. He was a highly educated man for his times. He wrote in Latin. He was a physician by profession and it was from his practice in the mining regions of Bohemia and Saxony that he secured the materials for his works, the most important being the *De Re Metallica*, a folio volume of 600 pages with many illustrations. Biringuccio wrote in his native tongue—Italian. The first edition of his book is a quarto volume of about 170 pages. Biringuccio was a practical worker in these arts, of the superintendent type. His book is badly written and the first edition badly printed. Both Agricola and Biringuccio were the reference books for chemists, metallurgists, and miners for centuries.

Agricola was a man highly regarded in his times. He remained a staunch Catholic although the Reformation thundered about him. That he was of substantial character and position is evidenced by the fact that, although a Catholic, he was repeatedly chosen Burgomaster of Protestant Chemnitz in Saxony and several times a member of Diets where Protestants dominated. Despite their differences in religion he and the great Erasmus were life-long friends.

Incidentally, he seems to have made a competence from his ownership in a gold mine called "God's Gift."

Mrs. Hoover and I translated his *De Re Metallica* from the Latin in 1912—after a five-year struggle trying to find out the meaning of his Latinization of German and Bohemian technical terms.

There is a record somewhere that an ironbound copy was chained to the pulpit in a Church at San Luis Potosí in Peru, where the priests with the aid of the illustrations translated the various processes for the miners.

These great Peruvian mines were discovered, or at least captured, by Pizarro about the time this book was published. For many years the Spaniards worked the native silver which capped the mines. Later they came into the difficult silver minerals and the processes adopted were those shown in *De Re Metallica*. These processes were adopted in Mexico and thence in the United States, and were the principles used on the great Comstock Lode in Nevada.

Agricola gives considerable space to description of the use of a forked stick used in discovery of metals and water. The performer grasps the two branches, which are supposed to twist irresistibly downward. Agricola, four hundred years ago, gives an elaborate argument showing that he believed it to be non-sense. But the belief that water and metal can be found that way has persisted down to this day.

That great American author, Kenneth Roberts, has recently published a book entitled *Henry Gross and His Dowsing Rod*, which gives a vivid account of this practice. It is a most entertaining book but there will be skeptics. At present it is used mostly for locating water wells.

Most engineers would explain its presumed successes by the physical fact that excluding obvious areas such as rocks, mountains, etc., the earth's crust contains water at some depth and the forked stick cannot miss.

Agricola paid a great tribute to the miners when he said:

Inasmuch as the chief callings are those of the moneylender, the soldier, the merchant, the farmer, and miner, I say, inasmuch as usury is odious, while the spoil cruelly captured from the possessions of the people innocent of wrong is wicked in the sight of God and man, and inasmuch as the calling of the miner excels in honor and dignity that of the merchant trading for lucre, while it is not less noble though far more profitable than agriculture, who can fail to realize that mining is a calling of peculiar dignity?

Engineers

*Address to the Columbia University Engineering
Campaign Center, New York City
[November 7, 1951]*

IT SEEMS appropriate for me to speak here. I was once a
nonresident engineering professor at Columbia University.
I gave a course of lectures that had all the wit of calculus,
the humor of a trilobite, and the joyousness of thermody-
namics. Somebody remembered it about ten years later and paid
me with an honorary degree. That entitles me to be on alumni
lists for solicitation of funds.

We are here to promote a great project in engineering education and research. Not all of you are engineers and thus
some have not heard me declaim on that profession. This, then,
is an opportunity not to be neglected even if I repeat a little.

Men never lose the love for the profession to which they
have given years of their lives. The recollection of its joys is
the more vivid if one has backslid onto the slippery path of
public life.

Within a little more than my lifetime, the training of engineers has risen from apprenticeship to a trade or secondary
technical schools, to the dignity of a University-trained profession. It was the American Universities who pioneered the
world in that breadth of training and endowed the profession
with great dignity.

As indicative of the distance the engineers have risen in
public repute, I might recall that some years ago while crossing
the Atlantic I took my meals at the same table with a cultivated

English lady. As we came into New York Harbor, at break-fast she said: "I hope you will forgive my dreadful curiosity, but I should like awfully to know what is your profession." I said that I was an engineer. Her involuntary exclamation was: "Why, I thought you were a gentleman."

Even yet the scientists look down on the engineers as being something earthy or at least very subsidiary.

As a profession, engineering has both joys and sorrows.

The engineer has the fascination of watching a figment of his imagination emerge with the aid of science to a plan on paper. Then it moves to realization in cement, metal or energy. Then it brings new jobs and homes to men. Then it adds to the security and comfort of these homes. That is the engineer's high privilege among professions.

The profession, however, does have woes. The engineer's work is out in the open where all men can see it. If he makes a mistake, he cannot, like the doctor, bury it in a grave. He cannot, like the architect, obscure it by trees and ivy. He cannot, like the lawyer, blame it on the judge or jury. He cannot, like the politician, claim his constituents demanded it. Nor can he, like the public official, change the name of it and hope the voters will forget. Unlike the clergyman, he cannot blame it on the devil.

Worse still, if his works do not work, he is damned. That is the phantasmagoria which haunts his nights and dogs his days. He goes to bed wondering where the bugs are which will inevitably appear to jolt its performance. He awakens at night in a cold sweat and puts something on paper that looks silly in the morning.

And the world mostly forgets the name of the engineer who did it. The credit goes to some fellow who used other people's money to pay for it. But the engineer himself looks back at the unending stream of goodness that flows from his successes with a satisfaction that few other professions can know.

Most people are not aware of it, but the engineer is also a political and economic as well as social force.

I asserted one time that he is the fellow who really dissolves monopolies, redistributes the wealth, and dismantles political platforms. Over our history, one generation after another, men have been elected to office by being sequently "agin" the monopoly of canals, or railroads or anthracite coal or kerosene oil or slums or private development of water power. There were no doubt great evils. But I ask you who really remedied these evils? It was the engineer. He upset the canal monopoly with the railways; he upset the railways with the automobile, the airplane, and the pipeline. He upset the anthracite monopoly with coke; he upset the monopoly in kerosene oil with the electric light. He assured that most of the streams would remain as scenery by making cheaper power with steam. Who makes possible the escape from the slums? It is the engineer with his parkways, his bridges, his satellite towns. Who provided leisure for the housewife to play canasta and attend political meetings? It was the engineer with his household gadgets. Sometime the engineer will be needed to put truth into propaganda. But I am getting off the track of amiability.

I hardly need add that it is the engineer who distributes wealth by creation of mass production and his many other devices to reduce costs of production, and thereby brings the prices of a thousand gadgets to the level of everybody's pocketbook. Thus all men become equal before gadgets.

The training of engineers instills character in those who would join its ranks. High ethical standards are the essential of all professions, engineering included. Technology without intellectual honesty does not work. Construction without conscientiousness soon crumbles. Those are the reasons you have seen no engineers before the Kefauver Committee. Nor in the headlines which these days pour forth from Grand Juries and District Attorneys' offices. In the main, engineers appear in public only to sit on juries.

And now after all this exposition surely you will agree that the engineer is an antidote to evil and the bearer of blessings. I hope you will also agree that he is worthy of your attention.

But here we meet a great national problem. We do not

have enough engineering teachers and we do not have enough students to carry on the nation's work. And we do not have enough research facilities to assure the needed flow of new inventions and improvements.

Our engineering graduates have dropped from 50,000 in 1950 to 38,000 in 1951. We need 60,000 a year to supply national needs.

And may I depart from our immediate purpose to make a suggestion? One reason for this drop is that a young mechanic with three years of training, during which he is paid, can earn more take-home pay after taxes than a young engineer with six years of training and three years more of experience. Too often the financing of such training is too expensive for his Dad. Could not more "somebodies" give more scholarships to needy boys who are willing to put in nine years with little reward?

But to return to our mission here, you are proposing not only an aid to education but also to research.

The job of the engineer is to take the discoveries of pure science and convert them into use for the good of mankind. To this end he needs laboratories.

At one time we got our inventions from the genius in the garret. Poverty, however, does not clarify thought. Nor does it provide a laboratory. Bread-and-butter diet has been discarded as the mother of invention. Today these gifts come from long years of organized search and experiment. Therefrom, like the cell-by-cell growth of plants, fact builds upon fact until there comes forth the blossom of discovery, the illuminating hypotheses, or the great generalization. And finally it finds fruition in a multitude of inventions and improvements in living. And it increases the power of a people to pay government debts.

This reminds me that there is one road to rapid recovery of the nation from our present burden of rearmament. That is to increase our productive power by new technologies and new inventions.

And there are spiritual consequences of research. From them comes the unfolding of beauty, the ever-widening boundaries of thought. Here is the invocation of veracity in a world sodden with intellectual dishonesty. From its discoveries comes the lifting of men's minds beyond the depressing incidents of the day. Here is confirmation of a Supreme Guidance in the Universe far above man himself.

Today the nation needs more and more research and more and more engineers.

Address at Dinner Honoring
Dr. Lee De Forest

New York City
[April 8, 1952]

THERE is no greater story of intellectual accomplishment, of adventure, of fabulous discovery than that of the world of electricity.

It has been a world where succeeding stages of research in abstract science laid foundations of fact upon fact, hypotheses upon hypotheses. Then, periodically, some scientifically trained genius has combined these parts into a great invention which has opened a new world to all mankind.

There have been, over 150 years, a host of scientists who have contributed the raw materials of pure science. Many men have made from them important inventions. But there have been especially outstanding men of genius who have transformed these mysteries of science into those great inventions which have shaken civilization into new channels. Greatest of these inventors were: Michael Faraday, Thomas Edison, Samuel Morse, Alexander Graham Bell, and Lee De Forest.

They stand out as a consequence of the effect of their genius on the living of all humanity.

There are others whom, perhaps, I should include but whose inventions have been less dramatic and less widespread in their effect. There is Tesla, who contributed the alternating current to power transmission; Marconi, with his pioneering in wireless telegraphy; Pupin, with his telephone booster; and others.

And I should not fail to mention even a few of the great

scientists who contributed in their research to the foundations upon which these great inventions were built. Perhaps the most outstanding are: Boyle, Kelvin, Davy, Hertz, Maxwell, Ampère, Becquerel—but I could not here name them all.

There are many parallels in the lives of these five greatest inventors. They were all men of scientific experience; long periods of struggle amid privation; then a dramatic triumph in the application of science to invention.

Faraday transformed pure scientific discovery into the key invention which transformed energy into electricity. It became the ancestor of all the dynamos and electric generators in the world. It is said that he exhibited his contraption to a political leader of the day who asked, "What practical use is it?" Faraday replied: "Sir, some day you will tax it."

Samuel Morse brought from pure science the invention of the telegraph. His memorable remark was: "What hath God wrought?"

Alexander Graham Bell brought the telephone from the realm of abstract science to a practicality. Bell's first message over the wires was to his co-worker: "Watson, come here. I want you!"

Thomas Edison's most dramatic triumph was the invention of the electric light. He also contributed greatly to the improvement in generation and transmission of power, and electrical improvements in a hundred other directions. And also he is the father of all movie shows, phonographs, and talking machines generally. There is a story, perhaps apocryphal, that when a political leader asked Edison questions about the phonograph, he is supposed to have replied, "The good Lord in the Garden of Eden invented the first talking machine and called it Eve—I, in my laboratory, invented the first talking machine that can be turned off."

The fifth of these great inventors is Dr. Lee De Forest, who ranks with the greatest. I need not tell you that most revolutionary of his many inventions was the electron tube. From it has come the radio, the television, the radar, and a thousand electronic controls in industry.

I can imagine that if Dr. De Forest had shown his contraption of the electron tube to an American political leader he
would have been asked the same question as had been put to
Faraday. I can imagine De Forest replying, "Sir, some day you
will try to regulate it with laws."

And now the managers of this six-billion-dollar industry
are haunted by day with summons to Washington and by night
theirs is the restless pillow of regulation nightmares in their
sleep.

Dr. De Forest, a few days ago, published an absorbing auto-
biography. From it I can give myself a little reflected glory.
Dr. De Forest and I were both born in Iowa and some part of
our boyhoods were spent within fifteen miles of each other.
He antedated me by 1 year and 16 days. I don't know that it
bears on the matters we are discussing tonight, but both of our
memoirs recall that we were induced by our own religious forebears to read the entire Bible before we were twelve years old.

We both were ambitious to enter the technological world—
and I gained a year on him by graduating from Stanford in
1895 and he from Yale in 1896. At that point the parallel stops.
He went on with vast contributions to science and new inventions, each with incomparable benefits to all humanity. I de-
serted the technological field for the slippery path of public
life. Some people think my gigantic invention was the great
world-wide depression.

Dr. De Forest brought infinite blessings to mankind by the
instant transmission into every home of the news, of great music,
of great drama, and great lifts in education.

But he has some grave matters to answer for. He has made
it possible to transmit the worst music on earth—and political
speeches. Perhaps the worst of his results is the singing commercial that plugs in when we try to get the news. And then
there is the fellow who cannot sponsor a program without periodic interruption of huckster chatter into the midst of an inspiring musical presentation or a great drama.

But Dr. De Forest could redeem himself if he would produce another great invention. That is the push button by which

we could transmit our emotions instantly back to the broad-casters. It would explode our feelings over the air instead of allowing their inner gnawing of our morals.

I do not lay the responsibility for the juke box or the Western movie, or for my neighbor's gramophone, on Dr. De Forest. The responsibilities for those lie with my friend, the great ancestor of a great man who is our other speaker tonight.

My friends, we are here to honor an unmeasurable benefactor of mankind. We honor ourselves by honoring him. He will be remembered when all the rest of us are long forgotten.

We Have Just Begun to Dream

The American Weekly
[May 25, 1952]

THE increasing capacity of the American people to produce things has saved the nation from repeated lost
statesmanship by their political leaders.

After the British lost statesmanship, which produced the
American Revolution, our people, rooted in a fertile soil by
hard and long hours of every member of the family, quickly
overcame its damages, restored the government credit, and
gained in living standards.

The ruinous inflation originating in the Jackson period was
finally overcome by the application of the steam engine to transport and factory power and the productivity of the Western
prairies.

Again after the lost statesmanship which preceded the Civil
War with its seemingly irreparable injuries, the expanding railways brought markets to millions of new acres which together
with growing skills in the industries soon overcame its losses,
restored the government credit, and the nation again gained in
its standards of living.

And then came a great period of invention—electric power,
the telegraph, the telephone, the gas engine, from which sprang
the automobile and the airplane; the electronic inventions which
gave birth to a vast new system of communication. From all of
these—and from a multitude of lesser inventions and increasing
skills—sprang higher and higher standards of living, reaching
far above those the world had ever known.

The lost statesmanship which produced World War I, with all its setbacks, was quickly overcome in the years that followed by a steadily increasing productivity per capita in the people.

Then came the '30s with a collapse of domestic inflation to which was added a hurricane from the collapse of the European economy as the aftermath of the War. Then followed the tampering with free enterprise by our government and we decreased in productive capacity for the first decade in our national history.

Then came the lost statesmanship which produced World War II and its evils, followed by the cold war for which we have turned from butter to guns. We have not yet recovered economic health—but we may.

What has created all this increasing capacity to produce civilian goods in the long era until the last two decades? Some people credit it to our natural resources. They are great, but the greater forces have been the freedom of mind, spirit, and enterprise which blossomed into great scientific discovery and their train of invention.

We need follow for a moment only one development—that is electricity. Michael Faraday discovered in 1821 that energy could be transformed into electricity through induction.

Samuel Morse in 1840 brought the telegraph into being. Then came James Maxwell in 1864 with the mathematical demonstration of the theory of electrical waves. Then David Hughes in 1878 invented a transmitter called a microphone. Then Alexander Graham Bell discovered that the human voice could be electrically transmitted over wires, and the telephone was born.

Then Heinrich Rudolph Hertz in 1887 discovered radio waves. Then came Thomas A. Edison in 1879 with his vacuum bulb with its filament and the practical electrical light was born. And from Edison the development of the dynamo and transmission of power came into being.

Then came Nikola Tesla in 1893 with his alternating current, and long-distance transmission of power became possible. Then came Sir John A. Fleming with the electron tube in 1904 and Lee De Forest in 1906 with his invention of the vacuum tube for transmission of electrical waves through the air. And from this came the radio, television, and a long line of electronic inventions.

While the engineer is also an inventor, his great job has been to design and build the great productive units of factory, transportation, and communication made possible by these discoveries and inventions. A rough estimate indicates that we have increased the skilled worker's aid from two or three horsepower per man until now workers average over 1,000 horsepower.

In agriculture, the scientist and the engineer, by better seeds, better animals, better machinery now enable 30 percent of our people to produce the abundant food of the nation which once required the labor of 70 percent of our people.

In the gigantic field of applied science, the trained engineer is now emerging into the executive field. It is said that the heads of more than one-half of the great productive corporations are trained engineers.

All this has been partly due to the fact that it was in America that about a century ago engineering was lifted from an apprenticeship trade to a highly trained profession by the incorporation of its training into our universities and colleges on equal terms with the other learned professions.

In what we call the American System, I, the son of a blacksmith, through the opportunities of the public schools and the university could grow into an engineer and serve in many high responsibilities.

At a recent luncheon I learned that the young man seated next to me had just enrolled in college. I asked him if he had decided on a career.

"No," he admitted. "I think I'll wait and see what kind of opportunities open up."

I was astonished.

"What if I were to tell you," I asked, "that the opportunity you are waiting for is right before your eyes and you must begin now?"

I suggested to him that in these troubled times there was

only one certain treasure he could keep—a definite training from his college stored in his head for some vocation. No man could take such from him.

I suggested he should begin to specialize at once in some direction in college, or he would be adrift with a little knowledge of everything and not much knowledge of anything. I suggested this did not mean no accompanying cultural training.

He asked about engineering. I inquired if he liked the exact sciences, such as chemistry, physics and mathematics. He did not. I advised him to choose some other vocation—but to *choose* one.

To youngsters with an interest in exacting technology, there are ever-expanding opportunities in scientific research and engineering. We need probably 70,000 newly trained technologists every year. We are training less than half that number.

All this is to lead up to the fact that the engineers are celebrating 100 years in the upward movement and accomplishment in the profession at Chicago, beginning on September 3d. One hundred years ago the American Society of Civil Engineers was incorporated.

At that time a "civil" engineer embraced all of the other branches so far as they were known. As specialization grew, the other great engineering societies sprang up until now more than two score of them will participate with the Civil Engineers in their birthday. There the engineers will present exhibits and discussions of engineering progress and knowledge that will truly mark so great an event. And the whole has been organized under the inspiration of Major Lenox R. Lohr.

Certainly, as this Centennial will remind us, there is glory in our productive past. The engineers can be proud of both the material progress and the cultural and spiritual richness which it has endowed. A possible vast field of scientific discovery and invention lies ahead of us.

The engineers and the scientists can save America again—if their minds and spirits are kept free from the stifling of government burdens and bureaucracy. Their Centennial of Engineering will teach these possibilities to the American people.

On Engineers

Address to Northwest Engineering Centennial,
Portland, Oregon
[August 9, 1952]

I HAVE said many times that if you want to know the truth about a man, ask the fellow members of his profession. I now have your certificate to flaunt before some people.

Men never lose their love for the profession to which they have been trained and have given years of their lives. The recollection of its joys is the more vivid if one has backslid onto the slippery path of public life.

THE ENGINEERS CAN HELP SAVE OUR NATIONAL LIFE

This is not a political speech. My first text comes from the agreement of both political platforms that the nation is mired down in a swamp of spending, inflation, and taxes. Both parties disagree on who-done-it. They seem to agree upon the obvious, that reduction of Federal expenditures would be a good step to get out of the swamp, but there is wide disagreement on where to begin and how much.

However I am suggesting something else which is a partial method of relief, and that is where the engineers come in. That partial remedy for our ills is with all our might to stimulate scientific discovery, invention, and their application by our engineers. That would increase productivity per capita and thereby mitigate these burdens. I do not guarantee it can work fast enough to save the American way of life—but it could help.

196

The basis of this hope lies in our experience from three great hot wars. By increased productivity after these wars the credit of our nation was restored and the prosperity of our people moved into high levels. That was true after the War of the Revolution, the Civil War, and the first World War. But this extension of the second World War into six years of cold war is where my belief comes from that this is now only a partial remedy. Otherwise a continuation of these spending, taxing, and inflation policies can have but one result. That is a national socialistic state.

After the War of the Revolution free initiative in expansion of our agriculture and the application of steam power in the factories increased our productivity, restored our national credit and gave a lift to the standard of living.

After the Civil War the expansion of the railways brought millions of new fertile acres into productivity. With this and with growing skills in free industry, the nation again recovered and marched forward.

After World War I, scientific discoveries and inventions, and still more growth of skills and improved processes found expression in the expansion of motor transport and electrification, radio, and airplanes. And from cheaper costs of production we remedied the ravages of war and rose to the highest average standard of living in all human history.

Since World War II we have again made great advances in science and invention. We have built many improved plants but we have not yet been able to catch up with the spenders and the tax collectors.

One warrant for my hope lies in the fact that we, with only six percent of the world's population, have today more trained scientists and engineers than all the rest of the world put together.

The application of new scientific discoveries and new inventions is always a business speculation. It is based on venture capital and plowing in of profits until production is in full bloom.

There are two obstructions in the path of such a solution of our economic problems. The first is unintelligent taxation and the second a coming national famine in technologists. I could enumerate a dozen other destructors but I said this would not be a political speech.

AN EXAMPLE

There is no better exhibit of what ill-considered taxation can do to our economy than our nonferrous metal industry in the West. That industry is founded wholly on venture capital and the plowing in of profits until a mine is equipped and producing. Today such venture capital from individuals is itself undermined and taxation prevents the necessary plowing in. That is not theory; it is a fact. Twenty years ago there were about 3,000 operating nonferrous metal mines in the Rocky Mountain area. Today there are only a few more than 1,000. I recently made a canvass of the operators of many of the large mines which were developed in a more favorable economic climate. I asked a simple question—"Could this enterprise have ever been developed and equipped under present taxation and other restrictions on freedom?" The answer was "No" in every case but one, and that case had been a bonanza so rich as to defy even the tax collector. But today even in most of these surviving enterprises the government takes from the stockholder about $85 out of every $100, earned before taxes, and if he received the remaining $15, there would be no fund left to plow into constantly needed improvements to treat decreasing grades of ore.

From it all, the nation is becoming short of these domestically produced metals.

By stimulated scientific research and invention looking to new engineering methods we can reduce costs and thus do something to aid this industry. But more intelligent taxes on mines such as those in other countries would sustain the industry. It would be cheaper than government subsidies.

The same problems apply to the other industries where venture capital and plowing in are their characteristics.

But there has arisen an alternative application of new ideas which bodes little good to our society. The established industries can and do undertake such risks in their fields. They can write off their losses against taxes, and the venture costs nothing. The inventor, the prospector, or the individual has little chance of this relief. The consequence is that existing enterprises absorb the new discoveries and inventions. They grow in size and monopolistic strength but the opportunity for the individual to establish his independent and competitive business is greatly diminished.

WE ARE RUNNING SHORT OF ENGINEERS

We have in our profession another great national problem. We do not have enough engineers in incubation to carry on the nation's work. We need 60,000 new technologists a year to supply national needs. Our engineering graduates have dropped from 50,000 in 1950 to 38,000 in 1951, and the students in training indicate less than 30,000 next year. Yet our universities have ample facilities to fill the demand.

One reason for this drop is that a young mechanic with three years of training, during which he is paid, can earn more take-home pay after taxes than a young engineer with six years of training and three years more of experience. Too often the financing of engineering training is too expensive for his Dad. And with increased tuition and living costs it is more and more difficult for boys by off-time work to make their way through college as many of you did.

The answer must come from the industries. They must consider their responsibility to aid promising boys. For it is upon such boys that future existence of industry depends.

THE ENGINEERING PROFESSION

But there are more cheerful subjects for discussion among engineers. I have reviewed them many times in the past.

Within a little more than my lifetime, the training of engineers has risen from apprenticeship to a trade or secondary technical schools to the dignity of a university-trained profession.

As indicative of the distance the engineers have risen in public repute, I might recall that some years ago while crossing the Atlantic, I took my meals at the same table with a cultivated English lady. As we came into New York Harbor, at breakfast she said: "I hope you will forgive my dreadful curiosity, but I should like awfully to know what is your profession." I said that I was an engineer. Her involuntary exclamation was: "Why, I thought you were a gentleman."

The engineer has a high privilege among professions. He has the fascination of watching a figment of his imagination emerge with the aid of science to a plan on paper. Then it moves to realization in cement, metal, or energy. Then it adds to the security and comfort of homes.

Engineering training by our universities has other great values to the country than its industrial consequences. It instills character in those who would join its ranks, for high ethical standards are the essential of all professions. Technology without intellectual honesty does not work. Construction without conscientiousness soon crumbles. Here is the invocation of veracity in a world sodden with intellectual dishonesty. These are the reasons you have seen no engineers before the Kefauver Committee. Nor in the headlines which these days pour forth from Grand Juries and District Attorneys' offices. The engineers' main appearance in public is only to sit on juries and committees for reform.

From the work of the engineers comes the lifting of men's minds beyond the depressing incidents of the day. And here is the rejuvenation of spirit and confidence in the future of our country.

In any event you will agree that the engineer is an antidote to evil and the bearer of blessings. Even including his antidote to inflation.

In closing, let me repeat a statement from a good engineer of just exactly four hundred years ago. He referred to the mining engineers but his general tolerance is warranty for its application to all engineers. "Inasmuch as the chief callings are those of the moneylender, the soldier, the merchant, the farmer, and miner, I say, inasmuch as usury is odious, while the spoil cruelly captured from the possessions of the people innocent of wrong is wicked in the sight of God and man and inasmuch as the calling of the miner excels in honor and dignity that of the merchant trading for lucre, while it is not less noble though far more profitable than agriculture, who can fail to realize that it is a calling of peculiar dignity?"

The Scientists' and Engineers' Promise to American Life

*Address Before the Centennial of Engineering,
Chicago, Illinois
[September 10, 1952]*

THIS celebration of one hundred years of engineering demonstrates the progress of our profession without any verbal supplements.

We are proud of the past. But our minds are turned to what may come to America from our profession in the future years. But before I mention these great hopes I must make a few reservations. Progress in scientific discovery, invention, and their application will depend upon:

1. The maintenance of a climate of individual freedom of mind, spirit, and action from which alone they can spring.

2. To achieve that, this nation must keep out of wars, avoid inflation, and unload our unbearable taxes. We might remember that ancient Athens, Rome, and some modern states by such practices bled white the intelligence and energies of their race.

THE PROMISE OF THE FUTURE

With these reservations I can say at once that the American people are on the threshold of a greater advance in living and comfort than ever known to mankind.

The promise of the scientists and engineers to America rests upon two foundations—the wider application of what we already know and the certainty of new discoveries and new inventions.

Even without any additional scientific discoveries or inventions we know these things:

The next generation will have less diseases and cure them faster than the last generation.

They will have less germs and insects to bite them.

They will have bigger and better food animals and plants, and less acres devoted to nonfood products. Add to this more food from the sea, and there will be an abundance for our people.

Already known synthetic fibers will give the next generation better and cheaper clothes.

Our new knowledge of highway, air transport, and diesel engines will expand easier, cheaper, and safer transportation.

Our improved industrial methods and processes and bigger labor-saving tools will be more widely used. The next generation will control their machinery processes more and more precisely and with less labor by our already known electronic devices.

The next generation will have wider application of our new chemical and mechanical processes for extracting metals from low-grade ores. They will have more synthetic materials and thus more abundant and cheaper construction.

From all this we will have better and cheaper housing with all the gadgets.

Our new knowledge of electronics gives promise of ever-widening communication by radar, radio, and TV. The next generation may need endure still more singing commercials.

And they already know more about how to kill fellow men than the past generation.

NEW DISCOVERIES, NEW INVENTIONS ALSO WOULD COME

Beyond all our accumulated knowledge which could be intensively applied by the next generation, we are assured of new discoveries in science and new inventions not now known. This is certain for several reasons. The next generation will have the advantage of already created better instruments and equipment for scientific research than the last generation.

At this beginning of the hundred years we celebrate, there were but a few scattered laboratories in our universities and colleges. Today, America has more than five thousand effective laboratories—more than all the rest of the world put together. And in a hundred of them, each staff is greater than the personnel in all of them put together a hundred years ago.

There was a time when we got our new inventions from a poverty-impelled genius in the garret. That time has long gone by. We have discarded a bread-and-water diet as the mother of invention. Our greater gifts from the last century came from long years of patient laboratory research and experiment by trained workers. We now have a new era in research by the co-ordination of teams of scientists who bring to our problems the combined knowledge of physics, chemistry, mathematics, and biology.

The result of scientific research in the future as in the past will be like the growth of plants, cell by cell. Some day there comes forth a new blossom of great scientific discovery, an illuminating hypothesis, a fruitful generalization, or a new instrument for enlarged research.

From this increasing raw material of abstract science the engineer will bring still more inventions, still greater command of power, still newer materials, and still more labor-saving devices, and new methods.

Out of his imagination, his blueprints, his construction will spring the new additions to human service and comfort, to leisure and recreation.

SOME ILLUSIONS

But we are even today plagued with two persistent ghosts which haunt the lay mind. The first is the fright of technological unemployment. That ghost has been summoned from his lair every year since Eli Whitney invented the cotton gin. Yet for every job in the livery stable of yesterday, there are a hundred jobs in the garage of today at four times the take-home pay. Moreover, a study of our annual flood of patents shows that two-thirds of them are for production of new or better methods and articles of use and with new jobs. Further, a study of our comparative occupations over years shows that three times as many work people are recruited into new occupations as those whose jobs disappear in obsolescence.

The other truculent ghost of space writers is that our inventions and mechanization create degenerative physical pressures upon those who work them. The contrary is true. Our engineering results are accomplished by making our machines and heads work harder—not our hands.

RECOVERY FROM LOST STATESMANSHIP

And the consequences of these advances produced by the scientists and engineers have another import.

From Watt's invention of the steam engine, down the long road of inventions to the latest electronic recorder, scientific discovery and the inventions by engineering productivity have periodically saved the world from impoverishment by the wars created through lost statesmanship. That is our hope for our nation today.

And let me add that bureaucracies do not produce these wonders in scientific discovery or invention. Governments can at times advantageously subsidize research or pioneering of the application of known discoveries.

However it is dynamic men and women, free in mind and spirit, who make these human advances. The decadence of scientific research in Germany under Hitler is a lesson to the world.

CONTRIBUTIONS TO MORALS AND THE SPIRIT

There also lies in these fields of science and engineering a contribution to the moral and spiritual welfare of mankind. Here is the "inculcation of veracity of thought" in a world sodden with intellectual dishonesty. For science and engineering must first be expressed in words of truth, or they do not work. And from scientists and engineers comes the harmonizing of the individual to the pattern of his environment.

Above all they bring the confirmation of a Supreme Guidance in the universe far above man himself.

On Engineering Standards

*Address in Response to Receiving the Howard Coonley
Gold Medal from the American Engineering Standards
Association, New York City*
[October 24, 1951]

A FEW days ago your committee invited me to accept this great honor. And I prize it, especially as it comes from my fellow engineers.

At once my mind traveled back to my Secretary of Commerce years, 1921–1928, when we all co-operated in a great crusade for the ideas you represent.

Many people probably even now do not appreciate in full the ideas which are embraced in your title of standardization and its subsidiaries, simplification and specification. Yet the philosophies behind these terms and the consequences of their application have played an enormous part in our whole economic development.

At that time the humorists sought to drown us in laughter over possible standardized women's hats. But in time we managed to sustain the conviction that we were wholly allergic to matters of style, for those vagaries were offsprings of joy, not of engineering. But we even helped to cheapen some hats by way of simplifying and standardizing parts in the milliners' machinery.

The ideas in our particular philosophy were concerned strictly with industrial products. Herein were standards of weights, measures, voltages, frequencies, heat, screw threads, spare parts, and what not. They included turbine generators, the parts of machine tools, automobiles, farm machinery, and hundreds of other items.

Simplifications were concerned with eliminating unnecessary varieties and dimensions in such sordid things as fishplates, bricks, lumber, lamp sockets, automobile wheels, bolts, nuts, plumbers' fittings, and a million other things.

And we were concerned with writing specifications which would assure the consumer quality and performance. This cataloguish statement, however, conveys no indication of their importance in our whole economic development. The public mostly assumes that this progress has come from scientific discovery of natural laws, new materials, inventions, and increasing skills. But you and I know that the increase in our living standards and comfort has received an enormous contribution from these related ideas of standards, of simplifications and specifications.

They are at the base of all mass production. They make possible more continuous employment by manufacture for stock instead of dependence upon immediate and specialized orders. They have made it possible to conduct our fabulous productive machine with the least amount of spare parts and inventories in the hands of the consumer industries. They have sharpened competition. They have cheapened the cost of production in millions of directions. Thus they have been a factor in our rising living standards. They have enabled thousands of different articles to be placed within the reach of everybody. They do not impose uniformity on the individual, because they make available to him an infinite variety of additions to his living.

This technology and its blessings reach unheralded into every household, not into industry alone. Before you engineers set to work, the housewife had to shop for special electric lamps that would fit her sockets, for special needles for her sewing machine. At one time she had to trim the bedstead or the springs or the mattress to make them fit with each other. But now they all fit, no matter what the breed. The workman at one time had to find a bolt of the same make before he could screw a nut on it and had to search among a hundred different diameters. Now the half-inch nuts screw onto all the half-inch bolts and there are but two-score of different diameters instead of two hundred. And the common man should be grateful that the three-score sizes of automobile wheels and tires have been replaced by about half a dozen standard sizes.

And the sum total of all these ideas has contributed to making thousands of machines which have lifted the burden from the backs of men and women.

This work of your Association has brought another invaluable accomplishment. Only a few of the literally tens of thousands of standardizations or simplifications have been imposed by law. The vast numbers of them have been the result of spontaneous, voluntary yet organized co-operation within highly individualized industry. To secure general acceptance of any one of them has been tedious at times. But their adoption has been playing a real part in the creation of the co-operation so vital among a free people.

Certainly it is true that the objects of organized society are to assure justice, freedom, respect for the dignity of men, and the improvement and security in living. And to this you continue to make a valuable contribution.

Engineering as a Profession*

Article in Engineer's Week, 1954

ENGINEERING training deals with the exact sciences. That sort of exactness makes for truth and conscience. It might be good for the world if more men had that sort of mental start in life even if they did not pursue the profession. But he who would enter these precincts as a life work must have a test taken of his imaginative faculties, for engineering without imagination sinks to a trade. And those who would enter here must for years abandon their white collars except for Sunday.

The profession means years on the lower rungs of the ladder—shops, works, and powerhouses—white collars are not a part of the engineer uniform. On the other hand, the engineer learns through work with his own hands not only the mind of the worker but the multitude of true gentlemen among them. And men who love a fight with nature, who like to build and see their building grow, men who do not hold themselves above manual labor, men who have the moral courage to do these things soundly, some day will be able to move to town, wear white collars every day, and send out the youngsters to the lower rungs and the frontiers of industry.

It is a great profession. There is the fascination of watching a figment of the imagination emerge through the aid of science to a plan on paper. Then it moves to realization in stone or metal or energy. Then it brings jobs and homes to men. Then it elevates the standards of living and adds to the comforts of life. That is the engineer's high privilege.

* Reprint of statement of 1916.

The great liability of the engineer compared to men of other professions is that his works are out in the open where all can see them. His acts, step by step, are in hard substance. He cannot bury his mistakes in the grave like the doctors. He cannot argue them into thin air or blame the judge like the lawyers. He cannot, like the architects, cover his failures with trees and vines. He cannot, like the politicians, screen his shortcomings by blaming his opponents and hope that the people will forget. The engineer simply cannot deny that he did it. If his works do not work, he is damned. That is the phantasmagoria that haunts his nights and dogs his days. He comes from the job at the end of the day resolved to calculate it again. He wakes in the night in a cold sweat and puts something on paper that looks silly in the morning. All day he shivers at the thought of the bugs which will inevitably appear to jolt its smooth consummation.

On the other hand, unlike the doctor, his is not a life among the weak. Unlike the soldier, destruction is not his purpose. Unlike the lawyer, quarrels are not his daily bread. To the engineer falls the job of clothing the bare bones of science with life, comfort, and hope. No doubt as years go by people forget which engineer did it, even if they ever knew. Or some politician puts his name on it. Or they credit it to some promoter who used other people's money with which to finance it. But the engineer himself looks back at the unending stream of goodness which flows from his successes with satisfactions that few professions may know. And the verdict of his fellow professionals is all the accolade he wants.

The engineer performs many public functions from which he gets only philosophical satisfactions. Most people do not know it, but he is an economic and social force. Every time he discovers a new application of science, thereby creating a new industry, providing new jobs, adding to the standards of living, he also disturbs everything that is. New laws and regulations have to be made and new sorts of wickedness curbed. He is also the person who really corrects monopolies and redistributes national wealth.

On Coal's Importance to the Nation's Economy

Letter to Mr. L. C. Campbell, President of the National Coal Association—36th Anniversary Convention, October 19–21, 1953
[October 2, 1953]

The Waldorf Astoria Towers
New York, New York
October 2, 1953

Mr. L. C. Campbell
President of the National Coal Association
Southern Building
Washington, D.C.

Dear Mr. Campbell:

There is no engineer who believes this nation can do without huge supplies of coal.

Despite the encroachment of water power, oil, gas, and the possible atomic power, the nation will need increasing coal production. There is in sight no ample substitute for much of our steam, a large part of household coal, supplies for metallurgical use, production of chemical materials, and other use.

Many uses will expand with every step of scientific discovery and increasing population.

Yours faithfully,

HERBERT HOOVER

211

Completion of the Cascade Tunnel

25th Anniversary Celebration
[December 22, 1953]

AS ONE who was present at the dedication of the Cascade Tunnel twenty-five years ago, I want to be present in spirit on this occasion. No one can measure the benefits that this great engineering triumph has brought to our people. They range the whole economic and social field. Even the political people can get around faster.

On the Development of Television

Letter to Mr. Herbert G. Moore, the National Republic
[March 6, 1954]

Dear Mr. Moore:

I have your letter asking if I can comment on what has happened to TV since I opened the first transmission twenty-seven years ago.

Any comment would be inadequate without giving the fabulous statistics of the growth of a new industry; or comment on its undoubted contributions to education, public understanding of national problems, the almost personal acquaintance with public figures; all this with some added remarks on the doubtful effect on children's minds from some of the shows.

You perhaps have more time to fill in all these developments better than I.

Yours faithfully,

HERBERT HOOVER

PART IV

THE REORGANIZATION OF THE EXECUTIVE BRANCH OF THE FEDERAL GOVERNMENT

(Mr. Hoover was chairman of the commission on this subject from 1947 to 1950.)

The Reconstruction Finance Corporation

*Statement Before the Senate Committee on Banking
and Currency
[April 30, 1951]*

Y OUR Committee has requested me to advise you of
my views upon the Reconstruction Finance Corporation.
I presume this request arises from the original creation of
the RFC upon my recommendation and from the investigation
into it by the Commission on Organization of the Executive
Branch of the Government of which I was chairman.

1. I believe that the RFC should be liquidated.

2. It should be liquidated by its new administrator.

3. I believe some facilities for loans in the small business
field should be continued under other organizations.

Starvation for credit in this area cannot have been very
great during the last five or six years. The five-year average
of the number of businesses operating is almost four million
and the new businesses started have averaged about four hundred thousand annually. From the number of loans under
$100,000 made by the RFC—and assuming they were neces-
sary—the relative figures indicate that probably 99 percent of
small businesses managed to finance themselves otherwise.

Be that as it may, the need should be tested out. The Federal Reserve Banks are already engaged in guaranteeing loans
for defense production. Therefore, I suggest their authority be

extended to a 100 percent guarantee (where necessary) of "small business" loans and to administering of them. The Reserve Banks should be indemnified by the Government against losses. A small organization should be set up in the Treasury Department to guide this purpose. But such loans should be restricted: (*a*) they should not exceed $100,000; (*b*) they must (as the Senate Banking and Currency Committee recommended two years ago) be made only where public interest is concerned and not solely in the interest of the borrower.

4. I believe the collateral activities of the RFC should be transferred to appropriate departments where definite responsibility of a Cabinet officer or single-individual administrator can be established. For instance, the rubber business should be transferred to the Department of Commerce; tin smelting to the Bureau of Mines of the Department of Interior; the functions of providing emergency credit for defense activities should be transferred to the Defense Department or to the Director of Defense Mobilization, who already have such authorities. The Federal National Mortgage Association should be transferred to the Administrator of Housing and Home Finance Agency.

REASONS FOR THESE RECOMMENDATIONS

1. Emergency agencies for defense production seem to be already in motion and the RFC is not needed in this field.

2. If a national emergency in credit should occur, such as a great economic crisis, the Congress, at any time of such need, can quickly create the necessary institution. Of great importance is the fact that in time of emergency the Government can command the best talent in the country. It can not maintain such talent in other times.

3. The last time the Congress was considering extension of the authority of the RFC, I recommended (May 30, 1947) that it be retained as an inactive stand-by institution for two or three years in a restricted field. Instead it has been most active.

When the RFC was founded in 1932 for the emergency of a national collapse of credit, stringent requirements were set by law as to security, purpose, and the absence of other sources of credit. Since that time, the requirements have been relaxed by legislation passed in January 1935, April 1938, May 1938, and June 1948. As a result, the institution now undertakes to finance, by so-called loans, almost anything, domestic and sometimes even foreign, on most any terms it pleases.

4. In my view when it enters the nonemergency area of loans in excess of $100,000, its social and economic purpose becomes submerged in support of risky business, and in bailing out creditors on a large scale. It would appear from the Fulbright hearings that the operation of the RFC for the past four or five years really shows a great loss. I see no reason why the taxpayers' money should be used to subsidize larger peacetime business.

5. This area of loans in excess of $100,000 is where the great dangers to the nation have occurred. That loans of this character have led to favoritism and corruption has been demonstrated by the exposures of the Fulbright Committee. Corruption in Government is far wider in effect than corruption in private business. Corruption in business affects only the pockets of employers or owners. Corruption in Government affects the pockets of all taxpayers, but far worse, it affects the morals of a people and lowers their respect for government.

6. The wisdom of the management of the RFC in recent years is seriously challenged by the infallible test of results. These results have been exposed by the Fulbright Committee. It is doubtful if wisdom can be maintained in such widespread Government action requiring the utmost good judgment. Under any new Administration a large part of the decisions must be delegated. And delegation by bureaucracy cannot always find such skilled and honest men.

7. It would appear that the test of public interest has been little applied. The public interest in several of the large loans has been questioned by the Fulbright Committee. I append some lists of a few samples.

a) 39 lesser-sized loans made for hotels, ranging from $9,000 to $1,500,000, in 23 states;

b) 14 loans made to hard and soft drink manufacturing distributors;

c) 18 loans to theaters and bowling alleys, ranging from $17,000 to $1,200,000.

Another list could be made of loans to beauty parlors, pool rooms, and a snake farm.

What public interest there can be in operations of these types of business at the taxpayers' risk is difficult to see.

8. The institution now has nearly 3,000 employees and a great overhead. The Federal Reserve Banks could administer the small business loans with a minor staff. The Federal Reserve personnel are of high order of character and ability. Also, they understand the loaning of money.

REPORT ON THE RFC BY THE COMMISSION ON ORGANIZATION OF THE EXECUTIVE BRANCH OF THE GOVERNMENT

The reports and recommendations of the Commission on Organization of the Executive Branch of the Government on the RFC are no doubt familiar to you.

THE TASK FORCE RECOMMENDATIONS

The Commission's task force for this examination was set up on the suggestion of Secretary James Forrestal, a member of the Commission. The Secretary recommended that Mr. Paul Grady of Price, Waterhouse and Company, public accountants, be made chairman of this task force. Mr. Grady was a former Assistant Secretary of the Navy handling finance matters. He was supported by an Advisory Committee of able men.

This task force recommended the liquidation of the RFC and the placing of any necessary lending of this character in the Federal Reserve Banks under a system of guarantees. They made recommendations as to disposal of the collateral activities. They made alternative recommendations in case liquidation was not possible. These recommendations called for a most vigorous reorganization with greater safeguards on loans if the institution was to continue.

THE COMMISSION'S RECOMMENDATIONS

The Commission itself made a number of recommendations in respect to this Agency.

The Commission did not agree upon liquidation but the majority of the Commission agreed upon a condemnation of direct lending by the RFC to persons or enterprises, except in national emergencies, saying that it:

. . . opens up dangerous possibilities of waste and favoritism . . . it invites political and private pressure or even corruption.

We recommended that Congress review at once the powers of the RFC so as to produce "economy, efficiency, and integrity."

It was further recommended that greater restrictions should be placed on loans.

We also recommended that the normal channels of credit should be used by guaranteed loans "through private or other established agencies."

We recommended the placing of some of the collateral activities in other agencies better able to administer them.

We further recommended that the whole organization be placed in the Treasury Department with responsibility for its administration vested in the Secretary of the Treasury.

The factual matter and recommendations of the Commission and the task force appear in several places in the Commission's statements. For the convenience of this Committee, I offer for the record an assembly of the scattered parts.

Selected Loans

to

Distillers, Brewers, and Bottlers

June 30, 1950

United Distillers of America, Inc., United Distillers of America, Ltd., New York, N.Y. Unpaid loan balance 6/30/50, $331,500.00.

James Distillery, Inc., Baltimore, Md. Unpaid balance 6/30/50, $315,000.00.

Harvard Brewing Company, Lowell, Mass. Undisbursed authorized balance 6/30/50, $300,000.00.

Old Rock Distilling Co., Joplin, Mo. Undisbursed loan balance 6/30/50, $29,936.48. Unpaid loan balance 6/30/50, $210,063.52. Total $240,000.00.

Morello Winery, Kerman, Calif. Undisbursed loan balance 6/30/50, $200,000.00.

Metz Brewing Co., Omaha, Neb. Unpaid loan balance (participating) 6/30/50, $178,125.00.

General Beverage Co., Inc., Oklahoma City, Okla. Unpaid loan balance 6/30/50, $145,-
000.00.
Coast View Winery, Inc., Fresno, Calif. Unpaid loan balance (participating) 6/30/50,
$117,750.00.
Clinton Distilling Co., Clinton, Iowa. Unpaid loan balance 6/30/50, $114,000.00.
Yakima Valley Brewing Co., Selah, Wash. Unpaid loan balance (participating) 6/30/50,
$99,562.50.
Scottish-American Distillers, Ltd., Peoria, Ill. Unpaid loan balance (participating)
$94,687.50.
Coca-Cola Bottling Company of Fargo, Fargo, N.D. Unpaid loan balance 6/30/50, $90,-
163.04.
The Wooden Shoe Brewing Co., Minster, Ohio. Unpaid loan balance (participating)
6/30/50, $65,040.00.
Sheridan Brewing Company, Sheridan, Wyo. Unpaid loan balance (participating) 6/30/50,
$60,000.00.

Selected Loans

to

Theaters, Bars, Bowling Alleys,

and Other Recreational Activities

June 30, 1950

Hal Roach Studios, Inc., Calif. $1,292,950.00.
Gersonde Brothers Recreation, St. Joseph, Mich. Authorized total, $377,212.28.
Hunt's Theaters, Inc., Wildwood, N.J. Undisbursed loan balance 6/30/50, $150,000.00.
Unpaid loan balance 6/30/50, $128,773.71. Total, $278,773.71.
Hollywood Stars, Inc., Calif. $172,600.00.
Coast Drive-In Theaters, Calif. $164,669.22.
Herndon Stadium, Inc., Atlanta, Ga. Unpaid loan balance 6/30/50, $164,038.46.
Collier Enterprises, Inc., Lowell, Mich. Authorized, $147,500.00.
Poulsen & Schock Theaters, Anchorage, Alaska. Undisbursed loan balance 6/30/50,
$100,000.00.
Gold Front Bar, Gold Front Theater, Gold Front Recreation, Cheboygan, Mich. Undis-
bursed authorized balance 6/30/50, $85,000.00.
Varden Park Bowling Club, Jackson, Mich. Authorized, $78,000.00.
Plymouth Rock Bar, Detroit, Mich. Authorized, $39,500.00.
Plains Theater, Lockney, Tex. Authorized, $27,500.00.
Eloia Theater, Calvert, Tex. Authorized, $25,000.00.
Samuel E. Evans (Rattlesnake Farm), Colfax, Calif. Authorized, $25,000.00.
Howes Lanes (Bowling), Clarkston, Mich. Authorized, $20,212.28.
Poormans Recreation, Buchanan, Mich. Authorized, $20,000.00.
Bronson Theater, Bronson, Mich. Authorized, $17,500.00.
Montcalm Bowling Center, Pontiac, Mich. Authorized, $17,000.00.

Selected Loans

to

Hotels and Other Hostelries

June 30, 1950

Sax Enterprises, Inc., Miami Beach, Fla. (Refinanced) 5/19/49, $1,500,000.00.
Mapes Hotel, Reno, Nev. (25% participation) 10/6/49, $1,300,000.00.
Simburg, Harry and Jennie (Hotel Sorrento), Miami Beach, Fla. 10/27/49, $1,000,000.00.
Civic Hotel Corp. of Odessa, Odessa, Tex. 2/27/50, $650,000.00.
Jack Tar Court Hotel, Hot Springs, Ark. Unpaid loan balance 6/30/50, $565,000.00.
Borger Hotel Corp., Borger, Tex. 1/30/50, $413,429.00.
The Virgin Isle Hotel, Inc., Thomas, V.I. Undisbursed loan balance 6/30/50, $400,000.00.
Tahoe Biltmore Hotel, Inc., Crystal Bay, Mo. SLP-RFC's portion, $45,000.00. Two BPA
loans, $300,000.00. Total, $345,000.00.
The Balsams, Inc., Dixville Notch, N.H. Unpaid loan balance 6/30/50, $300,000.00.

Community Hotel Co., Norman, Okla. Approved, $300,000.00.

Knutson Hotel Corp., Minneapolis, Minn. Undisbursed loan balance 6/30/50, $25,000.00. Unpaid loan balance 6/30/50, $270,000.00. Total, $295,000.00.

Grand Hotel, Billings, Mont. Undisbursed loan balance (participating) 6/30/50, $270,-000.00.

Bluebeards Castle Hotel Corp., Thomas, V.I. Undisbursed loan balance 6/30/50, $250,-000.00.

Muscle Shoals Community Hotel Corp., Sheffield, Ala. Unpaid loan balance 6/30/50 reported, $248,798.29.

Hereford Community Hotel Corp., Hereford, Tex. 7/14/49, $210,000.00.

Carlton Plaza Hotel Co., Detroit, Mich. Undisbursed authorized loan balance 6/30/50, $200,000.00.

Morningstar Hotels, Inc., Thomas, V.I. Undisbursed loan balance 6/30/50, $165,000.00.

Shore Club Lodge, Inc., Boise, Idaho. Unpaid loan balance 6/30/50, $164,500.00.

Tower Courts, Dallas, Tex. Unpaid loan balance (participating) 6/30/50, 158,165.92.

Bar Harbor Hotel, Bar Harbor, Me. 12/27/49, $150,000.00.

Independence Community Hotel Co., Independence, Iowa. Unpaid loan balance 6/30/50, $150,000.00.

Kennett Hotel Co., Kennett, Mo. Undisbursed loan balance 6/30/50, $150,000.00.

Clinton Community Hotel Corp., Clinton, Ohio. Undisbursed authorized balance (participating) 6/30/50, $125,000.00.

Plymouth Hotel Corp., Fort Fairfield, Me. Amount authorized, $125,000.00.

Saratoga Hotel Co., Saratoga, Wyo. Undisbursed loan balance 6/30/50, $125,000.00.

Henning Hotel Co., Casper, Wyo. Unpaid loan balance 6/30/50, $122,914.16.

Round-Up Lodge, Deming, N.M. Authorized, $95,000.00.

Titusville Hotel Corp., Titusville, Pa. Unpaid loan balance 6/30/50, $90,000.00.

Richard S. and Ellen H. Butler, trading as The Butler's Canvasback Inn, Perryville, Md. 2/23/50, $74,000.00.

South Parkway Hotel, Chicago, Ill. 4/6/50, $60,000.00

Island View Camp, Inc., Pottsboro, Tex. Amount, $56,000.00.

Woolsey C. Coombs, doing business as Casa Blanca Hotel. 4/3/50, $35,000.00.

Tower Trailer Park, Inc., Dallas, Tex. Authorized, $35,000.00.

Charles Fink and Vera Fischer, doing business as Sandpaper Inn, Fort Walton, Fla. 1/26/50, $32,000.00.

Frontier Motel, Willcox, Ariz. Authorized, $26,000.00.

Remora Lodge, Inc., Lyndon, Vt. Authorized, $16,000.00.

Cactus Courts, Carlsbad, N.M. Gross amount, $22,893.00. RFC share, $11,446.50.

Mission Trailer Park, Tucson, Ariz. Authorized, $10,000.00.

Rock Creek Camp, Whitesboro, Tex. Authorized, $9,000.00.

The Election of Federal Officials

Letter to The Honorable Guy M. Gillette in Response
to Certain Questions
[September 28, 1951]

My Dear Senator:

I have your note of September 4th in which you ask my views upon this point:

. . . there is a vital need for corrective or remedial legislation to make our elections to these federal offices more nearly a fair and honest expression of the will of the electorate. We have been concerned over the lack of accountability over huge expenditures of money in these campaigns. We have also been greatly disturbed over the expanded use of defamatory and scurrilous literature.

I am glad that your Committee is taking a strong interest in these problems. They have a vital bearing upon public confidence in our political system.

I do not have the facilities for the investigation which these subjects merit; nor can I presume to have the legal experience to draft actual legislation which the problems involve. I can, however, make some suggestions of areas which might be explored such as: (1) the extension of Federal law to cover primaries for Federal offices; (2) the reorganization of the existing law as to financial limitations on campaign expenditures; (3) the need of better definitions in these laws; (4) the political activities of civil servants; (5) the Government propaganda and political campaigns; (6) the "use of defamatory and scurrilous literature."

1. EXTENSION OF FEDERAL LAW TO COVER
PRIMARIES FOR FEDERAL OFFICES

It seems to me that one deficiency in our Federal election laws is that they do not extend to primaries for Federal offices. In many states primaries are equivalent to elections. In other states the primary is so closely a part of the whole election atmosphere as to amount to a part of a continuous political process. There are states which use the convention system and have no primaries.

While I would not have Federal laws take primaries dealing with Federal offices wholly out of the province of state control or party responsibility, I do think certain Federal laws regarding control of expenditures and safeguards against abusive or corrupt practices should be extended to cover such primaries. Where there are no primaries, there is little room for Federal action.

2. REORGANIZATION OF FINANCIAL LIMITATIONS
ON CAMPAIGN EXPENDITURES

I think it is fairly evident that the Federal Corrupt Practices Act of 1926, the Hatch Act of 1940, together with amendments and related legislation, should be overhauled. Congressional committees following almost every election have turned up violations and evasions of these laws, or failure of the law to cover every part of the problem.

The ceiling limitations placed on expenditures should be reconsidered. These ceilings were fixed when the purchasing power of the dollar was nearly twice what it is today. In the meantime campaign methods have evolved from local to more and more a system of nation-wide mass appeal. The ceilings were set when radio was less developed and television was not available at all. All of this results in a large increase in the cost of national political campaigns. For instance, with the increase in postage and mailing costs, a single letter to each potential voter in the nation would cost more than the allowed expenditures for all the parties combined. Existing law does not take these changed conditions into account.

Without more information I am not prepared to say whether ceilings should be lifted or how much. I suggest, however, that the Committee explore a formula of expenditure limits in which geographical area and population are considered. These factors obviously affect the cost of mail, radio and television time, newspaper space rates, printing costs for literature, reasonable party operating expenses, and reasonable travel and personal allowances. By such a formula, ceilings would bear some realistic relation to modern conditions.

By maintaining unrealistic limitations on campaign expenditures, the law invites evasion. If the law seems adequate to compel accountability for direct expenditures by organized political parties and individual candidates, it is only because it permits loopholes through which greater expenditures can be made by persons and associations outside the law.

The proper control of expenditures of the regular political parties is not so difficult a problem as the expenditures of organizations, clubs, etc., under the heading of "education," "information," etc. Yet very large sums are being used in such fashion to promote candidates or influence the trend of elections. These bodies can confuse the public and can defeat the control features of existing law. While the way must never be closed for our people to work in association for a particular candidate, for a political party, or for political ideas, there is no reason why these activities should not be required to identify themselves clearly, to report the source of their finances and the nature of their expenditures, and have the same published by public agencies, state or Federal, during a time period in which the force of public opinion could become effective.

Simultaneous with efforts to control campaign expenditures, it would be worth while to explore ways of reducing the total cost of campaigns. It might be possible to regulate the charges of radio and television and the time which should be given. Broadcasting is definitely charged with a public interest. This should be recognized in such matters of great public concern as national political campaigns.

3. DEFINITIONS

A part of the difficulties involved in lack of control of expenditures by "nonpolitical" organizations arises from the inadequate definitions in the existing law. It has been obvious in recent years that the definition of "political committee" in the Federal law is sufficiently ambiguous to permit associations to claim exemptions on the ground that their activities are solely "educational." Neither common sense nor political realities justify these claims. In the conditions in which such claims are made, they are pure deceptions.

The definition should be broadened to cover all bodies which receive contributions or expend funds bearing directly or indirectly upon the nomination or election of candidates for Federal office. Education on group interests and the relation of the candidates to these interests are inseparable parts of the political process. While such education is highly desirable and should never be discouraged, those providing it are not entitled to be exempt from any provisions designed to keep the electoral process fair, open, honest, and free from abuses.

The same is true of the definitions of "contributions" and "expenditures." Both provide loopholes for evasion of existing law. Not only should the nature of "contributions" and "expenditures" be accurately clarified, but their application should be extended beyond corporations and banks to labor organizations and all committees, associations, and other bodies active in the political process.

4. POLITICAL ACTIVITIES OF CIVIL SERVANTS

The growth of Government activities and personnel has a relation to these problems. I do not need to state that the selection of civil employees by merit examination was established partly in order to eliminate their influence in Federal elections. Many exemptions have been made in the past few years. It would be of value to determine the proportion of the present over 2,200,000 Federal civil employees who actually passed the Civil Service examinations before receiving their appointments.

Moreover, some Federal services such as postmasterships and some internal revenue appointments have never been incorporated within Civil Service requirements. Both to secure more merit and less politics, they should be placed under Civil Service selection and the whole civil personnel should be selected in this fashion except policy officials.

5. GOVERNMENT PROPAGANDA AND POLITICAL CAMPAIGNS

Another problem that will no doubt come before the Committee is the propaganda carried on by the various Government agencies in connection with the projects under their direction. Much of it is necessary public information or for educational purposes, but it can be deflected to political use.

The Government propaganda has grown so vast as Government operations have expanded, that I am at a loss to say what to do about it. To the extent that it rests upon the blurred line between legitimate education and information and plain propaganda, perhaps a code of ethics may serve to make the distinction clearer, and would enable the public to weigh the dangers of abusing the public service for political advantage. But it is a slender reed at best.

6. "DEFAMATORY AND SCURRILOUS LITERATURE"

As to the problems of "defamatory and scurrilous literature," I suggest that the Committee might examine the present effectiveness of the laws of libel and slander with the object of making the courts more effective agencies in these matters. In past years I have been advised many times by counsel that public men have little or no protection under these laws. They have stated that court decisions have practically reduced possible damages to pecuniary loss only. Public men can seldom prove such amounts. Successful verdicts, with only nominal awards, are neither vindication nor a preventive. In fact, public interpretation of nominal damages is that they are a condemnation. At one time (and still in England) heavy sums were collectible in moral damage from slander, libel, and untruthful defamation generally.

I greatly doubt the validity of any attempt to prevent untruthful statements, smears, or scurrilous publications except through actions in the courts lest it jeopardize the fundamentals of free speech and free press. However, if the laws of libel and slander are to be tightened, then some check should be placed upon their use for intimidation. It might be provided that plaintiffs shall proceed at once with suits, that on failure to do so or failure of verdict, they should be liable for double or treble the defendant's costs.

CONCLUSION

In the last analysis, no law will substitute for ethical standards applied as a matter of course by individuals in their daily conduct of the public business. There is a dangerous weakening of morality and of ethical standards in public life generally, the very area in which we should expect to find integrity and leadership on high principle. Without improvement in the minds and hearts of men, law and institutions are not enough to prevent deterioration in political behavior. And the people cannot be blamed if the bad example of men in public life leads to public toleration of corruption and abuse.

Yours faithfully,

HERBERT HOOVER

Reorganization of the Government

Address to the
Citizens Committee on the Hoover Reports,
New York City
[October 24, 1951]

I T SEEMS unnecessary for me to review the things we hope to accomplish in the Reorganization of the Executive Arm of the Government. You have been a potent force behind these reforms and you have participated in the realization of half of them. You have done wonders in effecting public understanding. I might mention one confirmation of your success. Over the past forty years we have seen many Government reorganization commissions, many proposed reforms, but never before did they have behind them a Citizens Committee of such capacity and devotion. These reports, for the most part, retired quietly into Government files. The legislation already enacted proves the worth of your efforts. Yet we have still more to do. We have about fifteen legislative acts now before the Congress. That body has been too busy during the past six months to give them much attention, but I hope for more success in the next session.

A few days ago a canvass was made of several responsible members of Congress as to whether you should continue or liquidate. They urged your continuance. It is a unique event when members of Congress ask a crusading group to continue.

It may be said that the further saving of two or three billion dollars by the enactment of our remaining recommendations is not much in a future Federal budget of $80 or $90 billion. But the larger the budget, the greater the savings to be made through a more efficient organization, a more efficient civil service, and the elimination of duplication and waste.

It is true that the purpose of your Committee is to effect Administrative reforms which would decrease our dangerous tax burden. In the wider aspects you are also interested in the whole problem of a balanced budget and the preservation of our economy from inflation and overstrain.

We are confronted with great plans for rearmament, European aid, and civilian expenditures. Even upon the recent basis of taxation, it would appear that the Federal Government is faced with a total deficit during this three-year rearmament period of somewhere between $40 and $50 billion. Unless something is done, we are confronted with one of two dangers— inflation, if we do not balance the budget; or the jeopardizing of our economic system, if we try to collect sufficient taxes to balance it.

As to inflation, if the Government borrows this deficit, a large part of it directly or indirectly must come from bank loans which are simply the creation of bank check money. And that inflation is rendered more potent because the suppression of civilian goods for guns creates scarcities.

Moreover with our labor organizations and farm parity every increase in taxes results in pressure for increased wages and prices. The inflationary effect is probably equal to or greater than the deflationary effect of the decrease in spending power.

Armament purposes require controls on production and distribution, but amid all these inflationary pressures price and wage controls are only temporary barriers at best. All this has been amply proved in ten major nations during two world wars. And ours is now a war economy.

OVERTAXATION

To attempt to cover such deficits by further taxes can so overstrain an economy like ours as to permanently injure it.

With these taxes the savings of a people are taken away from the re-creative enterprises upon which future freedom and progress depend. Such taxation can drive further toward socializing the income of the country and rendering the Government the only dispenser of capital either for credit or investment. We are already in or near the area of diminishing returns from our tax structure. Already it amounts to confiscation in the upper brackets and a hard pinch on savings in the lower brackets.

And in this connection I may remind you that Marx's Communist Manifesto of one hundred years ago outlined the road to socialism as, among other things, "heavy progressive income taxes," and "centralization of credit in the hands of the state."

THIS IS A LONG PULL

It is said that this is only a temporary situation; that, as soon as we are rearmed, the budget will be balanced, taxes will be greatly lowered and civilian production will be increased. No doubt a man can carry a three-hundred-pound weight across a room, but he will break his back trying to carry it around the block. Our load in this troubled world has got to be carried for miles to come. This Communist menace will be with us as far ahead as any man can see. Nor is rearmament a wholly temporary job which will be over in two or three years. Constant new invention in weapons and rapid deterioration in these machines of precision make rearmament, to a considerable degree, a continuous process.

A PARTIAL REMEDY

I state all this to emphasize the only way to at least a partial solution of our difficulties. The real protection from those dangers is obviously to reduce expenditures to as near a balanced budget as we can.

Your Committee's legislative proposals would be a contribution to these ends. Senator Byrd has demonstrated that in other directions some $7 billion per annum could be saved or postponed from civilian expenditure. And a further question arises as to whether some parts of the military program may be less urgent and that it could be stretched over a longer period.

Certainly we have to rearm. But it is equally certain that we are performing no service to the rest of the world if we over-strain American economy.

On Reducing the Federal Wasteline

Replies to Questions on Reorganization of the
Federal Government—Radio Broadcast,
New York City
[December 28, 1951]

First Question:

Mr. Hoover, will you first tell us something about the significance of your Commission?

Answer:

The work of the Reorganization Commission proves two main points beyond the shadow of a doubt. One, there is a constantly increasing amount of waste and extravagance in the Federal Government. Two, this trend can be reversed —something can be done about it.

All the cure calls for is a detailed plan—which was spelled out by the Commission—and public insistence on its application. If we all follow the principle of saying "I won't take 'no' for an answer," this job will be done.

These reforms could save us money—plenty of it—over $5 billion every year. Inflation is not the only reason why war is expensive. This waste represents enough money to buy approximately 16,000 modern tanks, or 1,650 heavy bombers. Putting it another way, it amounts to around $200 for every family in the Nation.

Only recently the Congress increased taxes. Perhaps it is a coincidence, but the amount of money that could be saved through better government is almost exactly the same as the amount of this latest tax increase.

Second Question:

Speaking of taxes, we have certainly heard a lot recently about how those particular laws are administered. What was the thinking of the Hoover Commission on the problem of how taxes should be collected? Did it get into this matter?

Answer:

It certainly did. The dangers of corruption in tax collection weren't news to the members of the Commission. Politics and tax collection are two nonsoluble substances. The ghost of Louis XVI could testify to that. So could most of the Roman Caesars.

We knew that the present method of selecting tax collectors was no good. They are selected by local political bosses. The determination of their fitness is pretty much based on their ability to get votes or rewards for doing so. Not competence in collecting taxes. These investigations in Washington are just getting started, but already it is quite clear that the prime factor in the selection of these officials has been often neglected—integrity.

Three factors make the present system unworkable: obligations to local bosses, the lack of professional competence, and the absence of integrity standards. These we have neglected. Now we find ourselves in a fine mess.

Proper tax collecting calls for the highest standard of morality. It is always unpleasant to "render to Caesar the things that are Caesar's." It is even worse when Caesar can't impose this high standard of morality on his own agents. Also, we should render unto Santa Claus those things that are his only province.

If our Commission's recommendations on collectors of Internal Revenue and on other minor political officials had been accepted two and one-half years ago—when we made them—*these scandals could not have occurred.*

We recommended that these posts be filled through the
Civil Service Commission. That is a bipartisan semijudicial
body. Its first and vigorous inquiry is into the background
of loyalty, character, and integrity of applicants. In this it
usually has the assistance of the FBI.

Then it requires a rigorous examination to determine their
competence for each special field. Thus appointments are
made on merit, not on ability to get votes or please some
local political boss. If such checks had been made, we would
not be finding so many rotten apples in this particular barrel.

Third Question:

This sort of scandal has—to my way of thinking—led to a
rising tide of citizen interest in Government. The validity
of the Hoover Report has become more and more manifest
as the months have passed since it was published. Will you
give us the benefit of some of your thinking, Mr. Hoover,
on what bases this reactivated citizen participation in Government should be founded?

Answer:

We must set our own house in order—re-examine the basic
blueprints of our Republic—readopt the traditional American principles and virtues—install good management.

We must conserve, and efficiently use, all our resources—
material, personal, moral, spiritual. We must not take democracy for granted—we must control the Government lest
it control us. It is an old but neglected saying that the Government is the servant, not the master.

Here in America today is the only remaining sanctuary of
freedom, the last oasis of civilization, and the last reserve
of moral and economic strength. Keep it we must.

Organization of Federal Government

*Address to the Citizens Committee for the Hoover
Report, Washington, D.C.*
[February 18, 1952]

D URING the last thirty years, I have said so many words
and written so many documents on reorganization of
the executive machinery of the Federal Government
that I can only add words of urgency to those proposals.

I can however, at once express my appreciation for the great
work of the Citizens Committee in keeping the problem before
the people and the Congress. I should mention not only the
work of President Johnson, Mr. Coates, Mr. McCormick, and
Mr. Ade, and their staff—if there were time I would mention
every single member of that nation-wide organization.

In the past forty years many recommendations and many
plans have been made by able men for reorganization of the
Executive arm. But it was not until we had this great citizens
movement that actual reforms were brought into being. Moreover, you have given the nation about the widest-spread education in civil government that it has had since the Constitution
was under debate.

We have made some progress in legislation. So much so that
upon the statements of Government officials, the savings up to
date amount to over a thousand times the cost of the original
Congressional Commission on Reorganization.

WHEREIN COMES GOOD GOVERNMENT

There are three parts to good representative government:
1. Good policies of government.

2. A system by which men and women of integrity, character, and competence are chosen for public service.

3. Efficient organization in which such good officials can function at their best.

I will not discuss policy questions lest I raise conflicting emotions among you. I do not wish to be partisan or to spread melancholy on so agreeable an occasion. However, bear in mind that the Reorganization Commission was the creation of the Congress. At times that body reminds me of a Dad who reproved his son for having taken the clock to pieces. The son replied, "If you do not like it, you can fix it. I want to play with my soldiers."

THE CHOICE OF ADMINISTRATION OFFICIALS

There are some eighteen major reorganization proposals still before the Congress. But recent events give especial urgency to one of them. That is the reform and reorganization of the Civil Service Commission and the whole personnel system. And for clarity I need first to define some terms. We have two distinct groups of Federal employees. There are perhaps a thousand at the policy-making level who must be of the political party which has the responsibility of administration. We can refer to the remaining 2,500,000 Federal civil employees as the Civil Service.

The first problem in administration of representative government is the choice of men and women to operate it. Manifestly, if they are to serve in the leadership of our people, their root qualifications must be:

First, probity. And by that I mean intellectual as well as financial honesty.

Second, character. And by that I mean courage to stand up for decent administration against all comers within or without.

Third, and not least, training and competence.

The most perfectly designed plans of organization break if any one of these fail. An imperfect plan of organization can function under good personnel even though it might be more costly.

No one can ignore the flood of exposures of less than sacred honor or real patriotism by employees in many agencies of the Government during these recent years. Daily, Congress and Grand Juries are turning up sickening conduct of Federal civil officials. These exposures can mean only one thing: That our method of selection and organization of Federal employees is badly at fault somewhere.

The American people have struggled to improve the methods of choice in Executive officials for over seventy years.

In reaction to the blatant regimes of "to the victor belongs the spoils" came the imperious public demand for the establishment of a civil service based upon nonpolitical selection by investigation as to character and loyalty, and examination as to competence, under a bipartisan Civil Service Commission. That system grew in application through both Democratic and Republican Administrations until, in 1932, over 80 percent of all Executive personnel came through that screening. In addition, another 10 percent, mostly post-office officials, although political appointees, had to pass through this screen before Presidents would present their names to the Senate.

I call your attention to the fact that there was a long period of practical freedom from dishonesty in the civil service. It was not the civil servants who failed the country in the scandals of the first World War and in 1923. It was political appointees.

Then came the period of the middle 'thirties. The Congress, in creating or revising over twenty-four great Executive agencies, specifically provided that these agencies were exempt from the provisions of law requiring selection of employees by the merit system under the Civil Service Commission. The percentage of civil servants who had been chosen through the Commission in seven years fell from over 80 percent to under 55 percent. In the years following it got worse. But thanks to Civil Service Commission Chairmen Fleming and Ramspeck the situation has somewhat improved.

I am far from believing that all the personnel problems were solved by the initial choice by screening under the bipartisan Civil Service Commission. The reforms in personnel management are wider than the initial choice if we are to have efficiency in Government. Our Commission, of which Dr. Fleming was a member, three years ago proposed such vital reforms in the whole personnel system. Your Committees have urged them upon Congress—so far without action.

I am convinced that had these reforms been enacted three years ago, they would have saved great grief to our country.

Surely the nation has a right to a better system of choice and management of its employees than one which has produced these months of humiliation. That humiliation extends to both the thousands of men and women who hold to the sacred honor of Government service and to the whole of a great and God-fearing people.

On the Reorganization Act of 1949

Letter to The Honorable Thomas B. Curtis,
House of Representatives
[February 25, 1952]

My dear Mr. Congressman:

I have your most thoughtful letter concerning repeal of the Reorganization Act of 1949.

I appreciate fully your reasons for suggesting the change. The growing abuse of the power of administrative discretion is also of deep concern to me.

However, I do not believe that the Reorganization Act of 1949 is such a grave departure. There are several good reasons for this retention:

First, the Reorganization Act does not permit the President to change policies, but merely propose reorganization of Executive functions. Second, the man who is responsible for administering the Presidency must have a method for such changes as the times may need. Third, the responsibility for bringing to Congress such organization changes is very definitely affixed on the President by the act. Under that act he is required to examine and re-examine the Executive agencies and to submit plans designed to increase economy and efficiency and he is given no choice in this. Fourth, while the Congress cannot amend the plans, the Congress can veto them; and it certainly is the duty of the Congress to exercise this veto power when objectionable features reach major proportions. And fifth, to come back to the constitutional question, the President is required under the Constitution to execute the laws faithfully, and he cannot execute them faithfully without a sound organization.

To these five specific reasons, a practical one must be added: the Government now has six million employees, counting the military, or almost one-tenth of the working population in this Nation. Obviously, if such a vast mechanism is to operate properly, the President has need of the machinery to propose improvements in administration to the Congress. The Congress cannot work out such details.

The Reorganization Act very clearly places the onus for good organization directly on the President's back; not on that of the Congress. Failures which breed corruption or waste are his failures, provided he has not attempted to correct them by using the authorities in the Act.

As you know, the President has had presented to him by the Citizens Committee fifty reorganization plans. Due to wartime emergencies, changing circumstances might make necessary many others. Yet only two have been submitted in over twelve months.

To follow this up might perhaps prove to be a more rewarding endeavor than attempting to repeal an Act which is intrinsically satisfactory, but which is beginning to atrophy. Knowing of your continuing interest and your diligent efforts on behalf of efficiency in the Executive Branch, I thought I would be perfectly frank with you on this matter. I do not wish to have this letter published at the present time for several reasons.

Yours faithfully,

HERBERT HOOVER

On Reorganization Proposals

Letter to The Honorable William L. Dawson
[June 2, 1952]

My dear Mr. Congressman:

I am most appreciative of your Committee's courteous invitation for me to appear before it in connection with the ten different reorganization proposals set forth in the bills on which hearings are now being held before you. I regret that previous commitments make it impossible for me to be present. I have instead prepared a few comments which I hope may be of assistance to you.

Your Committee and the Congress, six years ago, created the Commission on Organization of the Executive Branch, and three years ago the Commission made its recommendations. Many of them have been enacted. This six years' labor represents great progress in these problems.

There are before you some twenty-nine separate legislative measures, representing parts of the Commission's recommendations.

You will, as in all the enactments you have already made, be confronted with oppositions. They will have the familiar form: "Reorganize everybody but me." Or "Don't touch that agency. It's sacred."

I note below my comments on these bills—in groups related by the same purpose.

1. *General Management of the Executive Branch*
   (H.R. 3674, H.R. 3304)
   The most important part of this bill is Title I, Part I, which

states the organizational responsibilities of the President in executing the laws under Article II of the Constitution. The President is the only official of the Executive Branch to whom specific executive authorities are given in the Constitution. Were Title I, Part I, to be enacted, his authority over the Executive Branch of the Government (except in quasi-judicial matters) would be established as the Constitution intended and follows the Commission's Report on *General Management of the Executive Branch.*

Title I, Part II, provides for a realignment of the Executive Office of the President. This Part follows the recommendations of the Commission, but I would suggest that the authority be made permissive rather than mandatory, as it is in the present draft.

Title I, Part III, provides for a Federal Director of Personnel. Since the Civil Service Chairman is already fulfilling this function *de facto* under Reorganization Plan No. 5 of 1949, I suggest that this Part be deleted.

Title I, Part IV, would abolish the Council of Economic Advisers and would substitute in its place an Economic Adviser. That was recommended by the Commission. At that time the annual budget was about $40 billion and it is now near $90 billion. With this enormous expansion of Federal activities and their economic effects, I do not believe this action is desirable at the present time.

Title I, Part V, provides for the creation of a Presidential Staff Secretary. I commend this Part to you for favorable action.

Titles II and III, Executive Agency Management, would effect other beneficial recommendations of the Commission.

2. *Transfer of Civil Functions of Army Corps of Engineers to the Department of the Interior*

(H.R. 6243)

This bill conforms with the recommendations of the Commission. Effectuation of this reform is twenty-five years overdue. With the enormously expanded demands upon the Army

Engineers by our increased military establishment, this would seem even more urgent.

3. *Regulatory Commissions*
(H.R. 3678, H.R. 3307)
The important phases of this bill are those which provide for centering of purely paper work and office organization in the Chairmen of those four commissions which have not already been reorganized by Presidential Reorganization Plan. Such a change would expedite the work of these commissions. The bill also would extend the principle of bipartisanship to the National Labor Relations Board and to the Federal Reserve Board. I support that proposal.

4. *Intergovernmental Relations*
(H.R. 3893, H.R. 3303)
The Commission made certain recommendations to the Congress in this field. However, a majority of the Commission felt that a real solution of the problems involved in the relationship of the Federal Government to the States were not within its terms of reference. Hence, a further Congressional study was proposed. Such a study, successfully implemented, could solve many problems which have been plaguing us since the beginning of our Republic.

5. *To Establish a Department of Social Security and Education*
(H.R. 3689, H.R. 3306)
The recommendations of the Commission provided for certain fundamental changes in the Federal Security Agency without which I do not recommend any change in its name or status.

6. *Overseas Administration*
(H.R. 3697, H.R. 3406, H.R. 5879)
A fair and unbiased study of the method of administration of these vast expenditures beyond the continental limits of the United States is long overdue.

7. *General Services*
   (H.R. 3676, H.R. 3314)

The Commission recommended that minor Federal agencies in the District of Columbia and some floating functions of the Commissioners of the District of Columbia be co-ordinated through the General Services Administration in order to relieve the President of responsibilities he may have for personal supervision. I commend this to you for favorable action.

8. *Medical Services*
   (H.R. 3688, H.R. 3305)

I would suggest that your Committee defer action on this matter until the Senate, which has held extensive hearings and has drafted a substitute measure, takes action on it first. The Senate Committee has indicated that such action can be expected within the next ten days. It should be possible to put this substitute measure on the statute books before Congress adjourns in July.

9. *To Re-establish the Commission on Organization*
   (thirteen bills)

While many Commission recommendations have been adopted during the past three years, there are important reorganizations of the Post Office, Treasury, Interior, Agriculture Departments, the Veterans Administration, and the Social Security Agency, which are not fully dealt with in the twenty-nine bills before your Committee. We must also recognize the enormous increase in Federal activities since the Commission's recommendations.

I suggest, however, that these proposals to re-establish the Commission go over to the next Congress. It would be desirable that they should appoint a new Commission to examine these uncompleted tasks and to make recommendations upon them. Moreover, the increase in the Federal budget from about $40 billion annually to about $90 billion creates new problems of organization which should be studied.

Yours faithfully,

HERBERT HOOVER

On the Social Security Agency

Telegram to The Honorable Clare E. Hoffman, Chairman,
House Committee on Government Operations, and
to The Honorable Margaret Chase Smith,
United States Senate
[March 13, 1953]

I HAVE your telegram asking my views upon President Eisenhower's recommendation for the reorganization of the Social Security Agency. I wholeheartedly support his plan. It is a strong, constructive step in consummation of the reorganization proposals of the Commission on Organization of the Executive Branch of the Government and is vitally necessary at the earliest moment.

At some future time there needs to be an exhaustive investigation of the Federal hospital and medical setup, with a view to elimination of duplication and waste. Also, there needs to be an exhaustive investigation of the whole method of aids to the aged with view to simplification, elimination of waste, administrative overlaps with the States, if we are to reduce expenditure, and at the same time provide a better floor of support for those groups.

Such investigations would take time and should not delay approval of President Eisenhower's admirable and urgent plan.

HERBERT HOOVER

On Further Investigation Looking to Reorganization of the Government

Telegram to The Honorable Joseph McCarthy, Chairman, Senate Committee on Government Operations
[April 13, 1953]

I HAVE your telegram requesting my opinion and suggestions upon Bill S. 1514 introduced by Senator Robert Taft, and Bill S. 106 introduced by Senator Homer Ferguson and Congressman Clarence Brown. Both bills relate to further investigation looking to reorganization for economy and efficiency in the Federal Administration. Both bills are of great importance.

Senator Taft's bill provides for an investigation of Federal and State relations as to taxes and other important subjects.

The Ferguson-Brown Bill looks to the re-establishment of such a Commission on Organization of the Executive Branch of the Government as that over which I presided from 1947 to 1950 with powers to investigate and recommend *policies* as well as administrative methods. That former Commission was unable to report on *policy* questions.

A third phase of the reforms in Federal Administration before your Committee are the several "plans" being laid before the Congress by President Eisenhower. These "plans" are along the lines of the recommendations made by the Commission on Organization of the Executive Branch of the Government which have not been hitherto enacted.

248

There is, therefore, some overlapping in these bills and "plans" which, it seems to me, should be planned out by the Committee.

There are three vitally important areas which have never been adequately investigated and cannot be investigated except by adequate authority from the Congress and in which adequate technical assistance is provided. They badly need exhaustive consideration by Commissions in which the Congress and the Administration and public members are represented. These areas are:

1. An investigation as to Federal-States relations as provided by Senator Taft's bill (S. 1514).

2. An investigation of the Federal business enterprises in competition with private enterprises.

3. An investigation of all forms of Federal aid to the aged with recommendations designed to make them more just and effective; to save waste; to simplify their operation; and to avoid administrative duplications with the States.

The Ferguson-Brown bill (S. 106 and H.R. 992) covers the last two areas.

In order to avoid overlap with the President's "plans" and the Taft bill proposals, I suggest that the Ferguson-Brown bill be especially directed to the Federal business enterprises and the aid for the aged. There might be some provision for subjects later indicated by the Congress or the President.

I believe the Taft bill and the Ferguson-Brown bill (thus modified) should both be enacted. The Taft Commission should be kept separate from the Ferguson-Brown Commission as they involve a membership and technology which should not be confused.

HERBERT HOOVER

On the President's Reorganization Plan No. 2 for the Department of Agriculture

Letter to The Honorable Clare E. Hoffman
Chairman, House Committee on Government Operations
[April 21, 1953]

The Waldorf Astoria Towers
New York, New York
April 21, 1953

My dear Mr. Chairman:

I had prepared the attached statement, in compliance with your request for my views on the President's Reorganization Plan No. 2 of 1953, for the Department of Agriculture.

As I do not know what Senate Committee is now going to handle the matter, perhaps you might wish to send it to them.

With kind regards,

Yours faithfully,

HERBERT HOOVER

The organization of the Department of Agriculture is obsolete. To modernize it the Commission on Organization made sixteen recommendations. Very few of these have been put into effect.

The first necessity in good and economical executive administration now is to give responsibility and to fix that responsibility. That is the purpose of the President's plan. It is in full accord with the recommendations of the Commission on Organization and, in my opinion, the plan should be approved as soon as possible.

Major reductions in expenditures of the Department can be realized if the plan is approved and energetically implemented.

Among the advantages which would derive from the plan are these:

1. The plan would permit drastic reduction in the number of major units reporting directly to the Secretary. There are now more than twenty so reporting to him.

2. The plan would permit reduction of expenditures through elimination of overlapping of services within the department such as budgeting, personnel, supply, and research.

3. The plan would permit the Secretary to integrate related functions to the betterment of service for farmers.

4. The President's message directs that there be established closer working relationships between the Federal Government and State and local groups. The plan provides the machinery for making this possible.

5. The plan would make possible widespread streamlining and reduction in overlapping of Federal activities at the State and county levels.

I refer you to the recommendation of the Commission on Organization of the Executive Branch of the Government of February 1949, as follows:

We recommend a thorough overhaul of the organization of the Department, at State, county, and farmer levels.

Our comment on this recommendation was:

At the State Level

The State governments operate effective agricultural departments. They have in the past engaged in effective co-operative activities with the Department at State, county, and farmer levels. In recent years, the

Department has not taken full advantage of the established and effective State organizations in performing many agricultural programs and has thereby produced some duplication of national and State effort at local levels.

At the County Level

This Commission was unable to conduct a detailed survey of activities at the county level. Sampling inquiries, however, revealed that considerable duplication has developed. For example, 47 employees attached to 7 distinct and separate field services of the Department of Agriculture in one cotton-producing county in Georgia were working with 1,500 farmers; a fruit and grazing county in the State of Washington has 184 employees of separate field services working with some 6,700 farmers; a dairy county in Maryland had 88 employees attached to these field services working with less than 3,400 farmers. In these and other counties, representatives of each agency frequently advise the same farmers on the same problems. Farmers are confused and irritated, as climaxed in one Missouri county, where a farmer recently received from five different agencies varying advice on the application of fertilizer on his farm. There are many separate field services at the county level. These include the Soil Conservation Service; Extension Service; Farmers Home Administration; Production and Marketing Administration with its conservation payment program and school-lunch program; Farm Credit Administration through its Production Credit Associations and National Farm Loan Associations; and the Rural Electrification Administration. In addition, the Forest Service may be represented by Federal-State farm-forest management advisers; the Bureau of Animal Industry by Specialists on animal disease eradication programs; and the Bureau of Entomology and Plant Quarantine by others who work on plant disease eradication and insect control.

Separate from those of the Department of Agriculture, representatives of the Veterans Administration are usually present to administer the on-farm industrial training program for veterans. The farm labor representatives of the Federal-State Employment Service and Federal-State Department of Agriculture representatives may also be in the field at the county level.

A multitude of county advisory committees of farmers has been created and employed by these various activities at a cost exceeding $5 million a year. These local committees have been given administrative functions. The task force on agricultural activities believes that the local committees should be purely advisory on program formulation and operation. All administrative work should be done by departmental or State employees.

Our task force recommends that only one committee be set up in each county. It estimates their annual cost for the entire nation need not exceed $700,000.

Birthday Statement to the Press

San Francisco, California
[August 10, 1953]

UNENDING public chores seem to have become my privilege in life. One of these chores seems to be that I respond to a Press demand to make some remarks on each birthday. And that gives me the opportunity to thank the many thousands who have sent me greetings.

Our international situation is uppermost in the American mind. Obviously the situation is not good. But the many delicate and difficult negotiations in progress make it inadvisable to comment further than that our Government is doing its best.

On the domestic side, my main chore for the next year is to serve on the new Congressional Commission on Reorganization of the Executive Branch of the Government. This Commission will be called into meeting on September 29. In the meantime, preliminary preparations are in progress. They include a survey of the 230-odd recommendations of the 1947–50 Commission over which I presided. Some of these recommendations are still uncompleted; many were adopted during the Truman Administration; and still more adopted under President Eisenhower. The most recent moves in the direction of those recommendations are the sale of the Mississippi barge lines, the Congressional acts liquidating the RFC, and initiating reorganization of farm credit agencies.

Since the previous Commission, the Korean War and rearmament have intervened and the budget nearly doubled, thereby obscuring many savings made by that former Commission. The over-all picture is that during the last twenty years the Federal Government has expanded from about 400 different agencies to over 1,500 and from about 600,000 employees to over 2,400,000. Expenditures have grown from about $4 billion annually to over $70 billion annually.

I am in hopes that the new Commission can contribute something to lessen what President Eisenhower has aptly described as our "staggering economic burdens," will strengthen private enterprise, reduce the burdens of taxation, lessen bureaucratic tyranny over our citizens, and generally improve the efficiency of our Government.

On Reorganization of the Soil Conservation Service

A Telegram on Secretary of Agriculture Benson's Proposals to Congress
[October 30, 1953]

I NOTICE that the drive to alter or delay your reorganization of the Soil Conservation Service still continues despite the fact it will give better service to the farmers and effect real economies. Your plans of reorganization are along the lines of the recommendations of the task force of agriculturists and the Commission on Reorganization of the Executive Departments of 1949. They have been exhaustively debated since and favored by most of the substantial elements concerned. The opposition has apparently been misled or inspired by officials who will be displaced. If displaced officials are to counteract reorganization for economy and efficiency in the Government, all of us may as well throw up our hands in these efforts to serve the American people.

HERBERT HOOVER

On Opening the First Regional Division of the Postal Service

Statement Made Public by Postmaster General
Arthur Summerfield
[November 24, 1953]

I FEEL I have a right to congratulate you and your assistants in opening the first Regional Division of the Postal Service. We urged this solution in the report of the first Commission on Reorganization of the Government. The idea has remained dormant until your vigorous administration.

On Progress of the Commission on Organization of the Executive Branch of the Government

Letter to the President
[January 13, 1954]

January 13, 1954

The President
The White House
Washington, D.C.

My dear Mr. President:

We have made progress in the major setup of the Commission on Organization of the Executive Branch of the Government. The Commission was created by Public Law No. 108 of July 10, 1953. The membership of the Commission was completed in the latter part of August and the Commission held its first meeting on September 29, 1953.

The Presidential appointees to the Commission are: Attorney General Herbert Brownell, Jr., The Honorable James A. Farley, Director of Defense Mobilization Arthur S. Flemming, and Herbert Hoover.

The Vice-President's appointees are: Senator Homer Ferguson, Senator John L. McClellan, Dean Solomon C. Hollister of the School of Engineering at Cornell University, and Dean Robert G. Storey of the School of Law at Southern Methodist University.

The Speaker's appointees are: Congressman Clarence J. Brown, Congressman Chet Holifield, The Honorable Joseph P. Kennedy, and Mr. Sidney A. Mitchell.

The Honorable John B. Hollister is the Executive Director. Five of these members served on the Reorganization Commission of 1947–50.

As of the present we have created the following nine major Task Forces to undertake investigations and to make recommendations. They are: *The Business Organization of the Department of Defense*, Chairman Charles R. Hook and more than 10 members. The various Task Forces already at work on fractions of these problems will be represented on this Committee and another such Task Force will be created on Procurement; *Water Resources Development and Power*, Chairman Admiral Ben Moreell and 25 members; *Medical Services*, Chairman Chauncey McCormick and 15 members; *Personnel and Civil Service*, Chairman President Harold W. Dodds and 9 members; *Legal Services and Procedure of the Executive Branch of the Government*, Chairman Judge James M. Douglas and 15 members; *Use and Disposal of Surplus Property*, Chairman General Robert E. Wood and 7 members; *Subsistence Management*, Chairman Joseph P. Binns and 8 members; *Budgeting and Accounting*, Chairman J. Harold Stewart and 6 members; *Lending Agencies*, Chairman Paul Grady and 10 members.

In addition we are conducting staff investigations of certain other agencies as directed by the law. In all our work we have sought to avoid duplication with the work in progress for efficiency and economy by other Commissions, Committees of Congress, and the Departments.

The members of the Task Forces are chosen solely because of their experience in different fields. I have considered it in the public interest not to include representatives of any particular group interest. The representatives of such groups will be given full hearings.

The problems to be solved require a determination of fact and the deduction of recommendations therefrom. For the purpose of amassing the facts, each Task Force has been given adequate research staff. The recommendations of the Task Forces and of our staff will be reviewed by the Commission.

Due to the large proportion of voluntary service, the cash expenditures and outstanding obligations from September 29 to December 31, 1953 are $152,035. Our paid staff comprises three persons, an Assistant to each Commissioner, together with research employees of the Task Forces. Such clerical help as we require is mostly secured on a reimbursable basis from the Executive Departments so as not to create a permanent staff.

Thus far, over 115 leading professional and administrative citizens have been enlisted upon our Task Forces. I will forward to you a list of them and of the other men and women associated in the work.

Yours faithfully,

HERBERT HOOVER
Chairman

Lincoln Day Remarks

Washington, D.C.
[February 5, 1954]

I GREATLY appreciate your generous reception. Madame Patti, many years ago, established the procedure of repeated farewell appearances. With that great precedent, I might even appear again.

I am now once more a Federal official. During forty years I have served many times under Democratic as well as Republican Administrations.

But today again, I have the satisfaction of working with a Republican Administration. And may I say one word about that Administration.

The country has today a magnificent body of administrators of complete integrity under the leadership of a wise and courageous President. He has created for the Republican Party a great and constructive program which has restored faith and hope to the whole country.

That program in its economic conservatism, its liberal aid to the less fortunate among our citizens, and the building of a strong national defense against the dangerous forces that surround us, is in the best tradition of the Republican Party. With President Eisenhower's leadership and that program, you can enter battle with complete confidence.

On Legal Services and Procedures of the Commission on Organization of the Executive Branch of the Government

Statement to the Task Force
[February 5, 1954]

THE appreciation of the whole Commission goes out to you for your willingness to serve on this Task Force. There is no field in the whole government that so sorely needs remedies as the field you will study. I may mention that thirty years ago I made a public address upon exercise of the legislative and judicial powers by the Executive Branch of the Federal Government. This problem has been one of my aches ever since.

There has been no adequate clarification of this confusion of the three powers in the Executive arm since that time.

There are many executive agencies that through regulation exert legislative powers and many executive agencies that exert judicial powers of the utmost importance. Certain executive agencies even administer criminal law, where there is no adequate review by the Courts.

And this does not include the confusion of powers of review by the Courts of acts of the many regulatory commissions—and this is a sore subject in itself.

The legal procedures and staff arrangements on the legal

side of the Executive arm are likewise in great confusion with many overlaps, duplications, and waste of public money.

There are many procedures in other fields which you may sooner or later wish to consider—such as the procedures in criminal cases by the Courts, and the expansion of Federal authority over commerce, which today breaches the original concept of division of Federal and State powers and undermines many fundamentals of local government.

In any event, the whole field is open to you—and you are free to undertake investigations and make recommendations on any subject in the legal field.

The Commission and its Task Forces are not a part of the Executive branch. You are a part of the Legislative branch. The authority of the Commission, as you know, extends not only to investigation and recommendation for improvement of the structure of agencies and of the procedures of agencies, but to the determination of substantive changes in policies even to the extent of recommending amendments to the Constitution.

The whole field is yours.

Outlook for Further Reorganization

Address to the National Press Club,
Washington, D.C.
[March 10, 1954]

YOUR Chairman thought you would be interested in knowing how far we have gotten along with this Second Reorganization Commission. I may warn you in advance that if you can find high humor in reorganization of the government, you have that sense more highly developed than I have.

The major purpose of this Commission is to find ways of saving money for the taxpayers.

The First Commission of five years ago secured legislation or administrative action on about 70 percent of our recommendations. At that time the national budget was about $42 billion and our economies were badly obscured when the budget rose to $72 billion.

The First Commission removed most of the roadblocks against self-reorganization within the Departments. Therefore, this time we are mainly concerned with problems that involve several agencies, no one of which alone can solve the issue. Last time we had a limited authority. It did not cover policy questions. This time our authority to inquire and to recommend is almost unlimited. The law provides, however, that we leave the Congress alone. This time we are required to present the actual legislation which will express our recommendations in legal terms. This time we have some teeth. We can subpoena documents and persons.

264

However, ours is not a so-called witch hunt. This is a job of co-operating with the able men in leadership of the executive agencies and the Congress. Nor is this a star chamber performance. Any responsible person, who has a deep emotion over how to save money, is welcome to give us his views.

The First Commission developed the idea of dividing its work among Task Forces. The job of the Task Force is to determine exhaustively the facts, and to make recommendations based upon the facts. This Task Force method differs from most other governmental committees of inquiry. It provides for a more exhaustive determination of fact. Beyond this, it secures judgment and recommendations from men of ability and responsibility, all of whom have had experience in that particular executive field of the government. None of them represents any special interest.

No one would minimize the immense importance of inquiries by Congressional Committees. The difference is that they are seldom specialists in these matters. And among their multitude of responsibilities they have little time or staff for such highly technical inquiries. Moreover, few members of the Congress have served in the Executive Branch of the Government.

Up to date we have set up ten Task Forces, varying from 8 to 26 members on each. The 140 members of our staff, so far chosen, are solely from among professional men, business executives, or former government employees. They are all men in responsible positions outside the Government. Government spending and taxes are no academic abstraction to them. They cause them acute grief. The response I have had to requests for such service is a magnificent proof of Americans' public devotion. Practically all of them are giving their time without remuneration, other than out-of-pocket expenses.

These Task Forces already set up cover the Federal fields of:

Water Resources and Power
Business Organization of the Department of Defense
Medical Services
Subsistence Services

Procurement
Lending Agencies
Budget and Accounting
Civil Service
Legal Services and Procedure
Use and Disposal of Surplus Property

The theory and practice of the disposal of surplus property came down from the general who commanded the first army when gunpowder was invented. I have no doubt he kept his cross-bows in storage for thirty years thereafter.

All of the Task Forces are now in the midst of their inquiries and no horrid examples are ready for publication and no final recommendations have as yet been put on paper. However, we are learning a lot.

From discussions with officials and Task Force leaders, I am convinced that if we could secure all our desires from the Congress, we could save $5 to $7 billion per year without injury to the necessary functions of the Government. Those sums are equal to 15 percent or 20 percent of the personal income tax.

However, I never expect perfection on this earth.

Over the past thirty years I have taken part in four official efforts to reorganize the Federal Executive branch. Two or three years after the first commission on which I served, I made a public address over its funeral. I said:

Practically every single item has met with opposition from some vested official, or it has disturbed some vested habit, and offended some organized monopoly. All of them are in favor of every item of reorganization except that which affects the activity in which they are specially interested. In the aggregate, these directors of vested habits and propaganda surround the Congress with a confusing fog of opposition. Meantime, the inchoate voice of the public gets nowhere but to swear.

Here ended that funeral sermon of twenty-eight years ago.

But we did better five years ago, and I am confident that we will do even better this time. My confidence is based upon the fact that the tax burden is becoming highly annoying to the citizen—and he may neutralize some of the pressure groups.

I might dwell for a moment on this pressure-group problem.

There are probably 200,000 voluntary associations of some kind or another in the United States, most of which give voice for or against something relating to government. Except for the collectivists, they are one of the essential foundation piers under the American system of life. They perform millions of services in developing public understanding and public action. My rough guess is that about 200 of these groups occupy themselves pressuring the Government for more spending or in opposing any reductions. In this opposition, they are not always polite.

Nor do all these pressures come from the voluntary associations. The municipalities press the State governments, and the State governments press the Federal Government.

All pressure groups got their spiritual motto from Ben Franklin's remark that "God helps those who help themselves." If Ben were alive today, he would say: "Free men were not created by drives of pressure groups against the public treasury."

There is today a saving antidote which comes from that host of associations which do battle with the pressure groups. After the last Commission, the Press not only opposed them, but the citizens organized to oppose them, and other associations went into battle with them. Thereby we had more success. However, several pressure groups came out victorious in spite of these efforts.

If, by some unexpected dispensation, these 200 groups who seek more spending or who resist economies would take a holiday for two years, we could possibly get the $5 to $7 billion about which I spoke. And each member of these pressure groups would have a possible reward in Heaven and a positive reward in this life of reduced taxes.

One of the national problems is the growth of bureaucracy. Some of the gigantic expansion from 600,000 to 2,400,000 civilians in government during the past twenty years is due to the necessities of defense, some to the necessity of collecting immense taxes, and so on. But some of it is due to just the sheer exfoliation of empire which is a step to personal greatness. The

Commission will be pointing a finger when we get further along with our work.

No doubt life was simple about one hundred sixty years ago when our Government was getting under way. At that time there was less than one Federal civil employee to 1,400 people. Today there is one Federal civil employee to about every 70 persons in the population. If this trend keeps up, there will be more Chiefs than Indians.

The people in this city are greatly interested in the Civil Service. It is the greatest industry in the town. I may say at once that all my public life I have supported the idea of a professional, nonpolitical, protected, and pensioned body of skilled civil servants. I can claim some merit for legislation to that end. But any Civil Service to be efficient and to command public respect must be built upon competitive examination through the bipartisan Civil Service Commission, and promotion must be based on merit. But those principles have been badly messed up.

In the twenty years from 1932 to 1952, the Congress has enacted seventy-two laws exempting segments of the service from passing the Civil Service merit gate. Other entrances around the gate also have been discovered. How many got in without a pass, I do not know accurately, but the latest estimate I have heard is that the percentage who had passed through the merit gate had decreased from over 80 percent to about 50 percent. Some day I will give you a more accurate figure. You have heard that term "blanketing in." That term also connotes "to cover up."

There is a bothersome problem that involves about 3,000 to 4,000 Federal employees out of this 2,400,000. They are those occupying policy-making or confidential positions. Our system of government revolves around the two-major-parties system. When a party is newly elected to government, it comes in with a mandate from the people to carry out certain policies. It is of vital national importance that the policy-making employees shall believe in and give zeal to the consummation of those policies. That is important to both political parties. There are roadblocks in the way.

I have received a deluge of communications on how to make the Government more efficient. Many of them are wise and helpful. Some of them come from those who believe they are efficiency experts. They sometimes remind me of an efficiency expert who was sent from New York to improve the methods of a Western industrial operation in the middle of a snowy winter. An old Irish driver and his sleigh were sent to fetch the new-comer at the depot. The Irishman started to tuck the buffalo robe about the efficiency expert when his passenger reprimanded him for putting the hair side of the robe on the outside. The expert insisted that the leather should be on the outside as that would be more efficient in keeping out the cold. As they rode along, the driver kept chuckling. Finally the efficiency expert could stand it no longer and asked the Irishman what he was amused at. The Irishman replied: "Oh nothing, Mister. I was just wondering why somebody did not tell that to them buffa-loes."

Farm City Conference
Economy Award

*Nation-wide Broadcast Before the Government Economy
Rally of the Farm City Conference,
Town Hall, New York City
[May 25, 1954]*

I AM greatly honored to receive this "Economy Award"
from the Farm City Conference. Especially as I receive it
in company with Secretary Humphrey and Senator Byrd.

Those two distinguished public servants are every day in
the operating room performing surgery on Federal expenditures in the hope of maintaining national solvency. I am only
an old family doctor called in as a medical consultant. My job
is to suggest politely to Administrative agencies and pressure
groups, "You are a little bit heavy in the middle." The Secretary hourly has to say, "We just don't have any money for you."
The Senator's favorite prescription is, "Put Santa Claus in the
deep freeze."

In the fiscal field we have to contend with two delusions.
One is the John Maynard Keynes shell game that no matter
how much the public debt may be, it does not matter because we
owe it to ourselves. That theory includes the idea that the debt
never needs to be paid off. But it ignores the pain resulting when
the old and especially the young pay income tax for interest on
the debt. Twenty-odd years of deficits and consequent inflation
have produced another economic pain which the followers of

Lord Keynes did not diagnose. For the purchasing power of money has decreased by one-half.

The idea is that Blessed are the Young for they shall inherit the national debt.

I might observe generally that creating public debt through deficits is creating a dead horse. Private debt creates live horses.

The other delusion is that the Federal Government should do the homework of the counties and the States. There are two parts to this delusion. One is that the job will be better done if it is a long way off from local control. The other is that when the people in the States pay out money in Federal taxes, they get it all back in benefits. But the benefits idea omits the fact that there is deduction for the "kitty"—the real name of which is Federal bureaucracy.

While the authorities can carefully watch efficiency and waste in Washington, their influence seems to decrease inversely with distance. For instance, the Brownson Subcommittee of the House of Representatives reported that the Federal Government, in erecting certain quarters for American staff in Germany, supplied the following glassware at the taxpayers' expense to each four-bedroom apartment:

Twelve beer glasses, 12 champagne glasses, 12 cocktail glasses, 12 liqueur glasses, 12 white-wine glasses, 12 red-wine glasses, and 12 sweet-wine glasses.

There were also 12 water glasses, but it would seem this item might have been reduced. This happened during a previous Administration.

Another method for increasing the national debt and deficits is Federal lending of money and guaranteeing of loans. This flame can warm, but it also can consume.

Members of our Reorganization Commission of five years ago urged that there were great dangers when such loans or guarantees were made to anyone except public or government regulated institutions. We said it would lead to favoritism, waste, and corruption. As an example, I may mention that Senator Byrd and I once upon a time conducted a campaign to wind up the RFC for just those reasons. We did not immediately succeed, but we illuminated the subject. We showed that loans had been made to 11 distilleries and breweries, 8 theaters, 5 bowling alleys and beauty parlors, and 39 hotels. One hotel was named the Bluebeard. Also I should include a loan to one snake farm. The RFC is now in liquidation. But only after huge losses and the exposed corruption was a season's sensation.

I might also cite another example in the Housing Loan guarantees which are now under investigation for fraud—as ample proof of our rightness of five years ago.

I have frequently spoken on the consequences of pressure groups, both citizens and States and municipalities, operating on the Congress for huge spending. Of course, every pressure group and every Government agency wants economy for everybody else. But we three, who are speaking tonight, have difficulty in adding this up to unanimity for less expenditures. Today these pressure-group bills before the Congress would aggregate two or three billions of additions to the present authorizations.

My sympathy often goes out for the humble decimal point. He has a pathetic and hectic life wandering around among regimented ciphers, trying to find some of the old places he used to know when budgets were balanced.

Our Republic is beset by many dangers. But here is one which we can control if we have the will to do it. That is, waste, unnecessary spending and unbalanced budgets, and thus continued inflation. That will power can be provided by the citizens of the country expressing themselves in support of such leaders as Secretary Humphrey and Senator Byrd.

On Organization of the Atomic Energy Commission

Letter to The Honorable W. Sterling Cole,
Chairman, House Atomic Energy Commission
[June 8, 1954]

My dear Mr. Chairman:

I have your communication inquiring as to my views upon the organization of the Atomic Energy Commission. The 1947–49 Commission on Organization of the Executive Branch of which I was Chairman exhaustively examined the question of relative authority of members of all Federal Commissions except the Atomic Energy Commission. It did not investigate that Commission because of security reasons but the recommendations in my view equally applied to it.

It has been recognized for one hundred and seventy years that for effective administration the responsibility for executive functions must be placed in a single officer. That was established in the Federal and State Governments from the beginning. It is the universal practice of all business. In the Federal and State Governments, legislative and policy-determining functions of course rest in the Congress or Legislatures. The President or Governors are the administrative or executive officers. Likewise in business the president or chairman of the board of directors is as the occasion may be the administrative or executive head and the regulatory and policy-making functions must rest in the directors.

The Reorganization Commission Task Force of 1947–49 under Owen D. Young was unanimous that the administrative or executive duties of all Commissions should be lodged in the chairman and the regulatory or policy-making functions should rest in all the Commissioners.

The Commission on Reorganization itself also unanimously recommended this form of organization. That recommendation was: "We recommend that all administrative responsibility be vested in the Chairman."

That recommendation has been adopted by Congress in most of the Commissions and their performance greatly improved thereby.

The members of the Commission who approved this recommendation were: Herbert Hoover, Chairman; Dean Acheson, Vice-Chairman; Arthur S. Flemming; James Forrestal; George H. Mead; George B. Aiken; Joseph P. Kennedy; John Mc-Clellan; James K. Pollock; Clarence J. Brown; Carter Monasco; and James H. Rowe, Jr.

I suggest that some confusion has arisen in the current discussions by using the term "Principal Officer." It would seem to me to clarify matters if the term "Administrative and Executive Authority" should be used instead of "Principal Officer."

I unhesitatingly recommend that the authority in the Board should be thus divided; the regulatory and policy-making functions remaining in the Board as a whole.

The Atomic Energy Commission is an enormous enterprise and disorder and delay in its administration will surely arise if all Commission members are to exercise administrative and executive as well as policy-making functions.

HERBERT HOOVER

PART V

CHARITABLE ASSOCIATIONS

The City Versus Boys

The Rotarian
[April 1950]

TO ARRIVE at an understanding concerning the particular needs of our young boys and girls, we should proceed like scientists and examine the behavior characteristics of the animal. In this article I am particularly interested in the city boy. We must determine the anatomy of a boy's mind, and also what civilization has done to him.

This sort of boy, like all boys, is endowed with a dynamic energy and an impelling desire to take exercise on all occasions. He has tremendous potentiality even when he sits still. His every movement is a crisis. He lives in emergencies. Indeed, every boy must consider the world all over again. To his eyes it is a world filled with great adventures, discoveries, and vast undertakings. He does not come into the world with information on pains and penalties—he also must pick up these items.

Like all pups, he is born with a bounding instinct to play. Also his primary instinct is to hunt in a gang, and that multiplies his devices. He is a complete self-starter, and therefore wisdom in dealing with him consists mostly in what to do with him next. If he is to be a successful adventurer in life, he must grow in mind and imagination, and for that he must live at least part time in the land of make-believe. One of the sad things for him is that he must grow up into a land of realities.

He represents not only joys and hope, but also paradoxes. He strains our nerves, yet he is a complex of cells teeming with affection. He is a periodic nuisance, yet he is a joy forever. He is a part-time incarnation of destruction, yet he radiates sunlight to all the world. He gives evidence of being the child of iniquity, yet he makes a great nation. He is filled with curiosity as to every mortal thing. Every one of his body cells contains an interrogation point. Yet he is the most entertaining animal in existence.

Now, all that is mostly happy and encouraging, but modern civilization has bumped into this special group of boys. It has built up great cities. It has increased stupendously the number of boys per acre. It has covered up all the ground with bricks, cement, and cobblestones and surrounded it with brick walls. All the natural outlets for the energies of these boys have been upset.

The normal boy, a primitive animal, takes to competition and battle. In the days before our civilization became so perfect, he matched his wits with the birds, the bees, and the fish. Today he is separated from Mother Earth and all her works, except the weather. The outlet of curiosity in exploring the streams and fields is closed to him because of the city environment.

This pavement boy, in fact, has a life of stairs, light switches, alleys, fire escapes, bells, and cobblestones, and a chance to get run over by a truck. Inasmuch as he cannot contend with Nature, he is likely to take on contention with a policeman. There are about 4 million of these confined dynamos in congested districts of American cities.

The Constitution provides these boys, as well as grownups, with the inalienable right of liberty and the pursuit of happiness. His chief use of the Bill of Rights, however, is free assembly and free speech. We are not so much concerned at the moment, however, with his liberties as we are with his methods of pursuing happiness. He and his gang can go on this hunt for happiness either constructively or destructively. Therefore, our proposal is to channel him into constructive joy, rather than destructive glee.

I dislike to refer to these boys as "underprivileged." That is only a half-truth. My country provides the pavement boy with better schools and better health protection than any other in the world. He has more chance of becoming a policeman or a mayor or even an editor or a banker than he has anywhere else on earth. He suffers far less than his grandfather from mumps and measles and we heal his broken bones more quickly.

But we are more concerned at the moment with the privileges which this civilization has taken away; and the particular ones which concern us are those that influence or make his character and his physical stature. Now this brick and cement foundation of life is a poor soil for physical, moral, and spiritual growth.

Somebody will say morals are the job of parents, but the best of parents cannot keep him indoors all the time. His world in the streets is a distorted and dangerous world, which the parents cannot make or remake. So it becomes a job of public responsibility. That job hinges around what these boys can do every day between school hours and bedtime, on holidays, and on Sundays after church.

Ours is a problem of creating a place where these pavement boys can stretch their imaginations, where their inborn bent to play and where their unlimited desire for exercise can be led into the realms of sportsmanship—which is the second greatest code of morals. We must divert the boy's fine loyalties to the gang from fighting it out with fists to the winning of points. We must let off his explosive violence without letting him get into the police court.

It is a problem of creating a place in which his curiosity as to what makes the wheels of the world go around may be turned into learning how to make some of the wheels himself. All this will make the boy a citizen and not a gangster. Even the taxpayer can understand that the cure of a gangster is a thousand times more expensive than the diversion of a boy away from a gang. We can do the latter for $40 apiece, while the former costs $10,000 and often does not succeed at that.

That is why fourteen years ago I accepted the responsibility of becoming the chairman of the board of Boys' Clubs of

America. I am happy to say to you that there are many fine youth organizations serving not only the boys but the girls of my land, but I believe that the Boys' Clubs of America are doing a particularly fine job with this boy of the city pavements.

I have watched with great interest when the Boys' Clubs in Tampa, Florida; Amarillo, Fort Worth, San Antonio, Waco, and Wichita Falls, Texas; Binghamton, Jamestown, Utica, and Niagara Falls, New York; Washington, D.C.; Catasauqua, McKees Rocks, and Pittsburgh, Pennsylvania; Norfolk, Virginia; Rushville and Warsaw, Indiana; Cincinnati, Ohio; Salt Lake City, Utah; San Francisco, California; and Seattle, Washington, were established either through the direct sponsorship or initiative of the local Rotary Club.

In many other communities, including Fayetteville, Hot Springs, and Pine Bluff, Arkansas; Columbus, Indiana; Fair Lawn, Jersey City, Passaic, and Trenton, New Jersey; Bethlehem, Media, and Wilkinsburg, Pennsylvania; and Alpena, Michigan, the Rotary Club co-operated with other civic organizations in the establishment of Boys' Clubs.

These Boys' Clubs that Rotary has established offer outlets for that explosive energy in play and the land of make-believe. Their activities stretch all the way from checkers to sandlot baseball, from orchestras to bands. There are boxing matches, libraries, gymnasiums, and swimming pools. Boys are led into shops of the arts and the trades to discover their occupational bents, and, above all, they are taught the spirit of sportsmanship, co-operative living, and responsibility in citizenship. They are taught the rules of life and are given glimpses of the opportunities in this great land of ours.

From another direction these Clubs are proving of superlative importance. The totalitarian countries also adopted these benevolent ideas of handling boys. They grouped them, they systematically cured their physical defects, gave them recreation, and found their occupational bents. But they pounded in communist and fascist modes of thought. They built their minds into mental and moral submission and to a brutal mold. Their concept was that each boy was a molecule in a mass-directed State.

That is exactly the opposite of what our Boys' Clubs do. We build into our boys' personalities, personal responsibility, dignity, character, and moral discipline—not regimented minds. These concepts clashed on the field of battle, and ours proved the better of the two, man to man.

Dedication of the Lighthouse for the Blind

New York City
[April 25, 1951]

I T HAS been my misfortune to see suffering and human tragedy in every form. I have seen the tragedy to thousands of those living alone in endless midnight. There is no greater tragedy—lest it be blindness of the spirit.

But light to the spirit can come to the blind of sight. To bring that lamp into these lives has been your mission over these nearly fifty years. You have not alone served the blind in this city. You have pioneered in services and methods which aided the more than 300,000 blind among all our countrymen and women.

I am proud to be associated with you even so briefly in so great an occasion as this, because the dedication of this building is still another proof of the light you carry to those in darkness.

You have done something more than this building and its multitude of services. You have given opportunity to men and women of sympathy and understanding to expand their own spiritual lights by their gifts to you. Their souls have grown in the discharge of our greatest of all our social challenges—to be our brother's keeper.

You have done still more. In these days of clamor that the Government do it all, you have steadfastly maintained a most precious part of our American life. The work of voluntary institutions among our people can never be duplicated by Government bureaucracies. Governments do not build character.

Mass operations do not possess that solicitude for the individuals which comes from the serving human heart.

Today the world is in the grip of a death struggle between the philosophy of Christ and that of Hegel and Marx. The outstanding spiritual distinction of our philosophy from the other is compassion. It is the noblest expression of man. The day when we decide that the Government is our brother's keeper, that is the day when compassion will be lost to America. This greatest city in our land should give to you the resources which our Christian faith and our way of life demand—that you may carry more and more light to the blind.

On Medical Education

Address Before the National Fund for Medical Education*
New York City
[May 16, 1951]

THERE can be no question that this country is short of medical skills. Anyone who travels about to the extent that I do and has certain responsibilities in connection with institutions having medical schools must realize that the country is far short of its needed medical support.

I might say, parenthetically, that I have a theory that if it had not been for the so-called wonder drugs which have shortened the time required by the doctors to cure their patients, you and I would have to queue up to wait for somebody to die to get a doctor.

One of the evidences of a shortage in medical education facilities which those of us that have some responsibilities in these fields constantly meet is the fact that perhaps only one-third of the youngsters who have struggled through their pre-medical education are now able to find a medical school. Our medical schools taken all together face a deficit of about $14,-000,000 per annum. This deficit is being made up not only by uncertain contributions but by draining the resources of our universities and colleges away from their necessary other functions. Many of us who are trustees are torn in our budgeting of our institutions as to whether we shall not reduce the field covered by our medical schools.

* Mr. Hoover is Honorary Chairman.

Medical education is the absolute base of our national well-being. The medical men must conduct our hospitals, conduct our public health services, and cure our families. But their service is even greater than this. It is the trained technicians from our medical schools who must conduct our research. We must maintain this active research if we would advance skills and alleviate diseases. The discoveries in pure science are the raw material out of which we get our applied science. And that independence of mind which produces new discoveries in both the pure and applied science fields is to be realized fully only in the climate of our independently endowed institutions.

We must support these independent institutions over this very special economic crisis in which the nation is involved. We cannot leave all these things to a Government. If we do, the impulses of progress that bring discoveries and a constant rise in standards of education will be disastrously injured.

There are many economic aspects of our problem which I could discuss. But I will take your time on only one of them. I suggest to you that the efficiency of practically all of our industry and commerce today is dependent upon the health of their employees and their staffs. These institutions are obtaining their medical skills at the cost of public charity and at least of somebody else. Therefore, I have no hesitation in suggesting that they have a direct responsibility to support medical education. It should at least rest in part on the business community.

On Boys' Clubs

*The Dedication of the
New San Francisco Boys' Club Building
[September 25, 1952]*

YOU have done a great thing here. You have raised half a million dollars and built one of the finest Boys' Clubs in the world.

Behind you in this effort were the two clubs already many years in action under Harold Meyer, and his fine Board of Trustees, which have demonstrated their worth to this city.

But no new club springs up spontaneously. This was the work of a great civic committee of men and women under the leadership of Mr. Ernest Ingold, and always in the forefront has been your great Director, Harold Meyer.

This is an occasion of particular satisfactions.

It is a satisfaction to the thinking people of our city that such a step has been made in support of one of America's greatest character-building institutions. It is a satisfaction in a great accomplishment to the generous citizens who have brought it about. It will be an hourly satisfaction to the thousands of boys who will enjoy its service.

It is indeed a satisfaction to see such progress in an institution of which I have been national chairman for nearly eighteen years. I have had less responsibilities than William Hall, its devoted President, and David Armstrong, its magnificent Director.

I should like, for the benefit of those who are not familiar as you are with the Boys' Club movement, to say something about it. We are here concerned with pavement boys—the boys in our congested areas whose outlet after school and on Saturdays, Sundays, and holidays is the streets.

We are primarily concerned with building character. In this case it takes the form of creating an environment for the boy which reduces delinquency and builds him up morally and physically. And gives him a chance to find his bent in life. And above all gives to him a full measure of constructive joy.

To understand our problem we need some analysis of this very human person.

Together with his sister, the boy is our most precious possession. But he presents not only joys and hopes, but also paradoxes. He strains our nerves, yet he is a complex of cells teeming with affection. He is a periodic nuisance, yet he is a joy forever. He is a part-time incarnation of destruction, yet he radiates sunlight to all the world. He gives evidence of being the child of iniquity, yet he makes a great nation. He is filled with curiosity as to every mortal thing, he is an illuminated interrogation point, yet he is the most entertaining animal that is.

The whole world is new to him. Therefore his should be a life of adventure, of discovery, of great undertakings. He must spend much time, if he is to expand, in the land of make-believe. One of the sad things in the world is that he must grow up into the land of realities.

He is endowed with a dynamic energy and an impelling desire to take exercise on all occasions. His primary instinct is to hunt in a pack and that multiplies his devices. He is a complete self-starter, and therefore wisdom in dealing with him consists mostly in what to do next. He and his pack can go on this hunt for happiness either constructively or destructively. Our first problem is to find him constructive joy, instead of destructive glee.

To complicate this problem, this civilization has gone and built up great cities. We have increased the number of boys per acre. We have paved all this part of the land with cement and cobblestones. There are about twenty million of these human organisms in the country. Of these perhaps three million are crowded into the slums and poorer sections of our cities. They have to spend their spare time on these pavements, surrounded by brick walls. That pavement boy has a life of stairs, light switches, alleys, fire escapes, bells, and cobblestones, and a chance to get run over by a truck. Thus he is today widely separated from Mother Earth and all her works, except the weather. The outlet of curiosity in exploring the streams and the fields is closed to him. The mysteries of the birds and bees and fish are denied to him.

The normal boy is a primitive animal and takes to competition and battle. In the days before our civilization became so perfect, he matched his wits with the birds, the bees, and the fish. He cannot find battle with animal or plant life in zoos or parks. If he doesn't contend with nature, he is likely to take on contention with a policeman. And yet we cannot restore many of these constructive joys in a land of cement and bricks.

This is a marginal problem. It concerns only a minority of boys. And I may state generally that if the American people would only realize that our national problems are all marginal problems of eliminating evil, correcting abuse, and building up the weak, rather than the legerdemain of Utopia, we would make more progress.

I dislike to refer to these boys as "underprivileged." That is only a half-truth. The government provides even the marginal city boys with better facilities for education and better protection of health than any other government in the world. And we are today doing a better job of these things than ever before in our history. Far less than his grandfather does he suffer from mumps and measles; more quickly do we heal his fractures. Far less does he have to endure stench and filth. And the electric light has banished the former curse of all boys, of cleaning lamps and everlastingly carrying them about. The light switch has driven away the goblins that lived in dark corners and under the bed. It clothes drab streets with gaiety and cheer by night. And it is the attraction of these bright lights that increases our problem.

There are other privileges that the most lowly of them have.

It is a privilege to have been born in America. They live under a representative Government where they have more opportunity of becoming a mayor or a policeman or an editor or even a banker than in any other country. So they have some privileges.

But we are concerned with the privileges which this civilization has taken away; and the particular ones with which we are concerned bear on his character and moral stature. Now this brick and cement foundation of life is a hard soil for these growths. Somebody will say morals are the job of parents. The better the parents are, the better the morals; the worse they are, the greater our problem. But the best of parents cannot keep him indoors all the time. And the world in the streets is a distorted and dangerous world, which the parents cannot make or unmake. So it becomes a job of public concern.

But there is more than that. The fine qualities of loyalty to the pack, competition with violent zeal yet without bitterness, the restraints that cover the rights of others—these are the spirit of sportsmanship. They are not so good on the pavements. For here the pack turns to the gang, where his superabundant vitality leads him to depredation. And here we make gangsters and feed jails.

To demonstrate the worth of this movement which now has over 300 fully equipped clubs in over 200 cities I mention this:

1. Its facilities could not be replaced for 90 million dollars. It serves some 300,000 boys. It is conducted by some 10,000 unpaid devoted citizens and trained assistants.

2. I can best demonstrate the usefulness of this institution in reducing delinquency by relating an experience in Chicago. Some years ago the magistrate in the worst slum ward of that city asked if a Boys' Club could not be established in his ward. He stated the boy delinquency rate was over 80 percent—that is, 80 percent of the boys in the ward came into the hands of the police for something in a year. A club with full equipment was built by generous men and women in that city. Four years after the club opened the magistrate told me that delinquency had dropped to 15 percent and he accredited it all to the Boys' Club.

3. As to physical benefits I might mention that the national

rate of 4-F's is over 30 percent. A canvass of 200,000 alumni of Boys' Clubs showed only 4½ percent.

4. As to mental benefits I could point out a leading columnist, a leading editor, a leading sculptor, and five members of major league baseball teams who got their inspiration and their start from Boys' Clubs.

5. As to the value of the clubs to the working community I could mention a Connecticut city of under 100,000 people where there had long been two clubs. The industrial and business community in time awoke to the character of youngsters they were turning out. The business men in that small community raised one million dollars to build three more clubs. But I could go on endlessly.

San Francisco should be proud of your accomplishment. And I am proud to have taken a small part in this occasion.

Message to the
American Cancer Society

[*March 1, 1953*]

W HEN the problem of one individual is repeated in home after home throughout the United States, the problem becomes one of national concern.

Cancer constitutes just such a problem.

The American Cancer Society is devoted to these problems and has taken the lead in America's crusade against cancer through effective research, education, and service for cancer patients.

Because of the scope of the cancer problem, and the methods by which this independent, voluntary organization is facing the problem, I offer my wholehearted endorsement of the American Cancer Society.

On the Red Cross Annual Appeal

[March 7, 1953]

WHO can refuse to endorse the Red Cross annual appeal or fail to contribute to it? That institution is our insurance policy against suffering in our country. Greater than this, it is the expression of the American heart to those in trouble.

Statement on the Work of United Nations International Children's Emergency Fund

[*April 21, 1953*]

SEVEN years ago I was delegated to co-ordinate the forces of thirty-eight nations in the battle against the world's greatest famine—a consequence of World War II. I visited each of these countries in 1946. One of our special inquiries was into the situation of undernourished and subnormal children, the number of which in Europe alone we estimated at 20,000,000. During that year I emphasized this emergency concerning children, in public addresses in London, Paris, Rome, Warsaw, Cairo, Tokyo, Prague, New York, Washington, Chicago, and Ottawa. Shortly thereafter there was set up within the framework of the United Nations the United Nations Children's Fund. Maurice Pate, one of my assistants in both the famines of 1919 and 1946, was made Director.

The work of this organization in the first few years was done principally in those countries whose children had grievously suffered the hardships of six long years of war and occupation. Then UNICEF began to extend its work for the betterment of ill-fated children in the economically underdeveloped countries.

The wise part about this present work, and one appreciated by the countries that have been assisted, is that it is long-term work on a distinctly self-help basis. All the countries helped have increased their budgets not only for aid to their own children, but to the best of their means they have contributed to assist other children beyond their own frontiers.

The United States should be proud of the work accomplished and it should be continued as long as it is doing what it is doing at the present time. I believe that our Government should give its full moral and material support as long as other governments continue to do their part.

FACTS REGARDING UNICEF

1. All contributions to UNICEF whether from governments or from individuals are on a voluntary basis.

2. So far, the equivalent of approximately $180 million has been raised from 99 countries and territories.

3. About 8 percent of our funds have come from individuals; 92 percent from governments.

4. UNICEF-assisted programs so far have reached 60 million children in 72 countries and territories.

5. UNICEF is known as the most thrifty of all international organizations. It is also the freest and most flexible of all international organizations.

6. UNICEF encourages every voluntary effort and the utilization of voluntary agencies in field work in the countries.

7. About $60,000,000 of the $180,000,000 which UNICEF has raised has come from smaller countries, other than the United States of America. These countries would not have been able to participate effectively on their own except for the existence of a going mechanism like UNICEF.

8. Through UNICEF's principle of internal matching, the amount of aid actually extended to children and mothers will, when programs for which the $180,000,000 has been allocated are completed, have been built to a total figure of over $400,000,000.

On the Problems of Medical Education

Message Delivered at Dinner Meeting of National Fund for Medical Education, New York City
[April 16, 1953]

YOU have heard this cause from the ablest men in our medical world. Perhaps I can help sum up the emergency we face. We are short of doctors, technicians, and nurses to properly care for the American people. Our medical schools' capacity is inadequate to meet these needs. And today nearly every one of them faces a deficit. Many are threatened with a restricting of their efforts, due to rising costs, increasing requirements in teaching staffs and equipments, decreasing yield of interest on our endowments in the face of increasing purchasing value of the dollar. The result is this great deficit in our schools.

You have heard from one of the leaders in tax-supported institutions of the vital importance of maintaining the independent, voluntarily supported schools. By their standards, they spur the legislators to maintain similar standards. But beyond that we cannot maintain our American way of life if we are going to turn to the Government for these burdens. When we explore sources of support, we are faced with a decrease in individual giving due to oppressive income and estate taxes. We naturally turn to industry for help. These schools are training the staffs which directly increase industrial efficiency. I have today received a letter from a friend of this fund —and a friend of all Americans.

This letter reads:

THE WHITE HOUSE

Washington

April 9, 1953

Dear Mr. President:

I am extremely pleased to learn that you and Colby Chester will meet with the Educational Advisory Committee of the National Association of Manufacturers to discuss the problems of medical education and the ways in which the NAM can further the efforts of the National Fund for Medical Education to obtain the support of American business.

Certainly there is no organization better equipped to enlist the support of industry in behalf of our educational institutions than the Association. And certainly there are no two men who understand more clearly than you and Mr. Chester the basic issues here at stake.

As I see it, the mounting trend to rely on government for the fulfillment of responsibilities that properly belong to the individual citizen must be halted. It is high time that we reverse this trend. To take a stand now with the medical schools should set a fine example and establish a pattern for corporate support to all higher education.

Knowing something of the needs of the medical schools and their importance to the health, security, and productivity of the nation, I earnestly hope the National Association of Manufacturers will feel impelled to take direct action to place medical education in our country on a sound financial footing.

I am most encouraged that business leaders are discussing these problems with you, and I hope their decision will be to seize this opportunity as a turning point in American life.

With warm personal regard,

Sincerely,

DWIGHT D. EISENHOWER /s/

The Honorable Herbert Hoover
The Waldorf Towers
New York, New York

On Feeding People with the American Food Surplus

Statement in Reply to Press Inquiry,
New York City
[July 1, 1953]

PRESIDENT Eisenhower has made a most constructive recommendation to Congress in respect to our feeding hungry people with the huge American food surplus. Such a humanitarian program will bring results in saving human life and building friendships. An additional reason could be given. These surplus food accumulations of our Government are perishable and to withhold them until they spoil is unthinkable. Twice before, after both World Wars I and II, the skill and energy of the American farmer and the generosity of our people have saved uncounted lives.

On the Community Chest Drive

Washington, D.C.
[September 22, 1954]

A S A periodic Washingtonian I have had many occasions to
support the work of the Community Chest.

I propose to speak but a moment, and then only on
one phase of your noble work. That is a phase which also concerns every Community Chest in the country.

We have a steady expansion of government into welfare
activities. I am not here criticizing the expansion of these agencies. They have a place in American life—provided the cloak
of welfare is not used as a disguise for Karl Marx. But parallel
with this expansion, we have stupendous taxation to pay for
them and also for the former hot war and to support the present
cold war. That makes it difficult for the citizens to contribute to
the voluntary welfare agencies.

From all this, many citizens ask themselves: For what reasons must we continue to support the voluntary agencies? Why
not let the Government do it all?

The first short answer to this question is that you cannot
retire from the voluntary field if you wish our American civilization to survive. The essence of our self-government lies in
self-government outside of political government. The fabric
of American life is woven around our tens of thousands of
voluntary associations, the churches, the private schools and colleges, the research institutions, the professional societies, wom-
en's organizations, business, labor, and farmers' associations.

And by no means the least, our charitable institutions. That is the very nature of American life. The inspirations of progress spring more from all these agencies than from the also necessary agencies of government. If these voluntary activities were to be absorbed by government agencies, this civilization would be over. Something neither free nor noble would take its place. The very purpose of this Community Chest is to keep voluntary action alive in the spiritual and moral field.

The second answer to this question is that it is our privately supported and managed hospitals, educational institutions, and character-building institutions which are the spur to official progress. Without them, our governmental healing and educational agencies will lag and will degenerate.

The third answer to this question is that morals do not come from government. No government agency can create and sustain a system of morals. You perhaps are not working specifically in the religious field, but your works confirm religious faith and build morals.

There is a fourth answer. The governments cannot build character in our youth. With the brutalization which is inevitable from war, revitalized character building has never been as necessary as it is today. Over half the organizations for which you are appealing are, directly or indirectly, for character building.

There is a fifth answer. The greatest and, in fact, the only impulse to social progress is the spark of altruism in the individual human being. "And the greatest of these is charity" has been a religious precept from which no civilized people can depart without losing its soul. If governments practice charity, then it is solely because it rises from that spark in the hearts of the people. The day when altruism in the individual dies from lack of opportunity for personal expression, it will die in the government. At best, charity by government must be formal, statistical, and mechanistic. Yours is charity in its real sense—not obligatory but from the heart.

There is a sixth reason. The world is in the grip of a death struggle between the philosophy of Christ and that of Hegel and Marx. An essential part of the philosophy of Christ is a philosophy of compassion. The outstanding spiritual distinction of our civilization from all others is compassion. With us, it is the noblest expression of man. And those who serve receive in return untold spiritual benefits. The day when we decide that the Government is our brother's keeper, that is the day the personal responsibility for our brother has been lost. If you fail, Washington will have lost something that is vital to its material, its moral, and its spiritual welfare.

But a simpler answer than all this lies in the Parable of the Good Samaritan. The Good Samaritan did not stop to enter into governmental or philosophic discussion. It is said when he saw the helpless man "he had compassion on him . . . he bound his wounds . . . and took care of him."

That is your mission.

PART VI

ADDRESSES, LETTERS, AND COMMENT
ON VARIOUS INCIDENTS AND PHASES
OF AMERICAN LIFE

The American Dream

*Foreword to a Book, "I Like Protestants and Jews: A
Story of Brotherhood Told by a Catholic Priest,"
by Father John A. O'Brien,
Notre Dame University
[April 1951]*

NO NATION has drawn her citizens from so many lands
as has America. To her shores have come people from
every country; they bring with them their native languages, customs, and traditions. They are of different religious
faiths and diverse political creeds. In the great crucible of
American life they are fused into a national unity, displaying a
patriotism and a devotion to the land of their adoption which
have provoked the admiration of the world.

The numerous differences of her citizens in racial origin,
religious faith, and political creed have contributed greatly to
the enrichment of American life, to the fertilizing of our culture, and to the fostering of the ideals of religious and political
freedom. National unity in the midst of cultural pluralism has
become the ideal of our American democracy.

To preserve that ideal it is of supreme importance that tolerance, respect, good will, and friendship prevail among our
citizens of various racial origins, of different religious creeds
and diverse political faiths. When such differences are made
the breeding grounds of suspicion, antagonism, prejudice, and
hatred, they disfigure American life, impair the social order,
and menace the unity of the national effort in peace and in war.

By stressing the importance of understanding and friendship among these different groups and by showing how such good will can be maintained and fostered, this book renders a timely service to America at an hour when the need for national unity is so urgent. Citizens of all faiths and colors will welcome Father O'Brien's appeal for understanding, good will, and friendship among the members of all our diverse racial, religious, and political groups in order that the good-neighbor policy of our nation may prevail at home and abroad. Such internal harmony will make America not only a stronger and mightier nation but a better and happier one as well.

Great Quaker

Review of Book, Together with Felix Morley,
"Rufus Jones: Master Quaker,"
by David Hinshaw
[The Freeman, June 4, 1951]

I T IS now nearly three years since, on June 16, 1948, Rufus
Jones died at his home in Haverford, aged 85. The lapse
of time has not been sufficient for a final assessment of this
great Quaker spokesman and his role in a period when all the
values for which he stood were increasingly challenged or denied.

David Hinshaw, knowing that his work is premature as a
complete biography, has nevertheless laid foundations on which
all future students of the life of Rufus Jones will build. There
is little doubt that these will be numerous, and not confined to
members of the Society of Friends. As the philosophy of this
spiritual leader transcended the particularism of his sect, so we
may anticipate that some objective historian will eventually give
complete definition to Rufus Jones, against the background of
his times, as George Macaulay Trevelyan did for another great
Quaker in the *Life of John Bright*.

That classic biography of a Quaker statesman was published
24 years after Bright's death. Mr. Hinshaw reveals that he was
—fortunately, we must say—"gathering material for this book"
with Rufus Jones ten months before the latter died. It is this
intimacy with the personality of the subject that makes Mr.
Hinshaw's study delightful reading. But it is too early yet to

underwrite the bold assertion that Rufus Jones "occupies a place" with George Fox and Willian Penn "to form Quakerism's great triumvirate." There have been many others, John Woolman, John Greenleaf Whittier, John Bright not least among them.

Because hierarchical definition is dangerous, especially in the spiritual democracy of Quakerism, a caution as to the title of Mr. Hinshaw's biography is advisable. By "Rufus Jones: Master Quaker" the author does not mean that Rufus—as two of his friends may call him—ever ruled this highly individualistic sect. The suggestion, rather, is that Dr. Jones mastered not other Quakers, but the philosophy of Quakerism itself, just as a "master craftsman" was not, in guild parlance, a ruler of men, but of the materials with which he worked.

For members of the Society of Friends, as well as for the general reader with a mild interest in Quakerism, the Hinshaw biography does a great service in explaining how Rufus Jones, like all great spiritual leaders, rose above dogma and faction in order to unify through substance. As Harry Emerson Fosdick shrewdly observed of Rufus:

> He has gone to the root of the matter in religion, and emphasizing, as he has, the profundities, he has therefore emphasized the universals, and so, to an amazing degree, has been not sectarian at all, but the interpreter of Christianity to the deepest need of multitudes of people of all the denominations.

This spiritual insight is the more interesting because Rufus Jones was never an ascetic. All real Quakers, which does not mean all who call themselves such, base their faith on belief in a spark of the Divine in each individual, whether it be called "conscience" or "inner light." In some persons this sense of personal communion with God leads to an extreme of mysticism, but always it is as different from pantheism on the one hand as it is from positivism on the other.

Belief in the fundamental of "inner light" was the wellspring of the power that vested in this Quaker farm boy from the backwoods of Maine. The effect of that power was not merely to give Quakerism everywhere a new vitality, but also to make it a living, influential creed for tens of thousands, all over the world, to whom this sect had previously either been wholly unknown, or known only as a name.

It was not altogether easy, as Mr. Hinshaw shows, for Rufus Jones to reanimate Quakerism from within. And it is doubtful that Rufus Jones would have achieved so much if world upheaval and the friendship of worldly men had not made his task as a reformer easier. Certainly Rufus was not a nationally known figure prior to the organization of the American Friends Service Committee in 1917. This Committee is now famous because of many missions of mercy which have commanded world respect. The first of its great undertakings was the administration of regenerative feeding of several million debilitated German children in 1919 after the World War I Armistice, at the request of Mr. Hoover and largely financed by the Hoover organization. Dr. Jones in 1917 was 54 years old, an age at which both George Fox and William Penn had accomplished most of their active work. For Rufus, however, the middle fifties marked the beginning of thirty years of intense activity. Prior to that climacteric, he had been a remarkable teacher in a fine small college. The coming of world war somewhat paradoxically made this American pacifist a great international force.

Under present circumstances it is still too early to estimate the lasting influence of Rufus Jones, or of Quakerism as reinforced by his wise leadership, upon a world obsessed by fear and hate. David Hinshaw wisely does not attempt to do this, except inferentially. For instance, he relegates to an appendix the account, as told in an article by Rufus Jones himself, of an historic visit to Gestapo headquarters in Berlin in December 1938. The purpose of the visit, made by Rufus and two other prominent Friends, was to obtain permission for the extension of relief to Jewish victims of Nazi persecution.

As can be imagined, that was no easy task. Yet the trio of devoted Quakers won through to the inner citadel of Nazidom, delivered their message and were given "full permission to investigate the sufferings of Jews and to bring such relief as they see necessary." This could have been an action of great political moment except that a few months later war intervened.

The unfailing humor which always made Rufus Jones a very human character breaks forth in this story, as told in his own words. After their interview, while waiting for a decision from "Hangman" Heydrich, the three Friends were left entirely alone. Instinctively they bowed their heads in prayer— "the only Quaker Meeting ever held in the Gestapo." When the Nazi chiefs returned, one said casually that every word spoken in the room had been recorded. "We were glad then," wrote Rufus, "that we had kept the period of quiet!"

And his dry wit had all the pith and pungency one would expect from a real "Down-Easter." Rufus was speaking in Meeting, to college students, on the importance of individual effort. "Take the case of Methuselah," he said. "We have it on good authority that he lived 969 years. Yet, so far as we know, longevity was his only accomplishment worth recording."

The more modest 85 years vouchsafed to Rufus Jones were packed with subtle achievement of a nature that has lately been all too rare.

On the Purple Heart Decoration

Letter to Mrs. Edgar Mattocks, Tucson, Arizona
[August 17, 1951]

Stanford University
California
August 17, 1951

My dear Mrs. Mattocks:

I count it an honor to send a message to the wearers of the noblest and oldest of all Military decorations, the Purple Heart.

A deep significance of that decoration is that it was inaugurated by the first President of the United States. The newborn Republic in its conviction that all men are created equal banned all continued titles. Only those won by service were to be held.

I can add no praise to the honor these veterans wear. But I can salute them. I can especially take pride in them because, after nearly a hundred years of disuse of the Order, it was my privilege to revive it.

It gives me special pleasure to send my good wishes to the John J. Pershing Chapter, and its Auxiliary, honoring his memory at Tucson. He was a valiant friend to his country; and he was a friend of mine.

Yours faithfully,

HERBERT HOOVER

"Men Are Equal Before Fish"

Florida Speaks
[September 1951]

I HAVE met fish in many aspects. As Secretary of Commerce I dealt with their economic aspects. If anyone wants to know the need, the method or the urgency of conservation, I refer him to my reports of that time. They indicate the importance of fish in relation to food and employment, including the hotels, auto camps, and tackle makers.

But my emotional interest in fish, man and boy over seventy years, has been other aspects of this industry—which are also important.

The human animal originally came from out-of-doors. When spring begins to move in his bones, he just must get out again. Moreover, as civilization, cement pavements, office buildings, radios have overwhelmed us, the need for regeneration has increased, and the impulses are even stronger. When all the routines and details and the human bores get on our nerves, we just yearn to go away from here to somewhere else. To go fishing is a sound, a valid, and an accepted reason for an escape. It requires no explanation.

Nor is it the fish we get that counts. We could buy them in the market for mere silver at one percent of the cost. It is the chance to wash one's soul with pure air, with the rush of the brook, or with the shimmer of the sun on blue water. It brings meekness and inspiration from the decency of nature, charity toward tackle makers, patience toward fish, a mockery of profits and egos, a quieting of hate, a rejoicing that you do not have to decide a darned thing until next week. And it is discipline in the equality of men—for all men are equal before fish. And the contemplation of the water, the forest, and mountains soothes our troubles, shames our wickedness, and inspires us to esteem our fellowmen—especially other fishermen.

And the aspects of this sport have progressed with the march of civilization. Not only in improved tackle, but from spitting on the bait for magic and incantations, we have moved forward to cosmetics for artificial flies and wonders in special clothes and bags with pigeonholes for everything, including the mosquito repellents. We no longer call it a "pole," for it is a "rod"; and we no longer say that a fish "bites," he now "strikes."

Nor is fishing a rich man's regeneration. That boy with the worm and a grin is always a reminder that men are equal before fish.

Moreover, while we are steadily organizing increased production of leisure time, the production of what to do with it still lags greatly. And the more leisure, the more crime. We have great machinery for joy, some of it destructive, some of it synthetic, much of it mass production. We go to chain theaters and movies. We watch somebody else knock a ball over the fence or kick it over the goal post.

I do that and I believe in it. But these forms of organized joy are sadly lacking in the beatitudes which surround the fish. We gain none of the lift of soul coming from a return to the solemnity, the calm, and the inspiration of primitive nature. Furthermore, no one commits crime while fishing.

Dedication of the
Herbert Hoover School

Address, Kenmore, New York
[October 10, 1951]

NO GREATER honor may come to an American than to have a school named after him. I am deeply indebted to you for that distinction. And this occasion gives me an opportunity to express my obligation to the communities in several states which have done me the same honor. But the name on a schoolhouse is a trivial mark compared to the symbol of national progress which these modern buildings so well express.

There are many things which trouble us all these days. The future is dimmed by many gloomy shadows. But there are things in the nation from which we can take satisfaction and good hope—and it is good for our faith and fortitude that we occasionally take a look at some of our accomplishments. One of them is our Educational System, and some results that have flowed from it.

THE ASTONISHING GROWTH OF EDUCATION

The American people were the first on earth to undertake public education. Its monument is that today there are more than 30,000,000 youngsters enrolled in our schools and 2,300,-000 youth in our institutions of higher learning. And to this enormous task about 1,200,000 teachers and professors are giving devoted lives. We owe to them living standards which reward this devotion.

One amazing thing about this is its growth in the past fifty years. While the youngster age group in the population has increased 40 percent, school enrollment has increased about 100 percent and higher education has increased nearly 1,000 percent.

PRESERVING ITS INDEPENDENCE AND FREEDOM

This gigantic American cultural structure has a foundation from which comes its strength. It is the product of community responsibility and local government. It is a grass-roots enterprise. The Federal Government has had no important part in its origin, its growth, or in its administration. I hope it never will. And do not interpret that to mean that destitute communities must not receive even Federal aid to educate its children. I am saying there should be no strings on it. If we surrender the welfare of our children and the independence of our higher education to a Washington bureaucracy, we abandon the first obligation of parenthood, the foundation of local government, and we endanger an essential defense of freedom.

One of our oldest sayings is that "Eternal vigilance is the price of Liberty." But the vigilantes require education free of political influence if they are to be any good for this job.

SCIENTIFIC RESEARCH

And there is a by-product of our education system of which even its founders never dreamed. The stream of trained minds which this system pours into the nation has brought unprecedented skills in industry and the professions. It has made possible exhaustive research into natural laws and their use by mankind. Scientific discovery and invention are no longer dependent on the genius in the garret. They can come only step by step, through organized search.

Through such research we have been able to march triumphantly into new lands of scientific discovery and invention, new methods and devices. Here great burdens have been lifted from mankind. And in this land we Americans have increased the living standards and comforts to the highest levels in all history.

I will not labor you with many statistics, but one of the most striking in our civilization is the fabulous increase in the number of research laboratories and their workers during the last fifty years. At the opening of the century there were probably less than 300 institutions devoted to systematic research in pure and applied physical sciences. There were probably less than 3,000 scientists. Today these research centers probably number over 3,000, each bigger and better. In these institutions a probable 200,000 trained technologists engage in constant exploration and discovery. It is no accident that, parallel with this growth, our production per capita has increased about 300 percent.

This increased productivity has not come from Government, except in so far as Government contributes by protecting freedom of mind and action.

It is this increased productivity alone which has enabled us to carry the fearful Federal economic burdens so far imposed upon us by these times. If we emerge from these strains as a free people, it will be due more to our increasing productive power than to increased skill in Government.

THERE WILL BE GREAT JOBS TO BE DONE

And I can say something to the youngsters before me which you will perhaps appreciate more in a few years.

I, like you, sat at school desks. I too was the product of our free schools. For that I have an unpayable debt to my country.

Someday you will go out from here to take up your work in life. And there will be a job waiting for you.

Someday all the men and women who now direct this vast American complex of Government, educational and benevolent institutions, all those who direct the financial institutions, the factories, the farms, and the distribution of their products, all those who conduct the research and professional services and the intellectual life of the nation—they are all going to die.

Your generation, sometime, will need to take over the jobs in directing these vast mechanisms and leadership in these services.

Those who will get those jobs are those who are trained in our schools. But more even than school training will be required for these positions of leadership. These jobs will go to those who have ventured out into the battle of the competitive world. For that is the place where wits are sharpened and initiative is inspired. It will be the enterprising and self-reliant who will be chosen—not those who are leaners on Government or searchers for security.

These great jobs are all open to you. And do not think it is a cold, hard world you are going into. You will find a wealth of kindly help from your elders. For they want you to take over. They want you to succeed. And it is a world of constant new discovery and adventure to you if you have the will to enter it.

"This I Believe"

Radio Broadcast
[December 1951]

M Y PROFESSIONAL training was in science and engineering. That is a training in the search for truth
and its application to the use of mankind. With the
growth of science we have a continuous contention of a tribe of
atheistic and agnostic philosophers that there is an implacable
conflict between science and religion in which religion will be van-
quished. I do not believe it.

I believe not only that religious faith will be victorious, but
that it is vital to mankind that it shall be. We may differ in
forms and particulars of our religious faith. Those are matters
which are sacred to each of our inner sanctuaries. It is our privilege to decline to argue them. Their real demonstration is the
lives we live.

But there is one foundation common to all religious faith.

Our discoveries in science have proved that all the way
from the galaxies in the heavens to the constitution of the atom,
the universe is controlled by inflexible laws. Somewhere a Supreme Power created these laws. At some period, man was
differentiated from the beasts and was endowed with a spirit
from which springs conscience, idealism, and spiritual yearnings. It is impossible to believe that there is not here a Divine
touch and a purpose from the Creator of the Universe. I believe we can express these things only in religious faith.

From their religious faith, the Founding Fathers enunciated
the most fundamental law of human progress since the Sermon

on the Mount, when they stated that man received from the Creator certain inalienable rights and that these rights should be protected from the encroachment of others by law and justice.

The agnostic and atheistic philosophers have sought to declaim progress in terms of materialism alone. But from whence come the morals, the spiritual yearnings, the faith, the aspirations to justice and freedom of mind which have been the roots of our progress?

Always growing societies record their faith in God; decaying societies lack faith and deny God. But America is not a decaying society. It remains strong. Its faith is in compassion and in God's intelligent mercy.

Address to Youth

Mirror Youth Forum
New York City
[December 1, 1951]

I T IS a stimulating experience to become better acquainted with the work of the Youth Forum. Your many activities make for health and understanding of political, civic, and international responsibilities. Mr. McCabe and the staff of the *Daily Mirror* are making a real contribution to this community.

You are giving thought to the gigantic problems which confront the world. The greatest of all problems is peace.

East, West, North, South—over the whole earth—people are shuddering for fear that a world war may come again. Everywhere the people are praying daily that peace may come to the earth. And I am convinced this is the prayer of all peoples under domination of the Communist conspiracy.

I am not going to propose a solution for this international crisis, but I may say that whatever the road to enduring peace may be, it must include one fundamental concept. That is the full maintenance of the independence and the self-government of nations.

That is ofttimes referred to in contempt as "nationalism." There are fuzzy-minded people who contend that nationalism is an evil and must be abolished from the earth. That is not the road to freedom of mankind. I am not afraid of that word. Truly, nationalism can run to excesses. It can run to greed and desire for the domination of other peoples—or it can bring a thousand blessings which flow from the freedom of nations and men.

Nationalism as a powerful and progressive force has been witnessed by all of us in the creation of the State of Israel. We have seen history written. We have seen the survival and fruition of a national ideal which 3,000 years of dispersal and oppression could not dim.

It is nationalism in the Iron Curtain countries which will yet redeem them from the Communist tyranny of the Kremlin.

The co-operation of independent nations is the only foundation upon which international peace can be permanently built and sustained.

The independence of nations and the maintenance of self-government among nations is the basis of freedom. For in self-government lies the safety and guarantees of individual rights under law. It is said that vigilance is the price of liberty. It might be added that the seat of liberty must be near enough home to keep an eye on it.

And nationalism is something still more. It is a spiritual foundation which is essential to the soul of men. From it alone springs patriotism which, except for religion, is the greatest spiritual expression of mankind. Our patriotism springs from a thousand rills of pride of race. It rises from the long history of sacrifices that has gone before. The ideal of the independence of peoples and the freedom of men has been inscribed on our banners in the four great foreign wars which we have fought. In all our history our men and women have died with their national flag before their eyes and their national hymns upon their lips.

Some of you here come from other countries. Does not the very name of your nation stir something deeper within you than mere geography? Do not the suffering and sacrifice of your forebears, who fought for your independence, flash through your minds with every mention of your country's name? Was it not the independence which they created that brought free men and women? Was it not this freedom which gave the most expansive release to the creative spirit of mankind in all history?

Was it not the release of intellectual and spiritual freedom on
this continent that gave the moral strength and the self-reliance
which penetrated these plains and forests? Was it not these ideas
which brought independence to a score of peoples in the world
and through independence, the freedom of men?

Do not allow yourselves to be persuaded that nationalism
is an evil thing. Its other name is patriotism. In the wake of
these ideas run all freedoms, all reforms, all progress, and the
hope of peace to the world.

It is a satisfaction to meet with youth.

Our country and the world needs the courage and the new
vigor of youth as never before. Youth can yet bring the re-
newed strength, the ideals, and the confidence which can rebuild
America morally and spiritually from the debris of two world
wars.

We, the passing generation, who have lived deeply in the
great forces of the past may, perhaps, advise and counsel. Indeed the issues are not new, and we can distill some principles
from the experience of the years. But it is youth who must act,
and the past can never wholly point the way through the changing future.

You may well criticize the generations before your time for
the failures you inherit. I know you can do better, for at least
you can know what not to do.

But I may say this in defense of those who have gone before.
They pioneered for you the paths to freedom. They leave
youth great stores of knowledge and arts. They will leave you
millions of farms and homes which they have built. They have
prepared for your magnificent cities, great shops, and great factories. They have built great channels of transport and communications. You inherit magnificent institutions for health,
for research, and for education. You come into the literature
of ages and all the machinery of producing more printed words.

Just as surely as death comes to all men, you must need take
over and manage and lead these great political, economic, and
social agencies.

Also you in your own manner must lead our people away

from this jungle of dishonor and cynicism and these confusions which have haunted this nation from its failure to find peace.

We of the older generation know that you will carry forward. We wish you to carry the torch bravely and aloft. Carry it with the dauntlessness of your forebears who faced the peril of the ocean, the dangers of the forest and desert. Never forget the loneliness of those men and women who pioneered this continent and built here a great sanctuary of justice, of liberty, and of respect for the dignity of men. Vigilantly guard it. Protect it from foes within and without.

We who have lived long turn our eyes to your generation lovingly and with hope, with prayer and with confidence for our country and the world.

Greeting to the Radio Pioneers

Annual Banquet at the Conrad Hilton Hotel,
Chicago, Illinois
[April 1, 1952]

I WISH it had been possible for me to be in Chicago this evening—not only to accept the scroll with which you have honored me—but to greet my many old radio friends.

It is about thirty years ago that I, as Secretary of Commerce, called a general conference of the broadcasting industry. The Department had a minor authority to prevent interference in ship-to-shore communication, but no real authority to prevent interference in voice broadcasting. For four years we in effect conducted a voluntary regulation by annual conferences of the industry until the radio law was evolved.

I have looked up some of those records. The surprising thing in those infant days of the industry was the recognition at that time of its future potency in civilization. And it has filled all those anticipations of those pioneers.

Being with you in spirit, I can imagine the good fellowship of this evening, the warm greetings, the nostalgic reminiscences. I share them all with you. And I want you to know how deeply I appreciate your thought in awarding me the Radio Pioneers' scroll.

To you Pioneers and your younger brethren, I send my best wishes for continued success in your service to our country.

Fishing Auguries

Address to the Gridiron Club, Washington, D.C.
[May 10, 1952]

I DEEPLY appreciate the honor you have shown me. Ever since coming into this room and seeing your program, I have been mystified as to why I was so persistently urged to speak to you. I can understand your generous spirit of hospitality wishing to give me a good time but why a speech? I do not represent the Republican Party. Some of you are old enough to recollect that I was retired to the sidelines by that Party long ago. Perhaps I have been asked to speak because your Committee thought it would be a relief to just hear from the sidelines.

Forty years ago tonight I was your guest for the first time. I was young and filled with wonder and delight at your humor and your mockery set to music. I still wonder. Over the years I have painfully learned that you have a great motif. That is to lance the ego in Presidents, candidates, and lesser parties. Most of them can take it. At least they put on the same grin they use in press photographs.

Tonight, you have made some examination of the auguries of presidential candidates. In Roman times the people formed their political auguries by observing the flight of birds and the entrails of dead sheep.

I have recently been fishing. In the long time between bites I have come to the firm conclusion that today fish take the place of the flight of birds and the entrails of sheep.

Before I start to prove this, I should inform you that over

323

12,000,000 voters each year pay for a fishing license and most veterans fish for free. (That is a potent part of the electorate.) Candidates for nomination or election, and even Presidents, seem aware of this fact.

Also, I should inform you that from an augury point of view, there are two kinds of fish. There are the host of species of common or garden fish which are the recreation of the common man.

There are also the rare species of fish sought by the aristocracy of fisherman. They require more equipment and more incantations than merely spitting on the bait. They can be ignored as they are only landed the hard way and have no appeal to the common man.

Despite the fact that every great human advance has come from the uncommon man, every fish sign points up the validity of Mr. Wallace's assertion that we are firmly chained to the Common Man.

Now the augury process with fish is conducted by press photographs. A few years ago a press photograph showed my friend Senator Taft awkwardly holding a common fish, taken from many angles for all the common men to see. I knew without other evidence that he was a candidate. Two years ago my friend, General Eisenhower, burst into photographs from all angles, gingerly holding three very common fish. The augury was positive. A month ago General Ike stated that he was coming home to go fishing. Governors Warren and Stassen have not been in press photos with a fish! The augury swells up from 12,000,000 licensed fishermen that they are not likely to be nominated.

I have not had the time to study the auguries of the dozen candidates for the Democratic nomination. Many of you are members of the press. Your first duty in the morning is to report on all candidates. I suggest you keep your eyes on the fishy auguries of the Democratic side.

The political potency of fish is known to Presidents as well as to candidates.

Now you may think this fishing by Presidents has to do with

the 12 million paid license holders. It does not. Presidents have long since learned that the American people respect privacy on only two occasions: fishing and prayer. Some Presidents take to fishing.

Three Presidents, including President Cleveland, Theodore Roosevelt, and myself, fished from boyhood but we wasted all of our political time upon the uncommon fishes in places where photographers seldom come. However, in modern times all Presidents quickly begin to fish soon after election. I am told that McKinley, Taft, Wilson, and Harding all undertook fishing in a tentative way and for the common fishes.

President Coolidge apparently had not fished before election. Being a fundamentalist in religion, economics, and fishing, he began his fish career for common trout with worms. Ten million fly fishermen at once evidenced disturbed minds. Then Mr. Coolidge took to a fly. He gave the Secret Service guards great excitement in dodging his backcast and rescuing flies from trees. There were many photographs. Soon after that he declared he did not choose to run again. President Franklin Roosevelt caught many common fish from the military base of a battleship.

President Truman, prior to his 1948 election, appeared once in a photograph somewhere in a boat gingerly holding a common fish in his arms. An unkind reporter wrote that someone else had caught it. I can find no trace of the letter he must have received. It is reported also that Mr. Truman was fishing somewhere north of Key West when his boat was surrounded by sharks. It was decided that it might upset the boat if one were caught. There were no photographs. But sharks are always a bad augury. He subsequently announced he would not run again.

But the Gridiron Club expects from its speakers a moment on a more serious note.

When I first came here forty years ago, we were still in that quarter of a century of the world's last Golden Age. The long peace had buried the fear of war. The Four Horsemen seemed only a Biblical story. The dignity of men and personal liberty were spreading steadily over all nations. Slavery had long since disappeared. Men were able to move without restriction over the world's frontiers. There were black spots in the world but everywhere they were recognized. They were being lessened advancing human progress. Above all, there was a great growth in the human spirit. Confidence and boundless hope dominated the world.

After I was first your guest, the world stumbled into war and the great fear settled like a fog on the human race.

The only escape from this fog on men's minds is an occasional star shell of humor. And the Gridiron Club fires them —once in a while.

This is not an occasion for long discussion of the somber forces which have beset us over the years. But the dread shadows do lurk through all our minds. They are the fumes from the decay of liberty in all the world.

In these years, we Americans undertook two gigantic military Crusades to impose freedom on mankind. But they brought not more freedom to the world or to America itself, but less freedom. Even human slavery has come again upon the earth. We are today engaged in a third great Crusade. There were nine Crusades in the Middle Ages seeking the Holy Grail in some foreign place—and they failed. The Holy Grail of liberty lies in the hearts of men, not in any geographic spot.

But even to mention these things, no doubt, brings to your minds the old cuss words, "reactionary" or "isolationist" or "pessimist."

I will not take your time to argue over the moral aspects of this new art of blackguardism called semantics. But I may protest that I am no pessimist.

I am too much of a student of the thousands of years struggle of mankind toward the light to lose my confidence in the regeneration of free men.

The genius of our countrymen for productivity can even yet restore our economy from lost political statesmanship.

Liberty has survived great confusions before. And men have recovered their safety and freedoms. But how? Because some men stood solid. They stood not because they knew the solutions to all these confusions, not even because they had the power to find solutions. They held firm as they held up the lamp of true liberty. They held until these furies passed because they clung to certain principles of life, or morals, of spiritual values and free men.

And I may give you a further lift to your spirits. No doubt the bureaucrats now greatly limit our freedom to fish. But you are still free to pray.

On a Memorial to The Honorable James Forrestal at Princeton, New Jersey

Letter to Admiral Lewis L. Strauss
[May 16, 1952]

New York, New York
May 16, 1952

My dear Lewis:

I have followed with interest the project which you and other friends of the late James Forrestal have set in motion to establish as an enduring memorial to him a great research center at Princeton. I came to know Mr. Forrestal during his years of public service, more particularly during the period in which he served as Secretary of Defense. He worked with me on the Commission for the Organization of the Executive Branch of the Government, where his studiousness, his incisive intelligence, and his deeply rooted love of his country were daily evident.

The public record over the recent years attests to his realization and frequent emphasis upon the important place of both basic and applied research in the maintenance of American prosperity and American defense. For this reason it seems to me that the concept of a research institution as a monument to his life and achievements, and the location of that institution at his Alma Mater, is altogether fitting.

I wish the institution every success.

Yours faithfully,

HERBERT HOOVER

Admiral Lewis L. Strauss
30 Rockefeller Plaza
New York 20, New York

The Herbert Hoover
School of Neenah

*Letter to Mr. H. B. Mennes, Superintendent,
Neenah Public Schools, Neenah, Wisconsin
[March 6, 1953]*

New York, New York
March 6, 1953

My dear Mr. Mennes:

The greatest honor that can come to a person is to have his name placed on an American school house. The school is the symbol of everything good that America stands for—freedom of thought, of education, and of speech. Here one receives the necessary foundations which prepare one for life; for the school shares with the home the responsibility of moral and spiritual training.

Yours faithfully,

HERBERT HOOVER

On the Occasion of Welcoming Hawaii to Radio

Message for Radio Pioneers
[March 9, 1953]

I AM glad to join in the welcome to our Hawaiian colleagues to a free society of radio.

The radio pioneers can be proud of their fabulous accomplishment. And it is pride without make-believe. They have established great industries which give employment to hundreds of thousands of our people upon the highest levels of living standards. They have established a new medium of communication with its instant news brought to every home, its pictures of public events, its education, its entertainment, and music. But the radio and TV contain sorrows as well as joy. The pictures can dissolve the aura of great persons. However, that singing commercial and bum music may be the wild oats of youth.

And our American radio is a monument to private enterprise. Most countries have partly or wholly condemned it to the stifling land of socialism dependent upon the gift of gab by government employees. Bureaucracy has never been blessed with invention but they often seek to impose new methods, new programs on us.

Again, I welcome our Hawaiian colleagues.

On the Fiftieth Anniversary of Powered Flight

Foreword for Booklet, "Flight"
[March 17, 1953]

SOME thirty years ago I visited Kitty Hawk under a Congressional delegation to select a site and build there a monument to Orville and Wilbur Wright. While there the local telegraph operator showed me the original telegram of the Wright Brothers, dated December 17, 1903, to their devoted sister, saying as my note shows: "We have done it. Succeeded in four flights 31 miles an hour against the wind."

Thus began a new era for mankind. Soon, despite public skepticism, there came able men to the support of the Wrights with a vision of fulfillment of man's age-old dream of winged flight.

Year by year these far-seeing pioneers steadied the wings, flew faster, higher, longer and longer, with increasing safety. It has been a long road of brilliant invention and magnificent manufacture from the canvas biplane with a 12-horsepower motor of the Wrights to the all-metal monoplane and the gigantic Turbo Jets.

In the span of my generation alone there has come this magnificent revolution in transportation. With it, men's radius, their efficiency and effectiveness have been enormously increased, employment has been expanded, public health improved, and standards of living lifted. Penetration of inaccessible areas is no longer just an adventure; their resources are now added to world supplies.

The development of the military plane has contributed to the effectiveness of the commercial plane. It has become both a gigantic weapon of defense and a danger to our national safety. But the American genius which pioneered its development and its weapons can, with national will, make it our impregnable frontier.

This little book records in simple form some of the many steps that have led us to a new era of national and international communication and exchange. It is an unfinished story of courage and achievement—unfinished, because today we are on the threshold of new achievements, with airplanes moving beyond the speed of sound and with promise to double that speed.

Today we honor the pioneers of controlled flight—not only the Wrights and their determined disciples, but the pioneers who are projecting the airplane into unexplored realms of usefulness.

Remarks to the Bohemian Club of San Francisco

On the 40th Year of Membership
New York City
[March 19, 1953]

FELLOW Members and your guests. I deeply appreciate the touching evidence of your friendship marked by this occasion. And I feel greatly honored that President McLaren should have come across the continent to be here. And I am deeply moved by this call of the Red Woods which the Club sent to decorate this room.

Someone said that initiation to the Bohemian Old Guard was a tender push into oblivion. But your tributes surround it with an aura of glory. And this is a unique honor. Don't think any one of you can earn it through good conduct or merit. You just get it by being old enough. Moreover, the only place in the world where the Old Guard is still held in esteem is in the Bohemian Club.

Once upon a time the term Old Guard was regarded with esteem in every country and every avenue of life. Government, politics, business, drama, literature, and music all had their much revered Old Guards. But the Communists established the bad habit of periodically liquidating their sequent Old Guards in some dark cellar. A recent regime in the United States caught that infection, as witness their nasty smears and political tactics designed to liquidate the Old Guard in both political parties.

334

There is something to be said for all the Old Guards in the world. They are men past the time when they want anything on this earth but the welfare of those whom they guard. Their tempers have been softened in the solutions of experience. They have learned that virtue is a more stable currency than the commodity dollar. They are a menace to the fuzzy-minded, the foolish, and all New Deals. Some Frenchman mentioned over a hundred years ago that they never surrender. In Americanese, they die with their boots on. But those who enter Bohemia must take off their crusading boots. I might also mention that the Old Guards of the world are generally able to pay their own expenses, including their funerals.

Bohemia's consideration for its Old Guard rises to its high point by allowing them to explain themselves over a loudspeaker once each year for a few minutes while everybody is thirsting for dinner. The Old Guard on these occasions try to revive old memories and they concurrently express their hope for the Young Guard. Both these themes reflect something in the far, far distance. At this point there is applause. But on these occasions the Young Guard promptly insults them over the loudspeaker by calling them venerable. As one of them remarked, "Have they survived forty years of this? Gee Whiz!"

I came into the Club forty years ago with little recommendation other than that I had helped translate a huge Latin book. The awesome book was brandished before the Committee and they were told it weighed six pounds. Later on, after I had started to reform the world, I was made an Honorary Member. All members of the Club who become Presidents and Vice-Presidents of the United States receive that gracious honor. I recommend the Presidential bee to members, as success gives them generous freedom from annual dues. But make no mistake—they must contribute a Grove speech.

I have always wondered why the Encampment, having cremated Care himself, insists upon a speech every day before lunch, reviving and amplifying our national worries with very occasional spots of eloquence. But making a speech among those trees which were born before Caesar crossed the Rubicon dampens our emotions over our transitory themes. They hourly remind us that humility belongs here.

I do not know that I am particularly happy to have my age so prominently ventilated by this meeting. But this occasion recalls a host of memories. Over these years all the other founding fathers of my camp have passed on. Their wit and their blithe spirits brightened Bohemia's camp fires for a generation. But as is the way of Bohemia, new and good men come to carry on their places. And as is the way of Bohemia, we never refer to those who are gone in terms of sorrow but by recall of moments of happiness they spread among us.

There is wonderful compensation in life from having had forty years of such a happy association—and there has been the annual escape from this world of tumult into the land of make-believe. In that world of Bohemia there is a washing to the soul with laughter, with drama, poetry, and great music. That is an experience of precious days and precious memories. The rewards in friendship are beyond all measure.

How to Become President

This Week Magazine
[May 3, 1953]

(A letter written in answer to a young boy, who wrote:

Dear Mr. Hoover, I am a boy 10 years old and who would like to become a President like you were when I grow up. I thought that if I wrote to you that you can give me some information how you got to be a President. I wish you would send me an autograph. I would like that very much. Your friend, Martin Kainec.)

Dear Martin Kainec:

I am in favor of your ambition to be President. As to your request on the rules as to "how to get to be President," I suggest that:

The first rule is just to be a boy getting all the constructive joy out of life;

The second rule is that no one should win the Presidency without honesty and sportsmanship and consideration for others in his character—together with religious faith;

The third rule is that he should be a man of education.

If you follow these rules, you will be a man of standing in your community even if you do not make The White House. And who can tell? Maybe that also.

Yours faithfully,

HERBERT HOOVER

Commencement Exercises of Charlotte Hall Military Academy

Charlotte Hall, Maryland
[June 1, 1953]

I AM glad to congratulate and to express my good wishes to the graduating class. Yours is a great inheritance from this Academy. Founded at the beginning of our great struggle for independence, it witnessed the establishment of the Republic and the making of a land of free men. Over the whole span of the Republic it has participated in the ideals, the heartaches, and the successes that have gone into the making of our great Nation.

It is these ideals that must be handed on from generation to generation of its students—and no generation has a greater task than your own.

Statement in Support of
The Savings and Loan Foundation

[August 8, 1953]

I HAVE been following with interest the activities of The Savings and Loan Foundation and the progress which has been made toward reaching your membership goal, which, when attained, will make possible your going forward with a very challenging program. It seems to me that the education of our people to the benefits of thrift and home ownership is a constant necessity. In this undertaking the Foundation has my support and endorsement. I extend my congratulations to those institutions which already have become members of your organization, and my encouragement to these other associations which too are eligible for membership.

The savings and loan business already has attained a necessary and highly regarded position in the financial economy of the nation. They should be better known.

Having had the privilege of taking an initial part in the establishment of the Federal Home Loan Bank System in 1932, I am happy now to join with your organization in supporting the advancement of the objective of The Savings and Loan Foundation.

It is unnecessary that we review the history of this business —it is sufficient to recall that the organization of the first cooperative home-financing institution in the United States was something over one hundred years ago. Then followed the

creation of the Federal Home Loan Bank System and the establishment of a dual system of savings and loan institutions, with
Federally-chartered and State-chartered associations with insurance of accounts. Your present effort constitutes another high-
light in the development of this industry. The stimulation
which I am sure your organization will give to thrift, through
systematic savings and a stake in the permanent part of the
community through home-ownership, will be a stabilizing influence.

On the Dedication of the Monument to Powered Flight

Pikes Peak, Colorado
[August 26, 1953]

O N THE unrolled maps of History our world of 1953 will show as a deep and tortuous valley, with a few high peaks of faith and hope and accomplishment. The achievement of flight itself, with its widening possibilities in bringing men closer together in the peace of understanding, is itself one of those peaks.

Our hope is that the generations that come after us will find brighter paths to explore, meet lesser problems than ours, achieve more progress that will start their children to a finer life. But if they too meet discouragement in a darkened world, they can look back to our times for strength. We have kept the faith they inherit. Ours were somber times. They were times of intellectual, spiritual, and international confusion, which jeopardized free men everywhere. Free men survived great confusions before our times. And men recovered their freedoms. But how? Because some men stood solid. They have stood not because they knew the solutions to all these confusions, not even because they had the power to find solutions. They held firm as they held up the lamp of liberty—true liberty. They held firm until these furies passed, because they clung to certain rights of life and certain principles of morals and spiritual values.

Letter to a Small Boy Correspondent

(Published by the Boy)
[September 21, 1953]

The Waldorf Astoria Towers
New York, New York
September 21, 1953

My dear Friend:

I am glad to see that you are thinking about becoming President of the United States. That is the privilege of every American boy.

As to your questions about the job:

1. Is it a happy experience? There has not been as much joy in the job during the last forty years of troubled times as there may have been before. It is a job of hourly worries.

2. Does the President have much work to do? There is no other job in the country where one is compelled to spend as many hours every day. It is a job of about fourteen hours a day and a seven-day week. He has to carry on even at meals.

3. How do you go about being President? It takes too long to recite the political and legal mechanics, and that will require much study on your part. The main thing, however, is that you get an education—that is, high school and university. No one should come to the Presidency without that foundation. Moreover, you should not neglect the fact that you have a right to all the constructive joys in life as you go along—and that is also a part of education and preparation for dealing with your fellow citizens.

HERBERT HOOVER

The Importance of Voting

Reply to Press Inquiry
New York City
[October 5, 1953]

THE weakest link in the whole chain of protections to liberty is the vote. Other protections can be provided by law and officials designated to look after them.

The first step in protection of representative government is the vote. But that act is voluntary. If people do not go to the polls, freedom will die at its roots.

It is always a mystery to me why at every election there must be urging by a thousand voices: "Go to the Polls." Either our people must be absent minded or not concerned with their own safety. You may be sure that every fellow with an "ism" or a wild "do-not-like" will be there. If you want to neutralize him, then go and vote.

Message Sent to Dinner Honoring General Robert E. Wood

[*April 12, 1954*]

My dear General:

I would like to be present at the session in your honor in Chicago on April 12th. Unfortunately, that cannot be. However, I could make some observations for the record.

It is impossible for me to sum up in a letter my knowledge of your magnificent services to the American people. And my information goes back for thirty-seven years when we both served in executive positions in World War I.

Ever since, I have followed and admired your devotion to public interest, your courage, and your intellectual integrity. Not the least among your many services has been your membership on the Board of Directors of the Boys' Clubs of America, and, even more important, the leadership you have given to the establishment of the Boys' Clubs in Chicago.

Who can estimate the blessings that have flowed from such a life of service?

HERBERT HOOVER

Benjamin Franklin

Address Before the International Franklin Society, Inc.,
New York City
[January 23, 1954]

I DEEPLY appreciate the honor of receiving the gold
medal from the International Benjamin Franklin Society.
I am presumed to say something about Franklin, but how
can I add anything new to what has been said about him? The
members of your Society ought to know all about him by this
time.

The rest of the country has also heard of him. With appropriate remarks his name has been fixed to thousands of counties, towns, cities, and streets. Millions of parents have striven
to implant his qualities of character in their offspring by endow-
ing them with the surname of Franklin. That includes two
Presidents. One result is that his name appears in five thousand
telephone directories. To carry a conviction of integrity a thousand firms have labeled their goods after him. There is one
library alone of 10,000 items about him. There must have been
twenty million orations delivered about him.

Some members of your committee suggested that I should
say something about Franklin's influence on American life at
the present time. I investigated this subject a little but I came
up (on all but one great issue) with many frustrations, as I will
proceed to show you.

My first acquaintance with Franklin began early when, like
most schoolboys of my day, I received much drilling in Franklin's precepts. They at times seriously limited my freedom of
action and my projected enterprises. Especially objectionable

was his remark about early to bed and its consequences in health, wealth, and wisdom, provided we got up early in the morning.

Aside from human liberty, Ben's great design of American life or his ideology, as we would call it nowadays, had its central idea in frugality, thrift, and hard work. He conducted a propaganda campaign on that subject for over sixty years. His slogans sank so deep into the American mind that we practiced at it for quite a while. However, that was before we discovered the theory of spending ourselves into prosperity.

Franklin had definite ideas on the conduct of governments. His opinion of governmental borrowing and debts appears in his abundant command of the language. To him they were the road of sorrow and in general the destroyers of liberty. He knew none of the joys provided by Lord Maynard Keynes. However, this is not an economic debate and I believe it better not to pursue that subject further at this time.

Franklin also made some observations on money. He asserted that "The standard once fixed should ever be unvariable since any alteration would be followed by great confusion and detriment to the state." He was naturally unfamiliar with the theory and practice in the commodity dollar. But again that subject leads into a field of controversy not appropriate here.

Ben also observed that "It is impossible for government to . . . fix the extent of paper credit," and also that "no state or potentate can settle the prices of all sorts of merchandise [because] . . . plenty and scarcity must govern that." But this again raises questions which might be construed as controversial and must, therefore, not be pursued further at this time.

As to the industrial front he stated firmly that "God gives all things to industry," meaning hard work, and he intimated that you could save what you earned. But some people these days think the Government takes it away from you and then gives it away. However, this would also be a sour theme to pursue on this occasion.

Franklin made one remark that is of powerful weight today. He said that "God helps those who help themselves." That has become the motto of every pressure group in the country. But I will not pursue this pessimistic subject at this time.

Franklin had many notions of government. Using the architectural metaphor, he once said, "If the superstructure is too heavy for the foundations the building totters though assisted by outward props of art." I suppose the props of art he referred to was propaganda. He would have been even more forcible on this subject if he were in my place as Chairman of the Commission on Reorganization of the Government.

Franklin announced a formula for public office. He said, "Never ask, never refuse, never resign." The present Administration in Washington has found the "never resign" part is still in use.

But again I must not pursue such subjects here. I did think something might be done by way of comment on Franklin's fine stimulation to investigation and research. This seemed promising as the magnificent educational and research institutions which he founded have been fruitful of blessings down to this very day. But among institutions that he had a lot to do with creating was the United States Senate. Their spirit of education and investigation would seem rewarding to him, but perhaps also that theme is not profitable on this occasion.

Ben always referred to himself as a Republican but certainly in this nonpartisan meeting I cannot pursue this idea further.

On all controversial matters Franklin was a tolerant soul. He cautioned us that "By the collision of different sentiments, sparks of truth are struck out and political light is obtained." I hope so. But I will not illustrate it further.

He said, "It is true that in some of the states there are parties and discords; but let us look back and ask if we were ever without them. Such will exist wherever there is liberty; and perhaps they will help preserve it." I call your attention to the safety catch in that sentence—that is the use of the word "perhaps."

Ben made the emphatic remark that "They that can give up essential liberty to obtain a little temporary safety deserve neither liberty nor safety." Some way I feel Ben might be disappointed with the world on this subject. Indeed I have the feeling that staunch old emblem in his plain clothes with his radiating thrift would receive many shocks if he walked around on this earth for a few days. However, with his magnificent sense of humor, he might just laugh.

But to be more serious, we know the greatest inheritance that Franklin left the American people was his contribution to our liberties.

Franklin had sought and associated with men keen in devotion to freedom long before we gained our independence from England. Among his friends were Burke and Tom Paine. It is sometimes overlooked that it was Franklin who paid Tom Paine's shipfare across the Atlantic and set that firebrand of liberty on these shores. It was Tom Paine, then a soldier in the Continental army, who as a ghost writer for Washington composed that blazing document which Washington proclaimed to his dejected troops, revitalizing them to the victorious crossing of the Delaware. And Tom Paine, with his crusading spirit and his "Rights of Man," greatly stirred the emotions for personal liberty on this continent.

I scarcely need mention, however, that Franklin was one of the leaders among the Founding Fathers who riveted freedom into American life. We must never forget that Franklin helped frame and signed the Declaration of Independence. He negotiated the Peace Treaty of Paris, acknowledging our freedom from Britain. He contributed greatly to the framing of the Constitution of the United States. And in those great deeds he was inspired by both genius and determination to guarantee national independence and to secure the very foundations of personal liberty.

Franklin was an individualist. He held no belief in people's leaning on government. He contended they must have a sterner fare if the nation was to go forward. He insisted they must possess qualities and strength of character which would give them calmness and poise in prosperity and courage and vision in adversity. They must be guided not only by patriotism of the tribe, but by morality and religious faith, which belong alone to the individual spirit.

It was Joseph Choate who said, "When the spirit of Franklin decays the sun of America will have begun to set."

Address at the Westtown School

Westtown, Pennsylvania
[May 29, 1954]

IT IS a real pleasure to come to this school devoted for a century and a half to the faith of my fathers. My forebears landed in this city fifty years before this school was founded. They had been steadfast members of our faith even before they came to America.

It is also a personal pleasure to be associated with President Gilbert White, who was a distinguished member of the first Commission on Organization of the Federal Government in 1947, and Joseph Binns, one of your most distinguished alumni, who is a member with me on this second Commission on Organization of the Government.

When I asked what I should talk to you about, someone said, "Our Government." However, I will bore you for only ten minutes with some remarks hung on that hat hook.

You who are still boys and girls have already begun to find out some things about the Government. In any event, it is going to be all around you for the next sixty or seventy years of your lives. And you will need to look after it.

Also, some day you will inherit all the homes, the farms, the stores, the factories, the churches, and the schools in the United States—and you will need look after them at the same time. But if you have good government, you will find in all these places good jobs, great opportunities, and comfortable living.

I have lived in nearly forty different foreign countries under many kinds of government. I was not a tourist. I worked in their industries, their wars, in the terrible aftermaths of those wars and in the attempts to find peace from those wars. I was associated with their peoples, their officials, their statesmen, their writers, and their spiritual leaders.

In those foreign countries in which I worked there were despotisms and there were limited monarchies. There were socialistic governments where economic freedom is limited. There were Communist governments wherein the people were reduced to slavery. There were even many varied forms of representative governments elected by the people. The differences between those governments and ours and between the lives of their people and ours were before my eyes every day.

Our Founding Fathers did not invent the priceless boon of individual freedom and respect for the dignity of men. Your religious faith and the Declaration of Independence hold that great gift to mankind sprang from the Creator and not from governments.

Our Founding Fathers were profound students of history. From their learning of the causes of the decline and fall of free men into tyranny over thousands of years, they distilled new safeguards to our liberties. With superb genius they welded these new safeguards into the Declaration and our Constitution. Thereby they assured us a civilization of free men which has lasted longer than any other in all the human record.

The essence of it is that you are free to do whatever you like, choose any calling you like, and go into any enterprise you like, so long as you do not injure your neighbors and so long as you co-operate for the common good.

We hear much criticism of our Government—and it is often justified. No government is perfect because human beings are not perfect. But let me say that, despite many disheartening things, by and large the ideals of our country are still strong. And under our unique American system, we have given more opportunities to every boy and girl than any other government. And the proof of the rightness of the American system is that we have grown to the most powerful nation with the highest standard of living on the earth. But more important than all, we, more than most governments, respect the individual rights and personal dignity of our citizens.

You hear much about the many different breeds of socialism which are spreading over the world today. That anti-Christ and materialistic virus ranges all the way from bloody communism to the milder forms of legalistic socialism and the Welfare State. God has blessed us with a wonderful heritage. The great documents of that heritage are not from Karl Marx. They are the Bible, the Declaration of Independence, and the Constitution of the United States. Within them alone can the safeguards of freedom and religious faith survive.

You are sometimes told that the older generations have made a mess of things. I have often agreed with that idea. But we must bear in mind that it was the older generations who built for you all these millions of ways of making a living, obtaining an education, and of enjoying life. Above all, they gave you the greatest heritage that can come to man—national freedom and personal liberty. And some day you will be the Older Generation.

There are voices in our country who daily sound alarms that our civilization is on the way out. Concentrated on the difficulties of our times, they see an early and dour end for us. But civilization does not decline and fall while the people still possess dynamic creative faculties and individual devotion to religious faith and to liberty. The American people still possess these qualities. We are not at the bedside of a nation in death agony of its civilization.

Yours can be a bright future if we can avoid war.

With maintained free minds and free spirits, we daily open vast new frontiers of science and invention and new applications of older knowledge.

These new frontiers give us other blessings. Not only do they expand our living but also they open new opportunities and new areas of adventure and enterprise. They open new vistas of beauty. They unfold the wonders of the atom and the heavens.

Daily they prove the reality of an all-wise Supreme Giver of Law.

And one last word. When you go out into this complicated world to make your own way, you will find your elders anxious for your success. They will extend you more kindness and helpfulness than is the case in any other nation on earth. Do not be afraid for your future—and it is a bright future if we conduct our government rightly.

Remarks at Dedication of Herbert Hoover Public Schools

[*August 1954*]

Some thirty-two public schools have been named for Mr. Hoover. In 1954, he spoke at the opening of such schools at Kenmore, New York; West Branch, Cedar Rapids, Iowa City, and Mason City in Iowa; and Stockton, California. These addresses were mostly extemporaneous. A few paragraphs will indicate their tenor.

At Stockton, California, on August 3, 1954, he said:

It is indeed a great honor to have a public school named for me. And I deeply appreciate the affection which goes with this act. . . .

My first steps to learning were in a public school. To this day I have a lingering affection for my teachers of that day and many of my friendships made in school have been staunch over all these years.

.   .   .   .

We elders all of us have a responsibility for our educational system. With its 35,000,000 boys and girls and its 1,200,000 teachers, it is one of the foundation piers of our American System of free men and women. Its proper conduct is the guarantee of our national future.

.   .   .   .

And among these responsibilities is the adequate preparation and protection of our teachers. They are not only teachers to whom we entrust the instruction and moral development of our children. They must—each of them—occupy a position of community leadership. Theirs is a calling of great personal self-denial. They must be provided with adequate living and an assurance of protection to old age. . . .

At Iowa City, on August 10:

My steps in education came through the public schools and our free universities. Without those generous services from our country, I could never have attained my position in life. To these institutions of free men and the able devoted teachers, I owe a debt beyond any possibility of repayment. But I can prove my faith in the public schools because my two sons also trod that path in making their own successes in life.

Our Nation builds a secure future from you who are a part of the 35 million children in our public schools. Many of you will rise to great leaders, great artists and great baseball players. And more important, it is you who will carry on the America that we love.

And at Cedar Rapids, Iowa, on August 11:

I deeply appreciate the honor you have bestowed upon me. I seem to be making headway in my education. With the honor of five public schools named for me in Iowa and the additional honor of a degree from our State University, I am making progress.

I confess to you that when I was a boy in Iowa public school I did not incorporate these honors in my greatest dreams. In fact, those dreams were confined to finding an immediate outlet for my surplus energies.

.   .   .   .

When you begin to look backward, you will know that your school and college days were the happiest of your life. And these are not only the beginning of knowledge but of the friendships which last all your lives.

There are two roads you may take. One road is employment in the Government. It has the attraction of greater security in life. Staunch men and women are needed for public service who are willing to make the sacrifices which it entails and endure the heartbreaks which it brings. Our Nation cannot go on to greatness unless some of you are willing to give your lives to its many services.

Others of you will go into the great business of producing and distributing the necessities and luxuries of life. Ours is, or should be, a country of free enterprise. And free enterprise must make a profit. And a job in free enterprise also has advantages. It does not require qualifications as to ancestors, a particular religion, good looks, or ability to get votes. What is required is that you help your associates to make a profit. There is less security than in Government employment, but there is adventure in every day. If you have an employer, you are no wage slave in America—for if you do not like that particular profit-maker, you can choose another one.

Whatever calling you enter, I suggest to you that the real joy in life is from the creativeness of work. And success in your life will not come from watching of the time clock.

And one other word. When you go out into this complicated world to make your own way, you will find your elders anxious for your success. They will extend you more kindness and helpfulness than is the case in any other nation on earth. Do not be afraid for your future—it is a bright future filled with new opportunities and great adventures. Especially when you try to park your car! . . .

How to Stay Young*

This Week Magazine
[August 8, 1954]

T HE older I grow, the more I appreciate children. Now, as I near my eightieth birthday, I salute them again. Children are the most wholesome part of the race, the sweetest, for they are freshest from the hand of God. Whimsical, mischievous, they fill the world with joy and good humor. We adults live a life of apprehension as to what they will think of us; a life of defense against their terrifying energy; a life of hard work to live up to their great expectations. We put them to bed with a sense of relief—and greet them in the morning with delight and anticipation. We envy them the freshness of adventure and the discovery of life. In all these ways, children add to the wonder of being alive. In all these ways, they help to keep us young.

* Adapted from address at Constitution Hall, Washington, D.C. Opening session of White House Conference on Child Health and Protection, November 19, 1930.

Index